Breaking Clean

The twins and me on the front steps,
circa 1958

Breaking Clean

≠

Judy Blunt

Alfred A. Knopf

New York

2002

THIS IS A BORZOI BOOK
PUBLISHED BY ALFRED A. KNOPF

www.aaknopf.com

Knopf, Borzoi Books and the colophon are registered
trademarks of Random House, Inc.

The chapters "Breaking Clean" and "Lessons in Silence" and a
portion of "Learning Curves" were originally published, in
slightly different form, in *Northern Lights*. The chapter
"Salvage" was originally published in *Big Sky Journal*.

Library of Congress Cataloging-in-Publication Data
Blunt, Judy.
Breaking clean / Judy Blunt. — 1st ed.
p. cm.
ISBN 0-375-40131-8 (alk. paper)
1. Women ranchers—Montana—Biography. 2. Ranch life—
Montana. 3. Montana—Biography. I. Title.
CT275.B57984 A3 2002
978.86'033'0922—dc21   2001029861

Manufactured in the United States of America
Published February 12, 2002
Reprinted Twice
Fourth Printing, March 2002

For Margaret

And for
Jeanette, Jason and James—
growing roots, growing wings

A place belongs forever to whoever claims it hardest, remembers it most obsessively, wrenches it from itself, shapes it, renders it, loves it so radically that he remakes it in his image.

—*Joan Didion*

Contents

Acknowledgments

Missoula, Montana, is blessed with a community of writers, and I've been blessed to live among them as friend and colleague for the decade it's taken me to finish this book. There are no finer people. Special thanks to the women of the circle—readers, writers and healers of souls—who have sustained me and shared with me their strengths: Kim Barnes, Mary Clearman Blew, Frances Buck, Claire Davis, Robin Desser, Debra Earling, Martha Elizabeth, Kate Gadbow, Renee Wayne Golden, Linda Hasselstrom, Maria Healey, Rose Lynch, Deirdre McNamer and Patricia Swan Smith.

I am grateful to my parents, and to my brothers and sisters, for their unflagging support. They have accepted the millstone that is a writer in the family with grace and good humor.

Thanks also to the Montana Arts Council and the PEN/ Jerard Fund for their support of this book as a work in progress.

And finally, I want to acknowledge those who might choose a different version of the story than the one I tell. In sharing stories with others who were there, we discover how inevitably each perspective offers its own, sure version of events. I've long since made my peace with that variety of fiction we call truth.

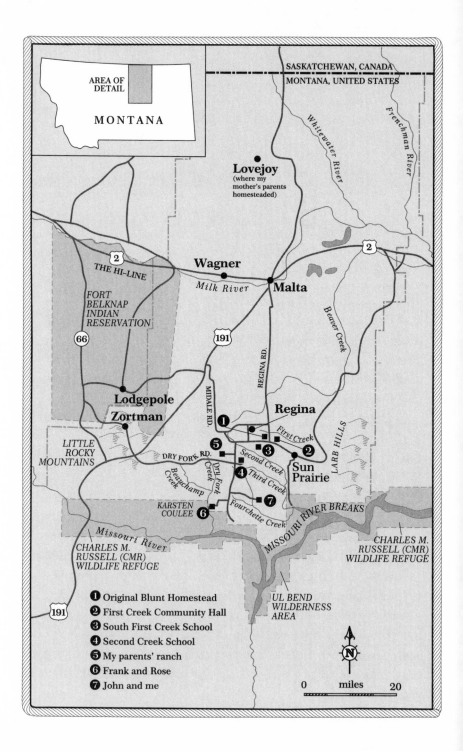

AREA OF
DETAIL

MONTANA

SASKATCHEWAN, CANADA
MONTANA, UNITED STATES

Whitewater River

Frenchman River

Lovejoy
(where my
mother's parents
homesteaded)

THE HI-LINE

Wagner

Milk River

Malta

FORT
BELKNAP
INDIAN
RESERVATION

Beaver Creek

191

REGINA RD.

MIDALE RD.

Lodgepole
Zortman

Regina

❶

First Creek

LARB HILLS

❺

❸

DRY FORK RD.

Second Creek

❷

LITTLE
ROCKY
MOUNTAINS

Beauchamp Creek

Dry Fork Creek

❹

Third Creek

Sun
Prairie

KARSTEN
COULEE

❻

Fourchette Creek

❼

MISSOURI RIVER BREAKS

Missouri River

CHARLES M.
RUSSELL (CMR)
WILDLIFE REFUGE

CHARLES M.
RUSSELL (CMR)
WILDLIFE REFUGE

191

❶ Original Blunt Homestead
❷ First Creek Community Hall
❸ South First Creek School
❹ Second Creek School
❺ My parents' ranch
❻ Frank and Rose
❼ John and me

UL BEND
WILDERNESS
AREA

N

0   miles   20

Breaking
Clean

Breaking Clean

I rarely go back to the ranch where I was born or to the neighboring land where I bore the fourth generation of a ranching family. My people live where hardpan and sagebrush flats give way to the Missouri River Breaks, a country so harsh and wild and distant that it must grow its own replacements, as it grows its own food, or it will die. Hereford cattle grow slick and mean foraging along the cutbanks for greasewood shoots and buffalo grass. Town lies an hour or more north over gumbo roads. Our town was Malta, population 2,500, county seat of Phillips County, Montana, and the largest settlement for nearly one hundred miles in any direction.

"Get tough," my father snapped as I dragged my feet at the edge of a two-acre potato field. He gave me a gunnysack and started me down the rows pulling the tough fanweed that towered over the potato plants. I was learning then the necessary lessons of weeds and seeds and blisters. My favorite story as a child was of how I fainted in the garden when I was eight. My mother had to pry my fingers from around the handle of the

3

hoe, she said, and she also said I was stupid not to wear a hat in the sun. But she was proud. My granddad hooted with glee when he heard about it.

"She's a hell of a little worker," he said, shaking his head. I was a hell of a little worker from that day forward, and I learned to wear a hat.

I am sometimes amazed at my own children, their outrage if they are required to do the dishes twice in one week, their tender self-absorption with minor bumps and bruises. As a mom, I've had to teach myself to croon over thorn scratches, admire bloody baby teeth and sponge the dirt from scraped shins. But in my mind, my mother's voice and that of her mother still compete for expression. "Oh for Christ's sake, you aren't hurt!" they're saying, and for a moment I struggle. For a moment I want to tell this new generation about my little brother calmly spitting out a palm full of tooth chips and wading back in to grab the biggest calf in the branding pen. I want to tell them how tough I was, falling asleep at the table with hands too sore to hold a fork, or about their grandmother, who cut off three fingers on the blades of a mower and finished the job before she came in to get help. For a moment I'm terrified I'll slip and tell them to get tough.

Like my parents and grandparents, I was born and trained to live there. I could rope and ride and jockey a John Deere as well as my brothers, but being female, I also learned to bake bread and can vegetables and reserve my opinion when the men were talking. When a bachelor neighbor began courting me when I was fifteen, my parents were proud and hopeful. Though he was twelve years older than I was, his other numbers were very promising. He and his father ran five hundred cow-calf pairs and five hundred head of yearlings on 36,000 acres of range.

After supper one spring evening, my mother and I stood in the kitchen. She held her back stiff as her hands shot like pistons into the mound of bread dough on the counter. I stood tough beside her. On the porch, John had presented my father with a bottle of whiskey and was asking Dad's permission to marry me. I wanted her to grab my cold hand and tell me how to run. I wanted her to smooth the crumpled letter from the garbage can and read the praise of my high school principal. I wanted her to tell me what I could be.

She rounded the bread neatly and efficiently and began smoothing lard over the top, intent on her fingers as they tidied the loaves.

"He's a good man," she said finally.

In the seventh grade, my daughter caught up with the culture shock and completed her transition from horse to bicycle, from boot-cut Levi's to acid-washed jeans. She delighted me with her discoveries. Knowing little of slumber parties, roller skates or packs of giggling girls, sometimes I was more her peer than her parent. She wrote, too, long sentimental stories about lost puppies that found homes and loving two-parent families with adventurous daughters. Her characters were usually right back where they started, rescued and happy, by the end of the story. She'd begun watching television.

"Do you hate Daddy?" she asked once, from the depths of a divorced child's sadness.

"Your daddy," I replied, "is a good man."

≠

In the manner of good ranchmen, my father and John squatted on their haunches on the porch facing each other. The whiskey bottle rested on the floor between them. John's good white shirt was buttoned painfully around his neck. Dad had pushed his Stetson back, and a white band of skin glowed above his dark face, smooth and strangely delicate. When I moved to the doorway, their conversation was shifting from weather and cattle to marriage. As Dad tilted back heavily on one heel to drink from the neck of the bottle, John looked down and began to plot our life with one finger in the dust on the floor.

"I been meaning to stop by . . . ," John said to the toe of his boot. He looked up to catch Dad's eye. Dad nodded and looked away.

"You figured a spot yet?" He spoke deliberately, weighing each word. Like all the big ranches out there, John's place had been pieced together from old homesteads and small farms turned back to grass.

"Morgan place has good buildings," John replied, holding Dad's gaze for a moment. He shifted the bottle to his lips and passed it back to Dad.

"Fair grass on the north end, but the meadows need work," Dad challenged. John shifted slightly to the left, glancing to the west through the screen door. The setting sun was balanced on the blue tips of the pines in the distance. He worked at the stiffness of his collar, leaving gray smudges of dust along his throat. Settling back, he spoke with a touch of defiance.

"If a person worked it right . . ." Then his eyes found his boots again. He held his head rigid, waiting.

Dad smoothed one hand along his jaw as if in deep

thought, and the two men squatted silently for several minutes. Then Dad drew a long breath and blew it out.

"Old Morgan used to get three cuttings in a rain year," he said at last. John's head rose and he met my father's steady look.

"A person might make a go of it," John agreed softly. Dad's shoulders lifted slightly and dropped in mock defeat. He placed a hand on each knee and pushed himself up, John rising beside him, and they shook hands, grinning. Twisting suddenly, Dad reached down and grabbed the whiskey. He held it high in a toast, then leaned forward and tapped John's chest with the neck of the bottle.

"And you, you cocky sonofabitch! Don't you try planting anything too early, understand?" They were still laughing when they entered the kitchen.

I talk to my father twice a year now, on Christmas and Father's Day. We talk about the yearling weights and the rain, or the lack of rain. When I moved away from our community, my parents lost a daughter, but they will have John forever, as a neighbor, a friend. He is closer to them in spirit than I am in blood, and shares their bewilderment and anger at my rejection of their way of life. As the ultimate betrayal, I have taken John's sons, interrupting the perfect rites of passage. The move was hardest on the boys, for here they were only boys. At the ranch they were men-in-training, and they mourned this loss of prestige.

"I used to drive tractor for my dad," the elder son once told his friends, and they scoffed. "You're only eleven years old," they laughed, and he was frustrated to bitter tears. He would go back to the ranch, that one. He would have to. But he returned there an outsider, as his father knew he would. He did not stay. The first son of the clan to cross the county line and survive found it easier to leave a second time, when he had to. Had he chosen to spend his life there, he would have had memories of symphonies and tennis shoes and basketball. When he marries and has children, he will raise them knowing that, at least sometimes, cowboys do cry.

I stuck with the bargain sealed on my parents' porch for more than twelve years, although my faith in martyrdom as a way of life dwindled. I collected children and nervous tics the way some of the women collected dress patterns and ceramic owls. It was hard to shine when all the good things had already been done. Dorothy crocheted tissue covers and made lampshades from Styrofoam egg cartons. Pearle looped thick, horrible rugs from rags and denim scraps. Helen gardened a half acre of land and raised two hundred turkeys in her spare time. And everyone attended the monthly meetings of the Near and Far Club to answer roll call with her favorite new recipe.

These were the successful ranchwomen who moved from barn to kitchen to field with patient, tireless steps. For nearly ten years, I kept up with the cycles of crops and seasons and moons, and I did it all well. I excelled. But in the end, I couldn't sleep. I quit eating. It wasn't enough.

I saved for three years and bought my typewriter from the Sears and Roebuck catalogue. I typed the first line while the cardboard carton lay around it in pieces. I wrote in a cold sweat on long strips of freezer paper that emerged from the keys thick and rich with ink. At first I only wrote at night when the children and John slept, emptying myself onto the paper until I could lie down. Then I began writing during the day, when the men were working in the fields. The children ran brown and wild and happy. The garden gave birth and died with rotting produce fat under its vines. The community buzzed. Dorothy offered to teach me how to crochet.

One day John's father, furious because lunch for the hay crew was late, took my warm, green typewriter to the shop and killed it with a sledgehammer.

A prescribed distance of beige plush separated us. On a TV monitor nearby, zigzag lines distorted our images. John's face looked lean and hard. My face showed fear and exhaustion. The years were all there in black and white. Mike, our marriage counselor, stood behind the video camera adjusting the sound level. We were learning to communicate, John and I. We each held a sweaty slip of paper with a list of priority topics we had prepared for this day. Our job was to discuss them on camera. Next week we would watch our debate and learn what areas needed improvement. We talked by turns, neither allowed to interrupt the other, for three minutes on each topic.

John was indignant, bewildered by my topics. I, on the other hand, could have written his list myself. Somewhere in a dusty file drawer is a film of an emaciated, haggard woman hesitantly describing her needs and dreams to a tight-jawed man who twists his knuckles and shakes his head because he wants to interrupt her and he can't. His expression shows that he doesn't know this woman; she's something he never bargained for. When it's over, they are both shaking and glad to get away.

"John," Mike once asked, "how often do you tell your wife that you love her?"

"Oh, I've told her that before," he replied cautiously. I cut into the conversation from my corner of the ring.

"You only told me you loved me once, and that was the day we were married," I said.

"Well," John said, injured and defensive, "I never took it back, did I?"

The break, when it came, was so swift and clean that I sometimes dream I went walking in the coulee behind the ranch house and emerged on the far side of the mountains. It's different here—not easier, but different. And it's enough.

A Place of
One's Own

Spring of 1954, my mother stood at the threshold of Henry Picotte's abandoned chicken house, a bouquet of hens dangling in either hand, and eyed the enormous prairie rattler coiled on the dirt floor. Killing the snake would be inconvenient, hampered as she was by a midterm pregnancy and the hysterical chickens swooping left and right around their new home, but a weapon would not have been hard to find. Stout diamond willow sticks leaned against every gatepost on the place, anywhere a man might step off a horse. Such readiness suggested an extended family of snakes with cousins and in-laws, generations of snakes, more than she wished to dwell on with her hands full of squawking chickens. Stepping back out, she hollered for my father to bring a spade. Once separated from the writhing coils, the snake's head would be buried in the soft ground outside the chicken house door, dirt tamped firm with the heel of his boot, the body flung over the weeds to the fence line as a warning to others. The wide rattles he would tuck in his hatband, perhaps for the same reason.

Margaret and Kenny bounced impatiently on the bench seat of the old truck while our parents swept a path to the shack, slashing the tall weeds with sticks to give remaining varmints the courtesy of a head start. Margaret was seven, a thin child, whose fair, delicate features stood in stark contrast to Kenny, a robust toddler about twenty months old. I was the child in her belly.

The story of my first days is embedded in stories of the land, for it was in the spring of 1954, the year of my birth, that my parents scraped together what money they had and borrowed more to make a down payment on a ranch of their own. They had married three years before, my father a rowdy young cowboy of twenty, my mother a no-nonsense divorcée of twenty-eight with a two-year-college degree and four-year-old Margaret. Dad worked those first years on his father's place and for neighboring ranchers, my mother sharing kitchen rights with a mother-in-law, then moving where the work took them, always with a common goal—a place of their own. They endured the setbacks, the added expense of a son born the day after the father's twenty-first birthday. The final delay occurred when they dealt for the land.

The retiring homesteader, Eric Anderson, had crops in the field, and they could not move in until after harvest, the end of August, first part of September. That summer, homeless and broke, they set up camp on the empty homestead of Henry Picotte, waiting out the growing season, awaiting my birth, awaiting the day the Anderson place would change hands and they could come, finally, home.

A sharp-featured little man with a lame leg and a strong French accent, Henry Picotte was one of several French Canadians who settled just over the border in southern Phillips County in the early 1900s. He was part of a second wave of settlers—the first having thrown up their hands and moved on—who bought up proven homesteads and combined them into more sustainable plots. A logger in his youth, Henry had "busted a leg in the timber" and it had healed badly. Drafted into the Canadian Militia during World War I, he soon washed his hands of army life and jumped the border south. It was a story he told my father with no apology. "Dey make me t-r-rot," Henry would sputter, slapping his short leg. "An' I can't t-r-rot!"

For the next twenty-five years, his work teams did his trotting for him, and he farmed his snake-ridden acres in peace until he sold out to my grandfather in 1945. His bachelor shack, more or less empty for a decade, became my mother's summer home.

Fenced off and ungrazed, the barnyard buildings were rafter-deep in weeds—fireweed, mustard, and pigweed grown rank and lusty on a diet of old manure. Henry was well remembered for the pies he baked and fed to visitors with cups of stout tea, and his patch of rhubarb, what the homesteaders called "pie plant," had not just survived, it had gone native. Last year's seed stalks rose chest-high over leaves as large as an elephant's ears, already thick as a hedge where the shed eaves had kept it irrigated. The artesian well seeped a sulfurous trickle through a gully near the barn, the ground around it crusted white. Dad knew Henry had tapped into an underground spring so foul his plow horses refused to drink it.

The day after they moved in, Dad trucked water from his parents' place to fill an old iron cistern Henry kept near the house, enough to last the summer if they were careful. The milk cow and my mother's saddle horse, Sox, were turned in around the buildings to battle the weeds. A couple of kittens took charge of the mice that sifted through the woodwork. Margaret and Kenny were given the standard lecture about snakes and set loose with the dog, Purp, to play for hours in the dim recesses of the log barn. Neither wired for electricity nor plumbed for water, the two-room shanty featured bare board floors, beaded ceilings and a twenty-year accumulation of dirt and grease that literally filled the narrow grooves of the ceiling panels. Although unusually strong and decisive when it came to making things right, Mother was not one to linger at pointless tasks. She gave it all a going-over, concluded that the devil himself couldn't get it clean and left it at that. The closest neighbors were miles away. Dad would be gone most of the summer, working on ranches to the north and south until the new place came empty after harvest. Mother dusted off her hands and settled in.

I'm not hard-pressed to imagine my mother as a young woman, for even in her seventies she remains independent, opinionated and fiercely practical. She'd been born late in the lives of her parents, one a homesteading schoolteacher up from the Dakotas, the other a Scots farmer who had emigrated from Canada to farm with his teams of horses in far northern Montana. Hers was one of many poor families in the Lovejoy community struggling to get by on white beans and garden truck, but being an only child afforded her opportunities she might never have known as a member of a large, hungry family. She learned at her mother's elbow. By the time she entered high school, she could sew expertly, cook adequately, milk a cow, break a colt, tend a garden and preserve the vegetables it produced. Unlike many women in her generation, she finished high school and went on to take secretarial and bookkeeping courses at a community college. From her gentle Scots father, she'd acquired a love of horses and from both

14

parents, a love of reading. Hardly surprising that in her thirties this woman waded into the summer without a qualm, not
only willing but determined to spend the third trimester of a
third pregnancy in a two-room shack twenty feet from the outhouse and a dozen miles from a telephone.

Freed from the notion of white-glove cleaning, freed of the
work of gardens and large meals, freed from the blistering
summer cycle of cattle and crops, my mother propped books
on her swelling belly and rested, sharing the shade of the
house with Sox and the cow, one ear tuned to the games of
her children and the vast quiet of the country around her.
Days ended with a flare of fire in the sky over the Little Rocky
Mountains and began again with the golden glow over the
prairie to the east. It was, my mother recalls in a fond and
misty voice, one of the most peaceful and pleasant summers
of her life.

In the next few years, she would have cause to look back
on that time with unbridled nostalgia, drawing up memories
like a comforter—the lazy afternoons that Sox thrust his great
sorrel head through an open window to mooch bread crusts,
Kenny's birthday cake rising to fill the tiny oven of the sheep-
herder's stove, a straggle of red and pink petunias she and
Margaret planted and kept alive by emptying the dishpan
water around the roots every evening. The growing season
parted and swept around them, weeks that passed like a
bloom of light in the eye of a storm, a sudden stillness made
all the sweeter for its brevity and the inevitable crash of thunder that followed.

That August, barnyards shook with the roar of threshing
machines tuning up for harvest, iron-wheeled monsters
pulled from behind outbuildings to be tinkered and tightened
until they bellowed. That August, the hay was up and the seed

crops fell to the blades of sickle mowers—wheat, oats and third cutting alfalfa raked into windrows to dry and gathered into maw-sized bunches to await the threshing crews. That August, with this one final harvest chore standing between my parents and their new home, it began to rain.

My father spent the month on a harvest crew north of Malta, cutting grain between rain showers, a day sitting for every day in the field, and finally ground his way home in disgust. He got on building fence for a neighbor, a job that lent itself to soft ground. Anderson's crop of alfalfa seed lay in the field as the days poured and dripped and spat and drooled into September. The roads turned to gumbo soup, rendering travel impractical when it wasn't impossible, and Dad knew time was running out. Margaret needed to start school. Mom, in her ninth month of pregnancy, was still stranded without transportation most of the week. Anderson was holding firm, waiting out the wet.

In September the family broke and scattered. The two kids were farmed out to Mons and Clara Veseth, who had a son in school as well as a little boy Kenny's age. Mom moved to a friend's house in Malta to be nearer the hospital. Dad camped in Anderson's front yard, helping him thresh alfalfa, borrowing Anderson's machinery to plant his first crop of winter wheat. My mother sums it up with a shake of her head, the disciplined cap of dark curls, the black snap of her eyes unchanged by the passage of time, although any real exasperation has given way to ironic humor. "You," she says in wry accusation, "*you* were the only damned thing that arrived on time that fall." And so I was born, landed, yet homeless, oblivious to the chaos, the second week of October, 1954.

The nights had turned cold, and when the new place finally came free, Dad traveled on the frost to fetch us from

A Place of One's Own

Wagner, a tiny community outside of Malta where Mom's parents had retired. She stoked up the stove at the Picotte place, stowed me in a basket with handles and started packing with her free hand. On moving day, I jounced along on the front seat of the farm truck, greeted for the first time by my older siblings as we plowed through the gumbo to retrieve them, then fishtailed up the road to our new home. We got stuck twice on the quarter-mile stretch leading to the house, but when the truck ground to a stop, we were home for good.

My mother bowed her neck and waded into the mess, building islands of boxes in each of the six small rooms. The next day, Dad returned to saddle Sox and drive the milk cow cross-country to the empty barn. By Christmas the house was put together, and my mother took stock. A new baby, a new ranch, a home of her own. Her name was on the deed next to my father's, the ink dry, the die cast. Time to settle in and hang on for the ride.

There are perspectives in my stories that I can only imagine, conclusions I come to based on the circumstances of the lives that led to my own. My family and the stories I tell are neither typical nor very unusual. My grandparents were part of the last wave of homesteading that began in Montana at the turn of the century. Their parents had been restless people, emblematic of a restless era. The Civil War, the economic shift from small farms to factory industry, the influx of immigrant labor and the discovery of gold all combined to create an upheaval, a ripple of movement like waves lapping a shore that pushed my ancestors a little farther west with each generation. Far back, the family stories track uncles and older siblings who caught wagon trains west, families coming apart as daughters married and followed their men to other states and sons followed their half-formed dreams over the horizon, always to the west. On both sides of my family tree, the women died young, both of my grandmothers' mothers succumbing to illness and overwork, giving birth to children every year or two until their bodies wore out. The men married again, and moved on.

Depending on the decade, I find the trail of my great-grandparents in Kansas, Oklahoma, Illinois, North Dakota, Ontario and Saskatchewan. Most were farming families of rather nondescript English/Irish/German lineage who would settle in one spot for a decade or more, then sell out and move a bit west where the grass seemed greener. My mother's dad was one of a large clan of Scots who followed the timber camps through Ontario to Saskatchewan and branched south. The Great Northern Railroad had punched a trail along the Hi-Line from east to west, leaving in its wake a string of sidings, or depots, spaced along the tracks. In 1887, a blindfolded clerk at the railroad's Minnesota headquarters named them all by spinning a globe and pointing randomly: Glasgow, Saco, Malta, Harlem, Zurich, Havre. The railroad advertised for merchants to make towns, farmers to grow wheat, people to order goods from the east and west, and they came. Within a few years of each other, each from his or her own direction, my grandparents crossed the border into Montana as young adults, took up homesteads independently of one another, met, married and stayed, rooted and grounded, through the great exodus of settlers that followed.

Nearly ninety years have passed since they cast their lot with the land locator and filed claims equally distant to the north and south of the cow town of Malta, Montana. Whatever drove them to see beyond the horizon grew quiet when they settled here. George Aikins and Pearle Watson, Alfred Blunt and Pansy Robinson McNeil stayed on, whether through optimism or exhaustion, to see their children raised and married, their grandchildren born to the same land, and in the case of my father's mother, Pansy, to admire upwards of thirty great-grandchildren. All four are buried in the same cemetery in Malta. Their legacy is a hardheaded independence still visible in the fourth and fifth generations of Montana-born children, and a restlessness that crops up every now and again, like the occasional head of red hair.

Ignorance allows for hope in any life, and if there was a mercy to my parents' first years on the ranch, that would be it. They couldn't see ahead. I imagine my mother laughing at the antics of her children that first Christmas on the ranch, applauding Margaret's performance in the school play with me tucked in the crook of her arm, Kenny wiggling with excitement on our father's knee, clinging shyly as Santa's weather-burned face smiled at him through the cotton beard, a bowlegged Santa with wide, chapped hands and little paper bags of ribbon candy. They shared that first Christmas with neighbors, holding paper cups of coffee by the rim to keep from scalding their fingers, laughter and the smoke of a dozen cigarettes ringing the schoolroom. They couldn't have seen then, the moment forecast for later that spring—a day in late March or early April—when my mother would wake to the changes in her body like a driver in a bad dream, fumbling for the brakes and feeling her feet sink all the way to the floorboards.

Exactly one year later, Dad attended the school program alone and within minutes of his return home, he and my mother were careening toward town on a sheet of black ice. Dad skittered and skated the old Jeep between ditches, pushing up to forty-five miles an hour when my mother's breath caught in her teeth, easing up whenever she could pull in enough air to yell at him: "I'd rather have them on the road than in the ditch." Traveling fifty miles in fits and starts took twice as long as the birth. My father received the news with his hat still crimped in his hands, his knees still rubbery. Gary came first, a sturdy seven pounds, and on his heels, Gail, two pounds smaller, but loud and healthy.

I imagine the trip back, the driver torn between celebration and exhaustion as he retraced the icy route to be home in time for chores. Some things couldn't be planned for, couldn't be gotten around. The birth of twins had been forecast by the old country doctor in August, but no one had predicted the hailstorm that had battered that first crop of winter wheat flat to the ground, the money for seed and fuel and taxes borrowed against time. There was no calf crop to make up the loss. They started that spring with fifty head of Hereford cattle, his father's cows, running them on shares. The heifer calves Dad would keep to start a herd of his own, but the steers, the bread-and-butter calves, belonged to his father.

My mother arrived home a few days after Christmas with a newborn on either arm, a year-old baby, a three-year-old and an excited schoolgirl waiting to greet her. Her life was already a serious business, but she stepped across the threshold to a logistical nightmare. Three babies in diapers, one climbing the rafters and one in school, her partner preoccupied with his own staggering workload, a young man jerked from boyhood into fatherhood still believing, as boys will, that a day's work earns a man the leisure of a night's sleep. Mornings he stepped out into the quiet of daybreak. Evenings he came in tired, set down a pail of milk and washed up. He pulled a chair to the table like a workhorse entering a stall, waiting to be fed, pushing his plate to the center of the table when he finished, shedding clothes as he made his way to bed. Just as easily, as predictably, he did not come home, but was gone playing tenor banjo or fiddle at a dance, or when he could scrape together a few loose dollars, gone to town for supplies in midafternoon, staggering home late or early or not at all until the next morning.

That first winter the teenage daughter of a neighboring family stayed to help with the twins. I became Margaret's baby, her after-school and weekend duty to change and feed. It was she who guided my first spraddle-legged explorations of our shared world, she who best remembers the contrast between the brightly lit, orderly schoolroom where she spent her day and the dimly lit chaos she returned to near dusk, lifting the solid bulk of me to one narrow hip as I greeted her with a six-toothed grin and raised arms. With me in tow, she played in the narrow alleys between cribs and cots, keeping me safe from the stove in the living room where the A-frame drying racks hung point down from hooks in the ceiling, swaying under loads of diapers. From these early years she acquired a view of motherhood that kept her childless into her thirties. When her son was born, she took a year's sabbatical from teaching and steeled herself for the onslaught, only to discover the delight of caring for one child in a modern home on an adequate income.

Our little house on the prairie was not charming, though by homestead standards, it was livable and remained relatively unchanged until we kids were grown and gone. From the outside, we entered a rough enclosed porch, passing between a row of muddy overshoes and a couple days' worth of split wood to the kitchen door. Over that threshold, linoleum cabbage flowers bloomed through the house, shades of maroon and green fading to black where the color had worn away in traffic lanes and doorways. In one corner of the kitchen built-in benches seated two sides of the square kitchen table, one step from the double-oven cookstove, one step from the washbasin, one step from the woodstove we stoked with white cottonwood logs, the sort of punky wood that churned out an equal measure of heat and soft ash. The dark-red linoleum covering the countertops peeped through its own covering of gallon milk jars, crockery and pots that wouldn't fit in the narrow cupboards. Small islands of work space around the sink and stove filled and cleared a dozen times a day.

My sisters and I slept just off the kitchen in one nine-by-nine room outfitted with a foldaway cot and a set of World War II army bunks. Two similar rooms crouched under the low eaves off the living room for my brothers and my parents. The girls' room shared a wall with another stamp-sized square that just fit a wringer washing machine, a claw-foot bathtub and the red iron pitcher pump where we got our household water.

In my grandparents' day, the term "running water" triggered a dozen witty definitions. Running water could refer to the pace a good wife set from well to house with a bucket in each hand, or the relative speed of the wildlife one found orbiting the bottom of those buckets. If shallow potholes and reservoirs were the source, water might run one morning, and scamper or dart or slither the next. Plumbing was another ripe topic. If the door worked on the outhouse, you had indoor facilities. The outdoor kind consisted of a tall sagebrush. We enjoyed one form of running water, in that one had to run the hand pump to get it, but it was a luxury compared with the bucket and barrel plumbing it replaced.

Anderson had modernized the house by burying a cement-lined cistern near the west wall and installing the hand pump. One slim pipe snaked through the wall over the tub and joined the pump. Another long swag of pipe connected the cistern to the well in one fifty-foot leap through the air. The artesian well was nearly a thousand feet deep, and the water that filled our cistern was softer than soapsuds and certified bug-free. It also carried enough sulfur and alkali to kill fish and plants. It reeked like a hot-water spa. Only fit for drinking, my father would say, finishing off a tall glass. Not always so. Anyone not raised on the stuff suffered cramps and diarrhea within an hour of drinking it.

Straight from the tap our water seldom made it past a visitor's nose, so very black coffee or murky gray lemonade were the seasonal offerings, and with these my father was insistently generous. A thick, rugged man, Dad was six feet tall and had hands like the paws on a grizzly bear. Just awkward enough in the kitchen to be endearing, he would lumber up from his chair and top off the coffee cups of unwitting hunters, salesmen and government officials every third sip or so. They, in an effort to be polite to their host, would ingest something akin to a triple dose of laxative at a kitchen table fifty miles from the nearest flush toilet. This was an unending source of amusement to my father.

Until I was seven years old, we drew water from the hand pump into pails and heated it on the stove for the weekly washing. On bath night the tub filled once and we children bathed in groups or by turns, the last one scrubbing quickly in the chilly gray residue of his siblings. Once filled, the old iron tub and sink drained by themselves—another relative luxury compared with the task of dipping it up and hauling it outside. Wastewater drained into a common pipe that shot out over a bank into a vile-smelling pothole behind the house, a private lagoon that flushed itself whenever the creeks ran. We dumped slops there, too. Coffee grounds, eggshells and kitchen waste heaved over the bank broke through an iridescent scum and sank out of sight, out of mind. The fireweed and cattails grew head-high in the driest year.

When the Rural Electrification Association (REA) strung electrical wires through southern Phillips County in the late fifties, the change was less dramatic than one might expect. Ours was one of the last areas in the nation to receive power, and by the time it arrived our community had long since become self-reliant where it mattered. In addition, for a farm or ranch to be connected to electricity required the expense of revamping existing home wiring and a pledge to use $45 worth of electricity each month. Many neighbors already relied on propane gas for cooking stoves and refrigeration. Wood and diesel fuel provided heat. Most had rigged up "light plants" for power, using windmill-driven or gasoline-fed generators to charge rows of wet-cell batteries lining a dirt basement beneath the house. A set of fifty-five glass storage batteries wired into the house provided enough 110-volt DC current to run lightbulbs and a few specially adapted appliances. The batteries that my parents inherited with the ranch were too old to hold a charge for long, and running the generator was a daily chore. In cold weather, the batteries could freeze unless they were fully charged. As a last resort, the old kerosene lamps and gasoline storm lanterns could be hauled out of the closet and pressed into service.

While the coming of electricity fell short of some night-to-day miracle in the south country, it did inspire a rash of indoor improvements and brought us within sight of the twentieth century. With electric pumps at the well, pressure tanks and hot-water heaters began to appear, which led to the advent of kitchen sinks and bathtubs connected to hot and cold water. Then septic tanks. And eventually toilets. For women, the largest single change occurred in the laundry chores. By 1960, electrical appliances were everywhere around us and the ranch wives still boiling shirts and cranking them through a hand wringer knew it. No one mourned the death of the scrub board, drying rack and flatiron less than the women who used them. Sheets that had once frozen dry on the clothesline could be hauled warm from the clothes dryer in January. Steam irons and sewing machines turned the drudgery of ironing and mending into a morning's work. As electrical appliances followed the power lines to our community, the old things found a new use. I remember flatirons acting as door-stops or used to weigh down the lid of the small coop where setting hens growled and sulked until the urge to brood passed. Tin washtubs held a summer's worth of geraniums or a week's stash of kindling. Come midnight, the dance crowds at the First Creek Community Hall ate sandwiches and cake washed down with gallons of coffee cooked up in an oblong copper wash boiler.

The coming of electricity made little impression on me, and of the issues surrounding its arrival, I recall only what affected me directly. For instance, I don't recall the exact moment we installed an indoor toilet, but I will never forget my unholy terror of the outhouse. I spent my young childhood the victim of an irrational, entirely impossible, yet firmly held belief that a mouse was going to run upside down, spiderlike, across my bare bottom as I sat there, feet dangling and unable to run. I don't know if this scenario had been suggested to me by a perverse sibling or if I invented it, but it needed little rein-forcement to bloom. Add to this an early and fairly generalized fear of the dark, and it's a wonder Mom managed to wean us off the potty chair at all. Margaret hated the chore of escorting the twins and me to the outhouse before bedtime. She would march us, coats over pajamas, down the path in the frigid winter dark, get us settled, then encourage us to hurry by clicking off the flashlight for a few seconds at a time, or by flicking the beam off into the bushes to highlight the beasts lurking there. We learned to hold our water like camels.

And I recall one day shortly after the power came, when I carefully latched the bathroom door and climbed up on a chair next to the old washing machine. The washer had two tubs, with a powerful wringer mounted between them. The wringer looked like two wide white rolling pins pressed tightly together, and it worked just like that, too. Shirts had to be fed through carefully so the wringer didn't pop off the buttons, and heavy items like towels and jeans were sent through more than once to squeeze all the water out. As a safety feature, a stop-bar ran along the bottom of the wringer, and when something got jammed up, a blow to the bar would pop the jaws of the wringer apart and stop them from turning.

I soon had the wringer running, and was mesmerized by the hum of the rollers and the splash and trickle of water. I fed dripping socks and washcloths in with my left hand and caught them with my right as they emerged from the rollers flat and damp-dry. I did this with a feeling of great maturity, for while I'd been allowed to feed socks and smaller items into the wringer before, I was not allowed to reach around the wringer as my mother did, and catch them. I was set to surprise her with my proficiency, when one of the socks stuck to the roller, as they sometimes did, going around and around instead of exiting the other side. When this happened to Mom, she loosened it with a flick of her fingers, and I reached to do the same, not thinking which side I was reaching toward, which side ate the socks, which side spit them out.

A Place of One's Own

The rollers caught my fingertips and steadily, mindlessly ate their way up my hand, squeezing my flesh flat as I hung back with all my strength, trying to pull free. Though I'd been shown how to use it, I never once thought to hit the stop-bar. And though I didn't think to call for help either, by the time the rollers were grinding past my wrist and up my arm I managed to produce a guttural squawk, the sort of noise that lifts the hair on a mother's neck two rooms away. The door seemed to explode before my eyes. The hook-and-eye latch flew apart, my mother charged through, and in one leap had hit the bar with the heel of her hand and dragged me back from the jaws of the wringer. While my pride suffered a devastating blow, my arm did not. Mom held me on her lap as I sniffled, and within a few minutes my poor flat, white arm had gotten back its blood and the feeling in its fingers, and was none the worse for wear.

The most profound changes brought by the electrical lines occurred outside the house, where darkness had always ended the workday and shop tools all came with handles instead of cords. Arc welders, power tools and air compressors made some repairs possible for the first time, and cut time and effort on the rest. Yard and shop lights extended the workday by allowing maintenance and repairs to be done after dark. Overhead lights in barns replaced the dangerous, fickle glow of lanterns on the straw for the predawn and after-dark rituals of milking and calving.

A more visceral change occurred as the community plugged in to the outside world. In one sense, we were simply catching up. Televisions and flush toilets, dial phones to replace the battery crank phones—every new gadget brought our lifestyles closer to those of our small-town neighbors. Modernization was touted as good business, a sign of progressive thinking, of success. But the exchange was more complex than the simple money-for-service contract offered by the REA. The old system implied a personal contract with nature, rather than an outside agency. Breakdowns affected one ranch only so long as it took one cursing rancher to climb the wind charger or tinker with the generator. All he needed was wind to turn the enormous fan blades of the chargers—this in a region blessed with four seasons of wind.

Wind was a fact of life. It swept from the slopes of the Rockies to the plains of Dakota without detour. It whipped down out of Canada in gusts and gales unhampered by mountains or trees. Wind blew for days on end, a relentless pushing at your back, a constant moan we listened around and shouted over without really hearing. Wind was dependable. Government agencies were not. With such a ready supply of one and such a chronic shortage of faith in the other, it seems odd now that the community changed over so quickly and completely. An entire community that had run for decades on muscle and wind fell silent now when the power lines went down. Nothing to be done but call in the outage and wait. Once wired in, there was no going back.

That the new electric power would prove unreliable was a given, for the poles were strung with salvaged World War II–era lines and the county line crew burdened with the upkeep of hundreds of miles of such line. Lightning searching for a target on the flat land more often than not found a power pole. Wind in combination with ice buildup or brittle cold snapped the old lines like dry spaghetti. Moisture wormed its way beneath the cracked insulation, shorted out connections. As a rule, the same weather that put the power down kept the repair crews away, our roads a grim stretch of mud or snow.

As a child I learned practical rules about electricity. One does not begin a baking project in a thunderstorm with an

Gorilla

© 1999 San Diego Zoo

#622

electric cookstove. When a lightning strike makes the phone jangle, don't answer. When black clouds boil over the horizon, unplug the television and fill the bathtub or a few buckets with water. No one depended on electricity for heat, and no one threw away the lanterns or tore down the outhouse when it arrived. For decades after real electricity came to the community the wind chargers remained in place, locked solid with rust or fanning loosely from one breeze to the next. Every farm kid I knew was forbidden to climb the wind charger, and the iron ladders leading up to the narrow platform on top always had the first section covered or removed to keep us off. We all got pretty good at it. Perhaps they were left in place because they filled a need in that relatively treeless landscape, some vertical element to balance the flat reach of prairie. More likely the huge angle-iron A-frames remained like crossed arms, waiting for the newfangled electricity to fail for good. Call it practicality or pessimism, it was common sense to expect the worst. No rancher made his reputation on how he handled good fortune. It took a few well-handled disasters to earn respect. There were usually enough to go around.

Anderson boasted of never losing a stalk of wheat to hail in all his years of farming that piece of prairie, but a creative combination of drought, grasshoppers and hail ravaged four of the first six crops my father planted. Dad picked up what work he could, leaving his own place to run a digger for the REA as the power poles marched south and the lines went up. A picture of the twins and me taken in '57 or '58 tells the story of those early years more frankly than any story told around the coffeepot. The three of us are posed on the front step of the house, a row of shapeless shirts and hand-me-down, hold-me-up pants clipped to suspenders. Our faces are clean, our hair clipped short and neatly combed. I am leaning forward, my shoulders hunched as if I am bashful or perhaps suspicious of this novelty of picture taking, my bare feet planted in the packed dirt of the dooryard. The twins face the camera intently, as though startled by the command to smile yet caught before they could fully obey. Gary sits solidly, the waist of his trousers nearly touching his armpits, the toes of his Buster Browns worn white. Gail's feet peek through gaps in her shoes where the soles have separated from the uppers. A stranger guessing the date of the photo would likely place it in the Great Depression rather than some thirty years later.

Around the time this picture was taken, there had been the promise of a good year, one golden summer when the wheat stood high and ripe under clear skies, an August day my father whistled to the roar of the combine as he greased gears. His own crop hovered on the brink of ripeness, not quite ready, and this morning found him a few miles from home working in a neighbor's field. Nearly done with the maintenance chores, he was checking the tension of the belts that snaked along the pulleys when his right hand caught and fed itself to the steel. For a second, two seconds, the sharp groove of the pulley spun like a buzz saw, slicing through the web between thumb and forefinger, grinding through bone and gristle. Halfway through the palm it spit him out. Just like that, harvest was over.

Dad braced his good hand against the side of the combine and drew the other against his stomach, taking in with a sort of numb detachment the rooster tail of blood and flesh spraypainted on gray galvanized metal. So fast. So hard to believe the look of this strong hand, the first two fingers severed deep behind the big knuckle, half a fist hanging limp across the other half. There was no thinking beyond the immediate need to remain upright, staggering weak-kneed around a machine he had no way of driving one-handed—not in the days of clutch and shift, stiff manual steering, gates to open and close—until he reached the front where he could shut it down.

It was the absence of noise that would save him, a hired hand pausing in the midst of an errand, alerted by the silence as he parked within sight of the field. The man stepped out of his rig and stopped to study the distant combine that stood silent when it should have been twice around the field, and in the miracle of that clear, windless morning he heard my father shout.

On that perfect harvest day, my parents drove fifty miles to the hospital in Malta. There, the doctor shook his head and administered morphine, while Mom called the local airport, one dirt strip at the edge of town. A small plane hauled my father to a medical center in Billings, where surgeons worked the puzzle of frayed nerves and tendons, cutting away mangled callus and muscle, arranging what was left into something near normal—a hand that would work for him some day, some year. Some other harvest.

I rely on Margaret's memory of those times, a child who came to my parents' union as an observer, old enough to remember the guided tour Anderson and his wife led through the house before the sale was complete, her excitement quashed by stern looks, clandestine signals, and when that didn't work, harsh words. *Will this be my room? Is this where I will sleep?* Our memories are separated by the eight years' difference in age, my own recall turning solid just as she left home, a shy, frail-looking child with thick glasses set adrift in Malta High School at age twelve, the sister who came home a visitor on weekends and vacations. She graduated from high school at sixteen, and then was off to college, working her summers away from home. Where our memories overlap, hers are balanced by the early years. She remembers parents I never knew—a mother whose dark eyes snapped with humor and play, girlish in her love for the dashing cowboy who wore his youth like a new hat, cocked over one ear, rakish and reckless. In the years to come, I knew that hat settled low over his eyes, sweat stains wicked up from the band like the layers of sunset, darkest at the brim, slowly bleeding out toward the crown. I knew the flash of my mother's eyes as a warning, like a flicker of lightning followed by the snap of fingers, a voice grown harsh and ragged as the skin on her hands. *Don't push me another single step,* those eyes are saying, but there are four of us clamoring for one lap, and we push.

Although the luxuries of indoor plumbing and electricity improved our standard of living in one sense, it was a standard that required cash to maintain. In the years that followed, my parents' grim, dark-to-dark pace barely covered the essentials. A typical workday left my mother little patience for the self-centered inefficiencies of children, since every careless spill, torn shirt or clutter of toys produced by four preschoolers in a cramped house created yet another chore, another interruption, another mess.

Some things were simply not allowed, and these included sassing an adult, making careless mistakes or questioning a direct order. To a child, these rules boiled down to "shut up, pay attention and do what you're told"; insofar as it showed on the exterior, we complied more frequently than not. Any lapse in judgment was dealt a swift flurry of open-handed slaps, twisted ears and the dreaded "shaking of sense" into the empty head, the hair being the most common handle for this wake-up call. It got to be a joke in later years when a parent eating dinner might suddenly raise a hand to bat at a fly, then stare in amazement at the answering wave along the table, the four of us ducking sideways with jet precision, the whole of it so automatic we never stopped chewing.

Although my memories are real, my interpretation of them is less trustworthy. Mine is a child's view of the walk to the woodpile, the four of us sent to select our own sticks, coming back to form a queue by age, oldest first, in front of my father's chair. The interrogation is brief. Sometimes the guilty child steps forward, sparing the others. More often we deny in one voice, refusing to give up what we know. We are whipped by turns, then, and threatened with another round if we cry too long or too loudly. My memories retain the vivid details of the second in line, her dread that the stick she's chosen is too small and will lead to more or harder blows; the agony of volunteering her frozen body across the knees, knowing it's worse to wait, unthinkable to resist; the humiliation of the worst-case scenario, the bare-butt spanking reserved for felony offense. What have we done? What rules flung aside, how many eggs smashed against the chicken house wall, barn windows broken with dirt clods or BB guns aimed at blackbirds? That part is lost to me. I remember feeling anger so intense it chilled me for days, but I don't recall a bad deed or a second of remorse. That is the memory of a child.

The less time our parents had to spend, the harder we fought for it, inevitably losing out to the demands of seasons and cycles. We turned on each other with explosions of rage I could never imagine in my own children—arguments over shares, turns or rules going silent in a frenzy of wild blows. By our middle years we had reached an uneasy truce, drawn together less by a sudden outpouring of sibling love than a set of pack rules. We stuck together to elude capture and avoid punishment, forming alliances based on mutual culpability, *you don't tell on me, I won't tell on you* pacts that came to include the unspoken clause *no matter what.* As we grew old enough to attend school, join 4-H and ride horseback cross-country to visit cousins, we discovered this sort of understanding to be universal among preadolescents. Our no-tell policy included preventative measures, such as posting lookouts to hang around the adults and keep track of their wandering while the rest of us puffed Pall Mall cigarettes and played strip poker in the loft of the horse barn—a thorny proposition if one is losing. Out of sight of authority, those neighborhood children who chose to do so experimented with impunity. We built campfires, made moonshine out of vanilla extract, aftershave and homemade wine, swapped sexual stories, rumors and show-me games and traded new dirty words and new combinations of old dirty words. We read and reread the porno paperbacks, skin magazines and *True Confessions* the luckier kids purloined from hired men and older siblings, then passed them down the line until the pages were soft and gray with wear.

Oddly, our strict upbringing bore the sweetest fruit outside the family. In public we were neat, clean, well behaved and polite to adults, and were rewarded when they laughed at our antics, told us we were full of the devil and treated us with kindness. Teachers liked us. In a swarm of kids at a ball game or a dance at the community hall, we would have stayed in the car rather than act like one of the babies who clung to their mothers' arms all night, but we also knew better than to join the undisciplined few who raced from one end of the room to the other, chasing and shoving and screeching. My mother had a hard job to sit on her hands in the presence of ill-mannered children, and she was not above cornering the whole lot of them if their parents remained complacent.

If I tell these stories now, I do so because so much of what I learned circles back and is lost in the way those lessons were taught, how I learned what I thought I knew until I had kids of my own. *Shut up, pay attention, do what you're told.* I was eighteen when I walked down the aisle on my father's arm. The groom was almost thirty, a man of simple tastes and few passions, staunch honor and little experience. I joined him at the altar, bristling with independence yet eager to please, desperate for attention yet filled with the fierce energy born of old anger—a riddle behind my homemade veil. From my parents to the unwitting hands of my husband I passed the terrible power of judgment and reward, the absolute authority I connected with love.

Salvage

The region we call the Hi-Line stretches the length of northern Montana from the foothills of the Rocky Mountains to the North Dakota border. Winter along the Hi-Line is all about wind, a cycle of wind. Cold wind brings the snow, whips it into place; warm chinook winds crust the snow, anchoring it until spring thaw. Between chinooks, wind levels the landscape, sweeping ridges bare, filling the low spots until creek beds and long, forked drainages seem to rise, exposed like a network of white veins against the wind-stripped hills. Ground blizzards shut down travel more often than fresh snow, dry winter storms, all variations on a theme: clear, cold nights with snow blowing knee-high, like a low fog streaming over the ground; cloudy days when the horizon disappears and wind pours sky and earth together into one seamless bowl; bright days you go blind trying to find the shadow-white of tire tracks under the continuous slither and glitter of moving white. In chinook country there is no snowpack. Instead, we talk about snow "on the level," a way of imagining a few inches spread out to an even depth. Only the drifts are measured in feet.

Winter mornings of my childhood take on a sameness in

my memory, every day a repetition of chores done the day before. The livestock waited, as hungry on Christmas as they were on everyday mornings, and our lives revolved around the responsibility of them. Every evening we had bum calves to feed, water and bed, a milk cow to be tended and milked, water tanks wanting cleared of ice and hay bunks pitched full for the yearling heifers in the feedlot, and two or three dozen chickens to separate from their eggs. As we children were broken in to the evening chores, our supper table took on the farm kid's version of *think of all the starving kids in China.* Fried round steak and gravy, boiled potatoes and home-canned green beans piled on my plate, I would lift my fork and center the first mouthful.

"Did you take care of the chickens?" my mother would ask, pointed in her tone, for she would know whether I had trailed through the kitchen for the pail of warm water. Like all our outbuildings, our chicken house was neither heated nor insulated, and in winter only warm water would stay liquid long enough for each hen to drink. The few times I had to admit I hadn't done chores were enough to cure me. How could I fill my face while the chickens that depended on me went to roost empty, trapped inside, unable to fend for themselves? "No, finish your supper first," Mom would say as I clambered up from the table, and I would have to settle back and clean my plate, chewing every bite, finishing my milk, asking to be excused, her silence a reproach, an accusation. No excuse covered the sin, no apology wiped it away. It was a small, small person who bellied up to the table while his livestock stood hungry, and in that lesson we were offered the best of role models.

I suppose there were ranchers who slept in on Sunday mornings after a night in town, or took winter vacations and let their cattle make do for a few days, but my father wasn't one of them. Every morning after barn chores Dad drove to the hay yard adjoining the winter pasture and pulled the pitchfork from its seat deep in the side of a stack. First cutting, second cutting, in rare wet years a third crop of alfalfa grew in the meadows along the creek, each fragrant forkful cut, raked and stacked by his own hand. Standing knee-deep in a stack, he pitched the wooden hayrack full, stabbed the fork into the mound and jumped down to hitch the tongue of the rack to the pickup. Some of the cattle bedded down on the feed ground, and these rose and stretched as the pickup pulled toward them. Others broke into a lumbering trot, bawling in chorus as the honk of the pickup horn called them in from the shelter of coulees. A hundred-yard path cut across the prairie north to south, the snow trampled flat and hard, colored with the residue of yesterday's hay, and here Dad stopped, rolling down the window as the cows crowded around him.

The first times I beat out my older brother as feed assistant, I was small enough to have to kneel on the seat to steer the pickup across the frozen ground, young enough to believe my father talked to his cows in their own language. *Come boss, comeboss, c'mbaaws*, his call melted into syllables bawled out the open window, and the cows answered in long, urgent drones, tipping up their chins and lofting streams of smoke into the bitter air. Planting the stick shift in compound gear, he would ease the clutch and push against their milling bodies to get the door open, jumping out as the pickup began to crawl forward.

Days we had school, the pickup made its own way across the feed ground, Dad keeping one eye on its direction as he pitched a trail of hay. The first forkfuls lit on the backs of the greediest cows, but as the feed stretched out along the path, the animals lined out alongside, and at the end it came out even—a thick line of green with red cattle, head-down on either side, a Christmas ribbon unfurled on a field of brilliant white. Swinging down from the rack, Dad trotted to catch the pickup, reaching out to grab the door handle and jump into the cab, settling behind the wheel in a gust of cold air, a flurry of fine chaff. He lingered after feeding, driving back slowly along the row of broad backs, stabbing the air with two fingers, lips moving silently as he counted the tally, squinting against the snow glare for signs of lameness, hocks cut on the sharp-crusted snow, a joint sprained in a slide on the ice. He judged health by their eagerness to shoulder and shove together, stopping to study any cow that held herself apart.

It's a luxury of the small rancher to look at a herd of uniform white-faced Herefords and see individuals, to know the old swing-bag cow from the Murphy heifer, or one 1,200-pound animal as the daughter of another, mother of a third. My father's cattle were not pets, but he knew them all, fifty big Hereford cows, the bulk of them descended from his father's herd. Each fall they lined up along the fence at the first sign of cold weather, bawling to be let into the winter pasture. "Spoiled old bitches," he'd grumble as we opened the gate and drove them in, all of them waddling fat, one calf weaned from their side that fall, another growing large in their bellies. It was good business to keep the cattle fed up, healthy, he would say, lest anyone accuse him of sentimentality. A person takes care of what's his. But his cows were far more than property, his connection to them more complex than the desire for heavy steer calves to sell and fine-quality heifers to keep. Their contentment was a measure of his own, their well-being a source of pride. Cattle that wore his brand spent their summers on good grass, their winters wallowing in hay, nursed their calves with sun rippling over sleek hides. They grazed fence lines along the county road, lifting their heads to gaze after passing cars, visible as any finely tended field.

The winter I was ten I would see my father as beaten as he ever got, though my recognition is one of hindsight. Children tend to observe catastrophe at their own level, maintaining a sort of cheerful indifference to those things outside their control. The blizzard of 1964 and its aftermath were adult problems, ones I assumed my parents were qualified to handle. For my part, the hard-packed drifts made great sledding. The snow could be chopped into blocks to make igloos, banks could be tunneled into or skated upon as the mood struck me. Plugged roads made school attendance an every-morning judgment call, and I went to bed each night in the thrill of uncertainty.

There was a lot of talk about death that winter, a lot of coming and going between neighbors as the community shoveled out and tried to piece together what was left. Though both were of vital interest to me, stories of birth and death had always differed in the telling. Birth happened, and whatever initiated the event was never discussed. Death, on the other hand, was caused. When animals died out of turn, the stories focused on exploring the reasons for it and assigning blame, either human error or that of the victim. As a cause of death, stupidity beat out old age by a wide margin. That winter the stories had a new twist—death just happened. "Sonofabitch just tipped over and died," a note of wonder leveling the voice, leaving the rest hanging in midair. By the end of January, birth and death ran together in a new combination as sick cows aborted, emptying their wombs months early. Calves born dead. In the telling, these births took on a nasty sound, both in the words used and in the bitter tone that spoke of betrayal:

Salvage

"That old red-necked cow sloughed her calf," they would say, or "She slunk a set of twins the size of jackrabbits."

That spring as the weather faired, Gail, Gary and I played around a deep trench gouged into the prairie a quarter mile from the house. We made games around the bloating carcasses it held, daring each other to cut pieces away with our jackknives, holding our breath against the sweetish stench as we jumped from one set of ribs to another, playing hopscotch on the bodies of half my father's cattle. We shivered with naughtiness, dancing on the dead. Some we recognized. The new Angus bull, Bellboy, was in there, and Inky, our milk cow. The rest were anonymous—at one end a dozen feeder calves dead of coccidiosis, the bloody scours, their eyes sunk deep in their skulls from the fever and dehydration, at the other, a layer of range cows, bigger animals that seemed sealed in death, eyes and mouths clamped tight.

Their loss was of passing interest to me, an event too large to grasp, perhaps, or simply dismissed because cows were not my job. My memories would have faded with spring thaw but for the community who got past the winter and kept the stories alive until children grew into them. They come down to me whole, stories of a blizzard that took the measure of any man, that became the measure of all storms to come.

December 14, 1964. Jackrabbits gather nervously at the edge of the feed ground, the first line moving in low to the ground, those behind rocking up on their hindquarters, ears flipping to the bedded cows and away, registering the stillness. A bad night for rabbits, twenty below zero under a sharp moon, every movement a shadow, every noise brittle, explosive. A good night for owls. But it's the flash of a spotlight the rabbits fear more than the shadow of silent flight. Their bodies are worth a quarter, and the men come hunting most every night. Every rancher has his pile of jackrabbits, his mountain of mad money, stashed in an outbuilding, frozen whole. Every couple of weeks, buyers arrive in Malta, collect the stiff corpses by the semi truckload, and sell them to mink farms.

Fifty Hereford cows and two bulls doze in the waste of morning feed, and the rabbits work around them, pulling alfalfa stems from the packed snow with nervous jerks, noses working the sharp air as they chew. The atmospheric pressure has fallen rapidly since dark. Strung tight, they scour the trampled ground, erupting in exaggerated leaps at the chalky crunch of snow under a cow's hoof. They've come on trails, hundreds of rabbits single file, and they leave the same way, following the paths beaten by cows coming to water, by pickups checking on cows. Off the trails, they leave body prints in the loose powder, no crust to support their weight. Scattering out of sight of the buildings, they settle in the shelter of cutbanks, under willows along the creek, in snow domes roofed by the spread of tall sagebrush, digging into the drifts and turning to face south. It's twenty-five below zero now and quiet, but something is coming. They can smell it.

Midnight turns with a sigh. A faint breeze eddies along the ruts of the county road, softening the channels cut by four-wheel-drives. More than a foot has fallen since Thanksgiving, and it lies in loose gathers across the fields, restless where the breeze touches it. Slack drifts taper across the grade, deepest where the road crosses a coulee. Where the lane is plugged, drifted straight across, it's been cleared by hand, a mother or a father with scoop shovel and a pickup load of kids heading for school. The snow shovels like sand or wheat, spilling off the sides of the scoop as it's tossed toward the ditch. The county plows come by every few days, kicking through drifts, shoving it all to one side, to the south or east, so the track will fill more slowly. Fifty miles west, a chinook has cleared the prairie at the base of the Little Rocky Mountains, but here the forecast remains cold, the warm spell overdue, and the ranchers grumble and shovel.

Past midnight, lights wink out to the northwest and the line spreads toward the moon, half the sky gone smooth as wet slate, half still rough with the jitter of starlight. The wind picks up, strong enough to scalp drifts and chase snow across the flats. Where the land pitches rough, snow streams flat off the ridge tops like foam spraying from whitecaps. On the lee side of the cutbanks, jackrabbits flatten their ears as snow fans over their bodies. The claws on their front feet are sharp enough to dig roots from dry sod. Those with full bellies may survive. But the prairie birds, the ring-necked pheasants and sage hens, dug their graves at dusk, burrowing under blankets of snow, insulated and invisible as the wind rises around them.

Within hours an inner alarm clock will rouse the birds, and they will shift and push against the solid roof overhead. Some will peck ineffectually at the snow until they tire, until they sleep from suffocation or starvation. Months later they surface untouched, head still tucked under a wing. The strongest die quickly, at daybreak. These manage to crack their sealed coffin like an eggshell and burst upward into the jaws of the storm. They drop within seconds, gaping, the air too thick to pull through the slim nares at the top of their beaks, too cold to breathe directly into the lungs for very long. These will be found first, in the top layers of the drifts, necks outstretched, wings spread as if for balance, or flight.

The big animals have nowhere to hide. The largest population of mule deer winter in the Missouri River Breaks, browsing where scrub pine and juniper mute the worst of the wind, but the pronghorn antelope live by their eyes. Winter and summer, they stick to the bench land where they can see what's coming, sheltered by distance rather than trees. This night, they gather in groups of twenty or thirty, pressing into draws and coulees. They are toughened to the cold, plush with winter hair, and still they stamp and shift against the bite. Well before dawn, the snow billows far over their heads, clogging the air, chilling their blood. They begin to move with the wind, walking to stay warm. The late fawns, a few wet does drawn thin from a summer of nursing, grow stiff and stop before morning, but the rest keep going, blinded by snow, pushed by the wind. They walk like machines, heads lowered to breathe in the shelter of their own bodies, slow and steady, a night and a day, another night. There's nothing to eat. Wind-packed drifts pave the prairie, sealing the grass like concrete. Where ramps of snow bridge the fences, they step over the wire, walking south. Hundreds cross the Missouri River on the ice forty or fifty miles from where they started, arriving at the edge of the storm front gaunt and hollow-eyed.

By two in the morning, the stars are gone, whether blotted by clouds or blowing snow there's no telling. On the feed ground, cows begin to rise, silent and miserable. They are range animals, bred for stamina, reared on the unsheltered prairie, and they weather storms on herd instinct. Guarded by layers of fat, thick hide, a dense coat of winter hair, they close ranks, shoulder to shoulder and turn tail to the wind. Those in the center of the herd stand quietly, heads lowered, surrounded by heat. Snow softens and refreezes in layers on their exposed backs, but inside where the bodies touch, they are warm. The outside ring is less content. Snow lodges under hair, sticks to the skin and builds outward. They clamp their tails and hump their backs against the sting of it until something gives, and they can push toward the shelter inside, stirring the group like a slow spoon. Warm flanks shoved to the outside turn white; cold ones entering the circle of condensed breath collect frost like magnets in a pile of metal shavings.

As the weather worsens, the cattle endure it as best they can, butts to the wind, aiming south like the arrow on a weather vane. With every change of the rear guard, the group shifts a few feet forward, away from the minimal windbreak of the stackyard, toward the open prairie. Icicles dangle from the guard hairs on their chins and bellies, from eyelash and ear fringe. A mile to the east antelope drift by on a twenty-mile wind, coated white, invisible but for the dark slits of their eyes. The air chill is some seventy degrees below zero, already cold enough to focus every creature, domestic or wild, on survival. At three, the blizzard hits like a freight train.

Thirty years after the storm I quiz my father about the wind, what does he guess? Forty, fifty miles an hour? Sixty, seventy? "Sixty," he says, "seventy." Shrugging. No one knows how hard the wind blew. Temperatures were a fact, measurable, recordable, though they varied a few degrees from ranch to ranch. Some reported twenty-seven below zero that first morning, others insist it was colder, thirty or thirty-five below. But the wind was a guess. They could only compare it to other winds, gales that hit with summer storms, times someone lost the roof off a shed or watched windrows of green hay roll like cigars across the meadow. All my father knows for sure is he never saw anything like it in winter.

I study the almanac open between us on the kitchen table.

"Wind chill charts stop at forty-five miles per hour. Says here anything stronger than that doesn't change the temperature much."

That draws a snort. He tips his head sideways, stubborn, thinking on it. "Matters if you're in it," he says finally. But I'm already testing my meager math skills, looking for a conservative estimate—let's say, thirty below zero with a forty-five-mile-per-hour wind. "That makes it one hundred sixteen degrees below zero," I say quietly, mentally refiguring the numbers: *minus 116?*

He's looking at his hands while I figure out loud, fingers as big around as a baby's wrist, opening and closing a fist as if limbering it up. "Hunerd n' sixteen," he muses. "Hell, it had to be at least that. Had to be." He studies at it a second, clenching, releasing, clenching, then shoves back in his chair, ready to get up and do something.

When it hit, the house bent and shrieked, a sound like nails pulled from damp wood. In the bedroom on the northwest corner of the house, my father woke, his breath visible in the air over his head. Cold enough to freeze pipes. He turned on the light long enough to find his jeans and socks. The window on the north wall rattled steadily, the curtains trembling, panes plastered with snow. The stove in the living room ran on fuel oil, #2 diesel, but there were no thermostats to kick on when the temperature dropped. In the dark, he made his way to the kitchen to hit the overhead light switch, then back to the oil heater. He turned the dial to "high" and pawed the litter of mittens and boots to one side. High meant cherry-red. The stove in the kitchen ran on cottonwood, a couple of logs ready on the floor beside it, a couple of days' worth stacked in the porch. He fed fires, turned on faucets, opened bedroom doors, made the necessary rounds with tense efficiency. The noise seemed impossible. Stovepipes hummed, beams creaked, snow blasted against the north windows like birdshot. Over-riding it all was the wind, an urgent moaning under the eaves that rose in sustained shrieks, like a cat fight.

He turned off the light, leaned over the cookstove and rested a hand against the kitchen window, trying to see move-ment in the wall of solid gray outside. Was the house drifted under? The frigid draft leaking through the frame said not, but there was no light, no shape of trees by the house, no way to judge the speed of the blowing snow. The illusion was one of stillness, a dark blanket held up to the glass. The window looked south, toward the feed ground, the stackyard. He stood a moment with the sound of the storm settling in his gut, try-ing to imagine his cows huddled against the fence, sheltered by the long row of haystacks. He might get them into the lot by the barn. He reached for the coffeepot, lifted the basket of used grounds, then stopped and leaned against the stove again. The wind was all wrong, north and west. The cattle were gone. He found his way back to bed in the dark. My mother's voice lifted in a question, and he answered her, "tougher than hell out there." He lay back, listening to the roar. Nothing he could do until daylight.

As what passed for dawn approached, only the prairie birds and children slept on unaware of the storm. Inside our house nine people curled closer to bedmates, drawing quilts over their noses against the chill. The boys had camped out on the living room floor, their bed given over to Granddad, our mother's father. Two neighbor girls were crowded into the cot-sized bunk beds with Gail and me, stranded at our house since school let out the day before. Their mom had buried her pickup in a drift trying to get them and had to dig out and turn back.

My parents rose early, before true light. The smells of bacon and coffee and backdraft smoke drifted through the house, sharpened by the nip of frost. Cold radiated from the bedrooms where the outside walls sandwiched a thin insulation of tar paper, old newspapers and Depression-era *Saturday Evening Posts*, and the household gathered as it woke, driven toward the roar of the woodstove. Outside the windows the air turned white as the sun rose, lighter but no less dense, no quieter. Breakfast occurred in shifts as places cleared at the table, adults tense, preoccupied, children hushed with excitement. As we planned our unexpected vacation from school, Dad dressed for morning chores in layers of long johns, coveralls, lined buckskin mitts, his cap pulled low over his eyes, earflaps secured by a wool scarf. Another scarf covered the back of his neck, a third wrapped the bottom of his face. He tucked his coveralls into the tops of his overshoes and buckled them down, finishing as Mom filled the milk pail with hot water for the chickens.

The barn lay a hundred yards south of the house, the low, red granary and chicken house a bit west of there, all of it lost in blowing snow. Stepping away from the porch, Dad aimed east for the yard gate, and then south, guided by the built-in compass of a man who has walked the same path at least twice a day for ten years. A big man, over six feet tall, over two hundred pounds centered in his chest and shoulders, and still it was difficult to stay grounded. The wind cut through the back of his coat as he braced against the storm and fought to keep his feet in the unfamiliar sea of hard drifts, digging in with his heels at every step.

The chickens met the cold by roosting with their feet drawn up, their feathers fluffed like chickadees. Dad fed them, poured water in their bucket. He left the eggs in one nest, their shells split lengthwise, the frozen whites bulging through like scar tissue. The milk cow, a thin-skinned Guernsey/Angus cross, could stay in the barn until the storm let up, he decided. The lack of water wouldn't kill her for one day. She was almost dry anyway, set to calve in March. The feeder calves would be huddled in the open-faced shed, safer there than if he tried to lure them out for grain. He saw no sign of the range cows. He could do no more.

Coming home meant walking into the storm, and within minutes his compass failed in the face of the wind. Eyes slitted against the stab of ice crystals, he breathed in shallow grunts, his airway clamping down as it would for a draft of pure ammonia. He couldn't get enough air. Every few yards, he swung his back to the blizzard and stopped to catch his breath, then turned into it again, walking blind for what seemed like too long. He corrected to the right and back to the left, trying to find northwest by feel, knowing he might have passed arm's length from the yard fence without seeing it. Sweat chilled on his ribs. A few more minutes and he would let the wind carry him south again. The windbreak or corrals would stop him and guide him back to the barn.

As he blundered left a last time, a single strand of No. 9 wire caught him across the chest and sprang him back in his tracks. He'd stumbled into the clothesline. He was halfway home. Keeping the wire in his left mitt, he bent his head into the wind and followed it until the end of the old house trailer, our bunkhouse, loomed out of white air in front of him. From there, another giant step west to the yard fence, the woven wire buried halfway to the top. Downwind from the house, he stopped a last time to strain air through a cupped mitten, then walked toward the light in the kitchen window.

Mom took the pail from his hand and set it hissing on the

woodstove to thaw out. The milk had slopped up and stuck to the sides, coating the inside with a thick rime, white ice on stainless steel. Above the scarf, Dad's face had turned the same blue-gray shade. The headgear had frozen together and came off in one piece. Under the scarf, the skin had stiffened in deep furrows that reddened quickly in the heat of the kitchen. I watched him as he thawed out, ice dripping from lashes and brows, his lips limbering to sip coffee. But his cheeks stayed rigid for a long time, stuck in a grimace or a scream. Over the course of the afternoon, the welts softened into frown lines as he passed from window to window, stepping around the card table where Granddad tried to keep us settled to a game of pinochle. They reappeared as he bared his teeth and squinted through the glass into the storm. We stayed out of his way.

Mom rattled pots and peeled potatoes, working at the logistics of three meals, nine mouths, descending with swift justice whenever our quarrels overrode the drone of the wind. Cramped up in the living room to stay warm, we six children grew quickly tired of cards, tired of board games, tired of each other. As a last resort, she hauled boxes of ornaments from their hiding spot and let us squabble over decorating the Christmas tree we'd hauled from the Breaks over the weekend. When the water pipes froze in the middle of the day, Dad grabbed the torch and headed for the basement like a man bent on tunneling out of prison.

That evening, he kept to his place at the table, drinking more coffee, feeding the woodstove, while Mom worked after supper. Their voices circled the kitchen, undercurrents of worry. The cattle were now more than twenty-four hours from their last full stomach, their last drink of water. They were heading into their second night of trying to breathe in the god-awful wind, their metabolism kicked into full gear, burning on high like the fuel-oil stove. When the tanks ran dry, then what? My parents knew.

In the years that followed, the ranchers in the path of the blizzard endured the second-guessing of those who were not, those on the edge of the storm, those favored by the early chinook. Where the snow had melted off, the wind and cold were fierce, but visibility remained good enough to see where you were going. The ones who weathered that version of the storm still insist my father and his neighbors might have tried riding out and bringing the cattle in. Why didn't they haul hay to them, or cut the fences to keep them moving like the antelope, keep the blood circulating? Half question, half accusation. The wound of them shows on my father's face, his defense arranging itself quietly across his features. The ferocity of the storm defies description, beggars the imagination of those who were not there. A part of him still wonders if he might have done something, the part that refuses to admit helplessness, refuses to be beaten. The rest of him sags with the burden of reality. It was just flat impossible.

The wind battered through the afternoon and into the night, and we rose the second morning nearly immune to it, voices pitched a notch louder to be heard over the steady scream. Midmorning, the air brightened and the gray shadow of cottonwood trunks appeared outside the kitchen window, then the fence posts further out. By noon, we could see the blurred outlines of the barn and outbuildings. Our voices rang loud in our own ears. In another hour the wind lifted and was gone like a curtain rising on an empty stage. Outside, the temperature held at a crystal thirty-five degrees below zero.

Nothing moved in the silence. Nothing showed above the hazy peaks of snow, no horizon appeared where the transformed landscape met the sky under a white December sun.

Dad organized with the urgency of someone held down too long. The shop door, a wide steel panel hung on rollers, had to be shoveled free to get the four-wheel-drive pickup. He picked his way around the worst of it getting to the stackyard for hay, but where the gates had plugged bumper-deep, he hacked the drifts with a spade, breaking the solid pack into chunks he could lift to one side with the bigger scoop shovel. The hay-stacks had made a perfect snow fence, capturing ten feet of snow on the downwind side, so he shoveled and floundered his way to the upwind side. The pitchfork crunched into the stack. In later years he would have a tractor with a hydraulic grapple fork, and perhaps those huge steel jaws could have taken a bite from the north side of the stack. But the wind had pounded snow so deeply into the hay and frozen it so solidly that one man heaving at a pitchfork could not free a wisp of it. It would take all day to shovel in from the drifted side. Climbing a stack of small square bales, he wrenched a few free and loosed them like toboggans down the steep slope toward the pickup.

Sound carries for miles in still air. He stood atop the stack and looked south, calling his cows, listening for the answering bawl. Silence snapped shut behind his voice. The winter pasture is relatively small, half a mile wide and a mile long, really more of a holding pasture than a grazing pasture, but rolling hills hide the south half from view. The county road borders the east fence line, and from the stack he could see the darker stripe of the raised grade, blown clear in some spots, covered in others.

Mom and twelve-year-old Kenny were bundled and waiting

when he pulled up at the house, and they struck off for the county lane. Low drifts held the weight of the pickup; the deep ones tapering toward the ditch could be avoided. Within minutes they spotted the first of them, four cows pressed against the east fence, just across the ditch. All four were down and drifted over, two dead and frozen stiff, the other two only half dead, unable to rise. They grabbed shovels to scoop the snowpack away from their heads, broke a bale and tucked squares of hay within reach, temporary measures. A minute later, they piled back in the pickup, fueled by a new sense of urgency.

Topping a low rise, the pickup slowed as the herd came into view. The cab was silent except for the warm blast of the defroster against the windshield. The fence corner was drifted full. One cow hung dead near the corner post, her hind legs twisted in the brace wires where she had walked up a drift and fallen through over the fence line. A few had made it out, pushing forward and stepping over the bodies of cows that had fallen and been buried against the wire. Some stood belly-deep in the ditch, others on the road. One had floundered on across, walking with the wind until her front feet slipped through the grate of a cattle guard. She had frozen standing up, still heading southeast. Forty head were still alive, the bulk of them gathered in the vee of the fence corner.

Dad turned the pickup around so it faced toward home and stepped out, his face flat and unreadable. Leaning back in to grab the fencing pliers from behind the seat, he started across the ditch, walking easily over the drifts. At the fence, he cut top wires and dug under the snow to get the rest, coiling the loose ends like a lariat and hanging them on the posts, out of the way. He needed a gate to get them to the road where they could follow the pickup home, a longer route, but faster than breaking trail across the dunes. At the sound of the engine revving, the horn blast, the cattle sheltered by the road shifted slowly, testing their strength against the drifts. Those in the pasture stood like a wedge of plaster statues, still posed as the storm had left them, heads low, backs humped, tails to the wind.

Snow had frozen a crust across each back, down each side, smoothing away evidence of the dark hair beneath. Pounds of ice sheathed their heads and hung in cones from their noses to the ground, breath grown solid in the bitter cold. What scant air they could draw whistled and puffed from slim vent holes half a foot from the tips of their noses. It was the only noise the cows made as Dad walked among them, struggling to find his own, some feature he recognized under the white cast. They stood motionless, though his steps creaked and squawked against the snow inches from their lowered heads. Eyes sealed tight under an inch of milky ice, they waited, blind and dumb, rigid with shock.

There was, he would say later, nothing to be done but what they did, an act both vicious and loving, desperate and calm. Pain, their pain, his pain, had reached the cold plateau that allows no more. The cattle couldn't hurt any worse. He could no longer do nothing. Raising the pliers in a wide arc, he swung them flat across a cow's face, shattering the ice that sealed her eyes, again across the bridge of her nose. Now there was motion, noise, as the animals fought to escape the crack of steel against their heads, grunting as their nostrils broke free and air rushed into their lungs. Mom stepped across the ditch where the fence was opened, a piece of board she had wrenched from the pickup bed clenched in both hands. Together they moved through the herd, the forty head of cows and both bulls still alive, and beat away the ice that was killing them, battering against the shields until the eyes jarred open, and again, until the whites rolled in fear and tongues hung from gaping mouths, until the cows began to struggle and live.

As the pickup crept home, my parents and my brother took turns driving, two following behind the staggering herd. Cows straggling to the side bogged down in the drifted ditches, and the procession would stop while someone fastened the log chain around the cow's neck and hooked it to the bumper of the pickup. The pickup eased the slack from the chain and kept going, dragging one after the other out where they could stand again. They lined out behind the hay, blood pumping warmth through their chilled muscles. The weakest formed a line to the rear where shouts and the slap of buckskin gloves kept them moving. These were animals whose eyes were glazed with something deeper than cold, the cows whose brittle hocks clattered like dry sticks as they swung their feet to keep up, the bulls walking gingerly, straddling the strange bulk of their frozen testicles.

Trailed to the buildings, the cattle spent their first day crammed together in the shed connected to the barn, the combined heat of their bodies melting the ice pack and revealing the gaunt frames beneath. Half a dozen went down as their feet thawed and began to swell. With the help of a neighbor, Dad drove back to rescue the two along the fence line still lying in their untouched hay. They winched them onto a stoneboat and dragged them home. They died that night, the Angus bull the next day. It took my father and two neighbors all of that afternoon to shovel out the calves, forty head of feeder steers and replacement heifers trapped in a straw-covered shed in the feedlot, another day to drag out the dead and treat the sick.

School started up and ran for a few days, but before Christmas vacation another storm dumped six inches of fresh snow atop the old drifts, and the wind had something new to play with. Once a week, plows cleared fifty miles of county roads from Highway 191 south, then cleared them again coming back north the next day. The Christmas play at the school was canceled. No company came for Christmas Eve dinner. On Christmas Day the milk cow died.

Technically, the blizzard blew itself out in thirty-six hours. The immediate marks were made in those first hours, while ranchers paced behind the vibrating windows of their houses and listened to it happening. But the worst of the storm lay hidden for weeks and months. The ranchers shoveled and fed and chopped water. They hacked trails into the haystacks, piled warm beds of straw on the prairie beside the feed, tending the sick and lame with single-minded intensity, as if making up for those hours of helplessness. Dad counted ten dead the first week. When the ground thawed, he would bury more than thirty.

Some of the stories that come down from that storm are framed in black humor, the polite way of stating something painful or horrible without burdening the listener. Even the cattle that regained their health turned black around the edges, as if scorched by fire instead of ice, and for months the dead pieces curled and dropped off. Made for extra chores, Gene Barnard remarked dryly, having to shovel the ears out of the feed bunks before he poured the grain every morning. And they found humor in the stories of neighbors like Sandford Barrett, blindsided by his own cleverness as he picked his way cross-country with a load of hay looking for live cattle, counting fifty head of dead ones. Wise to the ways of wind, he stuck to the high spots, breaking trail along the ridges where grass and sage showed above the drifts like a yardstick, going along fine until he mistook the tips of some four-foot willows for grass and sank his pickup to the windows.

The more delicate irony is found in the other stories, like the fate of the antelope, the hundreds that walked over the Missouri and lived to drop their fawns in new country. The river is a mile wide where the antelope crossed, on the tail of Fort Peck Lake, and the breakup of ice left them stranded. For years, the sight of a pronghorn was a rare privilege on our side of the river. The other side was crawling with them. But only for a few months. Antelope with the wit to outrun the storm died in a hail of fire that fall when Fish and Game gave in to pressure from landowners and staged a special hunting season to get rid of the surplus.

And there are the double-whammy stories, the farmer-rancher kind of storm that kills the cattle all winter, then washes gullies through the fields when it melts. April staged the spring thaw like a magic show, whipping the white cover to one side with a flourish. Water roared through dikes, washed out culverts and channeled across roads. Water stood in the meadows with nowhere to go as the alfalfa grew pale and greasy beneath it. Cactus bloomed red and yellow around the bloated remains of birds and antelope, fence corners sagged under the weight of dead cattle, corrals and sheds swam in a stew of decay and manure. The fields lay saturated, too wet to hold a plow. By June, only shallow puddles dotted the hardpan, all of them squirming with mosquito larvae. Until frost returned the next fall, the air hummed with a misery of flies and bloodsucking insects. Cattle submerged themselves in reservoirs or gathered on the hilltops where the wind could sweep their backs, twisting the useless pink stubs where their tails had been.

The stories are tempered by time, now, the drifts of dead cattle too deep to forget, the loss of faith too profound to call up in words. They talk about luck now, how lucky we were the storm hit when it did, no one caught out on the road, no kids stranded at school. Lucky the electricity stayed on, the phone lines up. Still salvaging what they can three decades later. But there is wonder, still, in the facts, in circumstances somehow unreasonable, beyond the logic we lived by. How could it be that a man did everything he knew to do and it wasn't enough, wasn't even close? What happens when good intentions fail, and the work that makes the man becomes worthless—not just wrong, but simply meaningless, without effect? The old-timers would squint through Bull Durham smoke and shrug, "Well, hell, every so often it's nature's turn." And so it was.

Like every other rancher in the path of the storm, my father kept badly frozen cows alive through the winter, trying to salvage the calves in their bellies. His decision was practical rather than humane, for the animals suffered for weeks as the flesh below their hocks swelled and turned black and their hooves dropped off. On the surface, it seemed a sensible business decision. If they could get a calf, if they could save the cow for hamburger, at least they'd have something. But he knew them, these cows that lay in their own waste and panted with pain, and I believe that part of him simply refused to give in, refused to turn loose. Saving them was the only way left of beating the storm.

"I guess if you had another lifetime to live, you would have learned something, anyway," my father tells me now. "One thing I learned, and that's for godsake don't ever . . ." He pauses, searching for words, his eyes grim or sad, then starts over. "If you have a froze-up critter, shoot 'em or haul them off or something. Get rid of them. It's cruel." He speaks the last word carefully, then lifts his head, steady, resigned to the fact of it. "They got a cruel deal to go through and they're not going to make it anyway."

The range cows gave birth that spring in the stench of decay, their tails gone, ear tips dried crisp, ready to fall. A few stood to wash their calves, murmuring and anxious, with milk pouring from them, milk streaming down their hocks, pooling around their feet, draining from holes in their udders where the teats had been. The calves were put on nurse cows, and the price of a good milk cow skyrocketed. Their mothers went to market, the milk still leaking, replenishing, no way to dry them up. The price of canner cows plummeted. Others were less fortunate still. All winter, in the gloom of outbuildings, those with no feet rose to their knees and fell back when men came to tend them, unable to stand on their raw clubs, unable to halt the poison that dripped from dead flesh to the straw, that crept upward through the blood. Penicillin kept the fever down, the rot slow.

The men tended them gently, expectantly, patient as drones around a gravid queen. We had four or five, bigger places twenty or thirty head plumping in rows in sheds, hours of hauling buckets in and manure out, betting on the get. Every morning they were turned, rolled out of their own muck onto clean straw, pans of grain and water, the best alfalfa hay shoved under their peeling noses. As spring drew near, one by one these cows lay back in the soured straw and strained, their bodies bent on self-preservation, and cast away fetuses that never drew breath. Downwind of the sheds, you could smell their progress, the ones who spent the winter dying.

For years, reminders of the storm lingered at the edge of

our vision like the glint of new wire splicing the old along the east fence. Scraps of stiff hide, darkened with age, turned up in manure as we dressed the garden, maybe an ear, maybe one of the buckskin boots Mom sewed to fit that crippled yearling, the one that kept trying to stand on his missing feet. At roundup and branding, we rode in the dust of survivors, cows with healed stumps for ears and tails, cows that grew old grazing lush grass over the mass grave of their sisters. The most lasting reminders were felt in the absence of things we had come to expect, the silence of summers without hearing the rusty-hinge crow of a cock pheasant, years without the harmony of pronghorns, the way they swerve and dodge over the cured grass like a school of fish.

Over time the artifacts went back to earth and the wildlife returned, nurtured and guarded by landowners who came to see the prairie as empty without them. Only stories survive, and a restlessness when wind rises on winter evenings. Every generation relearns the rules its fathers have forgotten. One rule is awareness, the need to see past the power of human hands on the land, to the power beneath it. Those who forget have the wind to jog their memory, wind slipping evenly through the sage, dusting across the fields. *Watch your back*, it's whispering. *This land owes you nothing.*

Church and State

In the days before laws mandated kindergarten, school started with first grade. I climbed the narrow wooden step and entered South First Creek School as a student at age five, proud of the new dress sewn for this day, mercifully unconcerned about the high-water bangs sheared into the front of my Dutch-boy haircut. I carried pencils, a gum eraser, a box of twenty-four crayons, a tub of paste with a brush built into the lid, a tiny bottle of Jergens hand lotion and a small packet of tissues—but my most prized possessions were a handkerchief with red and blue flowers and a *Gunsmoke* lunch box with a little thermos bottle that fit inside.

I started school every autumn for eight years with much the same collection of objects, but I would remember that day as the first time such possessions belonged to me alone—I did not have to share them with a sibling. Grace Nesbit, one of our near neighbors, taught my first year, and though she was familiar to me from dinners and neighborhood gatherings, at school she assumed the mantle of Teacher. She even looked different in school, her posture perfect, her hands folded—the only ranch wife I knew who kept her nails filed and polished. I sat amid the chatter of kids I'd known all my life, ten students from four families, my cousin Lois and a neighbor boy named Larry joining me in first grade.

South First Creek squatted on the prairie within driving distance of three rural communities, a stucco-covered shotgun shack with a steep pitched roof. It looked large to me only because there was nothing around it to compare—no trees, no boulders, no other buildings in sight except the outhouses. A barbed wire fence separated the grounds from the cow pasture surrounding it, enclosing the school buildings and some rudimentary playground equipment—a welded-pipe swing set with four swings and a slide. The school was a mouse-infested bungalow entered through a bare stud-and-siding porch, and though the schoolroom was wired for electricity, the site had no well, and therefore no plumbing. Twin outhouses sat in opposite corners along the western fence, boys' to the right, girls' to the left. Parents took turns hauling water to fill the Red Wing drinking crock that occupied the low bench on the left wall of the entry, while hooks for our coats formed a row along the right wall. A basin and towel shared the bench, and over it a scattering of hooks and bent nails held our collection of mismatched cups, one for each of us brought from home every autumn and returned, black with grime, in May. We pushed a spigot at the base of the crock to get water, and when we finished with our wash or our drink, we tossed the dregs out the front door.

At the far end of the building, a tiny unheated room acted as living quarters for the teacher. Mrs. Nesbit commuted from her ranch home, but even when vacant the teacherage was kept closed off. A peek through the window from outside revealed a bare cotton-tick mattress on an old iron bed, a battered dresser and a small table with a hot plate. The only time students were allowed in the teacherage was during the Christmas play, when it served as "backstage" for the performers.

The main schoolroom held it all—students, teacher and eight grades' worth of books, materials and supplies. Bookcases and shelves lined the walls below the windows and rose to the ceiling in places, every inch of space crammed with books, paper, flash cards and art materials. A large blackboard dressed the north wall, and strung along above it was a permanent display of the Palmer Penmanship alphabet, the uppercase letters made grand with a fat swirl at the start, a bit of flourish at the end. We used the flattop heating stove as a storage table until it had to be lit in October. Standard-issue portraits of George Washington and Abe Lincoln glowered down upon us, and before Health Inspection every morning, we stood beside our desks and pledged allegiance to a flag propped in the corner behind Teacher's desk.

Decades after the fact, I tell my children about Inspection, and they are aghast at what they consider a huge violation of privacy, if not basic civil rights. We had no such frame of reference, of course, and first thing in the morning every student, from big, sulky eighth-grade boys to barely housebroken first graders, pulled out a clean hanky and unfolded it on the desktop for Inspection. Spreading our hands flat on the hankies to display our fingers, we sat up straight, feet flat on the floor, and waited our turns in silence. Teacher began at one side and walked slowly up and down the aisles between rows, pausing at each desk to check the posture, the cleanliness of the hands and fingernails, the neatness of the hair, and to hear the student say, "I brushed my teeth." Occasionally one of the big boys sported black crescents under his nails or someone owned up and said she hadn't brushed her teeth, in which case that student did not get a gold star on the Health chart. From our performance during Inspection came our Satisfactory or Unsatisfactory mark in Health on our report cards.

Inspection probably originated as a means of reinforcing cleanliness and civilized hygiene habits in rural communities before the advent of plumbing and electricity, a way of keeping disease contagion and body odors to a minimum in the congested schoolroom. The ritual continued in my era, despite the fact that every family in our community had some variation of running water and at least four or five changes of school clothes. By then, however, we were far less conscious of the basic hygiene lessons than we were of the institution of Inspection itself. We intoned "I brushed my teeth" like we did the Pledge of Allegiance, words with slender connection to that morning's ablutions. Older girls competed to have the nicest handkerchiefs, and although we were each required to have a handkerchief on hand at all times, we never, never used them to blow our noses. We rubbed away sniffles on our shirt cuffs or were directed to the box of tissues on Teacher's desk when she got tired of hearing us snort. Handkerchiefs were for Inspection.

The first day of school, someone's father stayed awhile to work the special wrench required to adjust the desk's height, fine-tuning the fit as we sat straight in our seats with our forearms level on the tops. Once it was customized, the desk became private property. To open another student's desk without permission was unheard of, except for Teacher, who had access to all. Each row began with the smallest desks directly in front of Teacher's desk and ended with the eighth graders' desks at the rear of the room. Each fall desks were swapped around with other rural schools to accommodate the year's crop of growing students, so certain coveted desks circulated through our school only once every couple of years. Desks we had never seen before popped up occasionally, and we studied them for familiar names or signs that spoke their origin, deciphering them like archaeological sites. We interpreted initials or cattle brands, more rarely a first name, carefully, always searching for a sign of an ancestor or a now-grown neighbor. Small drawings etched into the oak with the sharp end of a compass might take the bulk of a year to complete, and almost always were done by older students—the ones at the back of the room, the ones required to have compasses for their arithmetic, the ones able to work furtively and persistently and not be caught. Finished, the etching was rubbed full of fountain pen ink, which soaked into the wood and lent a tattoo-like appearance; we copied it by laying a sheet of tablet paper over it and rubbing with a pencil until the design came through in relief.

We had no say in which desk we got, for the decision was based on size and availability, and the teacher had the final say. A really bad desk, one worthy of a winter's sulking, might feature a slick Formica top—no carving, no graffiti—with a tarnished metal rim that turned white cuffs black, an inner cavity lumpy with dried-glue puddles, and sprung hinges that no longer held the desktop up when you raised it. With these desks, a student propped the lid on her forehead to rummage for items and risked it slamming shut on her fingers if it slipped. The best desks were varnished oak with slots along the top to hold pencils and enough carving to both add historical interest and mask additional etchings.

It's true what they say about the rural school experience—the ranch kids who attended one-room country schools saw both the best of education and the worst it could offer. At best, we received one-on-one attention, with every assignment marked and returned to us to be corrected; spelling bees, learning games and elaborate Christmas programs; and of course we had the advantage of all grades in one room—this last lending the effect of having lessons presented subliminally for a year or two before being called upon to master them yourself. At worst, we had chaos. A school taught by only one teacher is bound to reflect the strengths and weaknesses of that teacher, and indeed, if the weaknesses were of the sort that encouraged rebellion and disorder, then students were in for a long year.

For decades, our county relied on a dozen or more regular schoolmarms, women with local ties who had taught for years in one or another of our rural schools. Most schools made it a rule to switch teachers every year or two to promote diversity, but by the time my education commenced in 1960, practicality made this impossible. Many of the regulars were nearing retirement age, and the local school board had difficulty finding new teachers willing to live in one side of a shack and teach in the other for less than ten thousand dollars a year. When they found a good one, they kept her as long as they could. My favorite teacher, Mae Bibeau, taught two of my eight years, her wry sense of humor and enthusiasm for writing lending me courage long after she left. Another great educator, Grace Nesbit, taught me two more grades after the first. In between the good years were a couple of teachers with lessons that extended beyond the covers of a book. My second grade at South First Creek School, for example, was one fall-to-spring lesson in anarchy taught by the Peigneux boys and sponsored by the distraught and ineffectual Mrs. Hughes. The chaos of the classroom and the bullying permitted during recess prompted an exodus during Christmas break, as parents who could manage it pulled their students out and sent them to other, more distant schools. Those who left never came back. After second grade, I would not have another person in my grade again until I started high school. A few years later, with the old school near collapse, the board wrangled the funds to erect a small prefab two-room building on a new site between Second and Third Creeks. It was in the inaugural year of this new school, my sixth-grade year, that I was introduced to God and Cary Grant by the venerable Mr. Saxton.

Nine kids attended Second Creek School that first year, four of them boys in the seventh and eighth grades, and for the first time the board cast the net wide to find a male teacher, who would offer discipline and keep order. They caught Daniel Saxton, a retired high school teacher from Minnesota. When I read *The Legend of Sleepy Hollow* that fall, I patterned my mental picture of Ichabod Crane after Mr. Saxton: tall, lanky and stoop-shouldered, with a shock of yellowish-gray hair, thick spectacles perched on a thin, beaky nose, a neck with wattles, and huge flat ears that flushed when he lost his temper. I believe he had taught at a Catholic or private high school, but whatever his experience, there was no direct transferal from that to our rural school and the six elementary grades we filled that year. He lost the older boys, the very students he'd been hand-selected to teach, in the first hour of the first day. Blinking and baring his tarnished teeth, he made us all stand and introduce ourselves. Then, waving a baton of chalk, he led us with great gusto through a song that was to become a hated morning ritual:

> *Good morning to you!*
> *Good morning to you!*
> *We're all in our places*

67

Breaking Clean

With sweet, smiling faces,
For this is the way
To start a new day!

The year progressed with few smiles. Joyce, our sweet little redheaded first grader, was the eldest in her family, the first to attend school, and had been exposed to few strangers in her life. Along with us, she had never seen anything like him at all. For weeks he tried to teach her to count, and for weeks she stood trembling at his desk carefully reciting numbers as far as she could go. Beyond the number seven, she winged it, poised to run for the safety of her desk if she guessed wrong and he lost his temper. The alphabet progressed at about the same pace, her dread palpable from the moment she was called forward to the moment she scurried back to her desk, where she was allowed to draw and color in peace for a while.

The seventh- and eighth-grade boys occasionally disappeared into the fields around the schoolhouse during morning recess, staging elaborate snowball battles and feigning deafness while Mr. Saxton rang the brass handbell and shouted, red-faced, from the porch. He taught in his bedroom slippers and changed into boots only when he visited the outhouse. He didn't go after them, though he fumed until they returned. Polite, well-behaved little girls must have seemed a blessing in the midst of this warfare, for Gail and I soon became his favorites. After finishing our own sandwiches at lunch, we often wandered out of the schoolroom through the open door of the teacherage to lean against the little wooden table where he ate, answering questions he posed to us, wrinkling our noses at his everyday fare of hard cheese and strong, rust-colored mustard. We'd never seen a human eat something that smelled like that, and its origin was a matter of much whispered speculation.

Church and State

Being singled out for attention was a new experience, and the wonder of it lured us back to the teacherage day after day, curious and repelled by equal measure. He took no more liberties than a grandfather might, circling an arm around our shoulders to hold us still as he offered a piece of cheese on the point of his paring knife, laughing delightedly as we pinched our noses and ran from the smell of old socks. Still, his behavior made us uneasy. We hated having our ears chewed on, a tease he initiated with a tight one-armed hug that brought us within range, while he pretended to attack the exposed ear, gnawing and growling comically as we shrieked and twisted away. But as an elderly male teacher, he enjoyed the benefit of fitting into three categories of People We Trust and Obey. We put up with it, or more likely Gail did, for I was far less outgoing and trusting by nature and she was more often found within arm's reach of his affection. His grandfatherly presumptions didn't seem wrong, exactly, in and of themselves, aside from the rather glaring fact that he was not our grandfather. But they felt wrong enough to trigger a wariness. We knew instinctively that these things would not be mentioned at home. Had it occurred to us, we might have given his unseemly actions a truer context by imagining some other teacher, say the proper Mrs. Nesbit, growling and nibbling our earlobes—a thought that causes my scalp to ripple even now.

Late that spring, during an interrogatory session at Mr. Saxton's lunch table, he dredged up the fact that neither Gail nor I had ever attended church. When further probing revealed that we likely hadn't been baptized, he simply gaped at us. I'd already forgotten the conversation a few weeks later when he called to ask our parents' permission to take us on an outing. If Mom was surprised by this request from a teacher I'd heard her describe as "an odd old duck," she didn't let on to us. Teachers commanded great respect in our community, and having her girls singled out for special attention must have been something of an honor, albeit a strange one.

Early Sunday morning, Mom hushed our wiggling and buttoned us into our good dresses, fashioning little hats for us from scraps of netting cut from an old cancan slip. She packed our lunch and saw us off as Mr. Saxton's old sedan lurched off toward the Catholic mission in the Little Rocky Mountains, a two-hour drive. I could always depend on Gail when a situation required entertaining adults with conversation, but her chatter dwindled as we drew away from the familiar confines of family and school. For miles we rode without speaking, the silence made no less profound by Mr. Saxton's idle humming and the thump of dirt clods on the floorboards beneath our feet.

Each spring, the end of the school year coincided with a change of wardrobe, as I outgrew the last round of dress alterations and stepped into jeans for the summer. On this warm spring day I tugged at my skirt, conscious of the old hemlines, a double tier of faded rings encircling the bottom edge. The backs of my thighs were stuck to the plastic seat covers. Coached about proper behavior, Gail and I sat unnaturally straight, glancing sideways at each other, eyes bright with nervous laughter that we didn't dare let spill. We watched out the side window as county road gave way to highway, and the Little Rockies rose up from the prairie, their familiar distant blue turning to green as we neared.

Well into our journey, Mr. Saxton reached across and twisted the dial of the AM radio. Blips of sound filled the car until he settled on a station. I was riveted as his lips began to move in perfect sequence, making words from what sounded like the moans of a hundred ghosts: *Hail Mary, full of grace, the Lord is with thee.* The flesh on my arms puckered into bumps as the faraway voices chanted full circle and began again. Catching myself staring, I quickly lowered my eyes. Surely it was rude to watch this. Surely I wasn't hearing correctly, but no—there it was again, echoed by the man beside us. "Blessed art thou amongst women," he intoned, "and blessed art the fruit of thy womb, Jesus."

Holy moley! I risked a sideways glance at my little sister. She looked furtive, eyes darting right to left, like Mom had the day I was helping fold clothes and had asked, out of the blue, what part of the cows came out when they prolapsed. I'd been preoccupied, replaying events I had observed in the calving shed, and my question was an idle one. She had continued folding clothes; her face grew still as a mask except for her eyes, which skated back and forth as if looking for a way out of her head. "The womb," she said finally, her tone deliberately casual. "The womb is where the calf grows." The eyes darted toward me and away. Realization hit with a rush, a bloom that rose from my throat to my ears in one heartbeat. "If you ever have any questions about that . . . stuff," she went on, "you can ask me." Her eyes fell to a T-shirt and settled as she shook it out, creased it in half. *Womb.* Mentally I was pounding my forehead with one fist at this blunder. I had read the word, I knew what it meant. *Womb.* Now here was this man who said "woman," "womb" and "Jesus" in the same breath. I slouched lower against the car door.

Despite Mr. Saxton's concern for our immortal souls, we were not the little pagans he imagined us to be—at least not entirely. We did not attend church, and at that point we had not been baptized, though a couple of years later the twins and I received this rite when the Reverend Fred Fox and wife, Phoebe, made an evangelical swing through the south country. Almost every summer, a couple of high school girls from a church in Malta organized a Bible school for the children in our area, and Mom was more than glad to haul us back to the schoolhouse for five days of free child care. We learned to parrot children's prayers, sing Jesus songs and do all manner of crafty projects while our devout and genuinely kind young teachers taught us the familiar Bible stories—Adam and Eve, David and Goliath, Noah and the Ark, Jesus and the Miracles.

Mother's week of freedom was a mixed blessing. Because there were four of us attending, she was bound to admire, and somehow display, four of every craft project the school offered, and we were very speedy workers with glue and Popsicle sticks, paper plates and colored yarn. Her vacation ended abruptly on the fifth day, when she was called upon to bake goodies, don a dress and join other mothers at the Program, where we performed the skits, recited memorized Bible verses and sang songs we had practiced all week. Our religious instruction would be hard-pressed to own that title, but it had served to introduce the main players and basic story line of Christianity. However, in no verse, story or song at Bible school had we addressed the Main Players in the familiar vein taken by Mr. Saxton and the radio's Mournful Crooners. There followed a day of revelations no larger and no less amazing, events strung together like prayer beads on a thread of unfamiliar highway, the whole of it finally drawn full circle long after our ability to decipher the world around us had gone stone, and only shortly before our parents would have called the sheriff.

Whether our teacher had misunderstood the time of the service or planned to arrive after the traveling priest had moved on I never knew, but he didn't seem perturbed to find the church empty. As we entered a long room filled with benches, he dipped one knee and crossed himself. From there he ushered us into a bench and knelt beside us. I kept a wary eye on his hands as they clasped and rose and danced in the dim light, for they seemed to have much to do. He tapped his forehead with the tips of his fingers, he tapped his chest. Once he appeared to kiss his fingers.

At last he settled into whispering with his eyes closed while we sat on the polished boards and gathered information from the walls around us. The hall was silent now, but the air felt warm and expectant, as though a crowd had just stepped out and might be back. I retain a fragile sense of the scenes or pictures on the walls, men and women with dark faces barely discernible from the background, the style of their robes recognizable from Christmas cards and the flannel-board figures at Bible school. The statues seemed wildly colorful by comparison. Ceramic blood congealed on Jesus' stomach and dripped from his head, which appeared to be wrapped in barbed wire. Holy Mary wore a blue dress and held the Babe on her lap at arm's length, precariously close to falling, I thought, or perhaps she was offering him to someone else to hold. Little fat candles bloomed at her feet, unattended. Who had lit them? Who would blow them out?

I had given up trying to figure it all out as we took our cue and slid along the bench to follow our slow-moving teacher back up the aisle. He paused at the doorway, and when he stopped, I nearly ran over his heels in my eagerness to see daylight. His gentle smile never faltering, he dipped his fingers into a container of water and turned to us. He drew a small cross in the air over my sister's head, then touched her forehead with his wet thumb. He dipped again for me. We stood quietly until he was done, reading his face for signs that we could move on again. By then, he could have dragged a live chicken from his vest and bitten off its head and neither of us would have flinched. We followed him quietly to the car.

The next station of our journey found us puttering along a

73

narrow blacktop through Mission Canyon, pulling off the road into a campground or parking area, where we unpacked our picnic lunch. Gail and I raced around, shrill with the exhaustion that comes from hours of being still and alert at the same time. Mindless of our slippery shoes and short dresses, we climbed sandstone boulders at the base of a natural bridge, shouting from the top to hear the canyon's echo. We ate our sandwiches perched on rocks, our skirts tucked modestly around our legs while Mr. Saxton sat in the front seat of his car far below us, watching with passive benevolence. "Like talking monkeys out of the trees," he chuckled, when he finally coaxed us back into the car. On our way once more, conversation came more easily, my confidence renewed by the final leg of our journey. As far as I knew, we had survived this strange outing and were heading home the same way we came.

Secondary Highway 66 runs roughly parallel to the mountains, connecting Montana's two major highways like the crossbar of an A. A driver with large time and no purpose might begin in Malta, drive west down 191, turn off on the connection route 66 and follow it to its juncture with Highway 2, turn east and return to Malta—a round-trip of 150 miles. Of course there are miles of mountain trails and ranch roads as well, and given the options, any number of routes might have gotten us home, or as easily have gotten us lost. Whatever his decision or inspiration, instead of arriving home in midafternoon as expected, I found myself blinking out the side window as the sun streaked through the cottonwoods along the Milk River and the town of Malta came into view.

The rest of the afternoon we spent in still another rich, dark room hung with exciting scenes, this one featuring folddown seats instead of pews and a stage instead of an altar.

Malta's Villa Theatre was no more familiar to us than the church in the mountains, but we were quickly settled in with a bag of popcorn and transported via big screen to a tropical island, courtesy of *Father Goose* and the antics of Cary Grant. Gail would recall her rapt immersion in this romantic comedy about a drunken recluse stranded on an island with a French woman and a flock of schoolgirls. I would not. At the end of the matinee, one of us had the sense to call home and let them know we had not been kidnapped.

We rode home in silence, both of us full of new experiences and drained by the work of not knowing what came next. By the time we rolled into our barnyard, my throat was tight with self-pity. We had been sold down the river, sent off with an Odd Duck. If we returned, I thought mournfully, it was no thanks to Mom. Gail drooped beside me, trying to stay awake. Mr. Saxton whistled contentedly, tunelessly. At the house he chuckled at their concern for our late arrival, their state of mind having been downgraded from near panic to irritation by our phone call, then bid our parents good evening as they resumed charge of us. Prompted, we thanked him for the good time.

The school year ended a couple of weeks later, and we saw the last of Mr. Saxton as we packed up our desks and cleaned the school. But it didn't end there. He sent us greeting cards for a while, and a heart-shaped box of chocolates the next Valentine's Day, addressing it all to the Regina Rascals, his nickname for us. Our brothers were off and running. "Hey, Rascal! You got a letter from your boyfriend!" Gail and I shriveled under the torture of this teasing, for we didn't know what to think of it either.

We spoke little about our day with Mr. Saxton, even to each other, until we were grown women, a conversation that began just as it might have back then, in a wondering tone: "That day trip with Saxton, you remember? . . . that church thing . . . What was that about?" We still don't know. By and large, men simply did not seek the company of little girls in our community. Dad had never singled us out and taken a day off to drive us anywhere, and neither had our grandfathers. Mr. Saxton wasn't even kin. But we agree on one thing—he never stepped beyond the bounds of propriety. A lonely old man, perhaps, who thought to save our souls and broaden our horizons in one fell swoop—but not a predator. Still, something tells us we shouldn't have been there, even now—something that recognizes the intimate nature of religious worship, the sensual mixture of darkness and popcorn, the blast of color and sound and big-screen romance that held us tight against our seats until the very end. We still cannot accept his gift. "The crazy old goat was probably perfectly innocent," my sister sighs, "but you know, if he did those things today he'd get thrown in jail." For better or worse, she's right.

Lessons in Silence

The first week of school the indoor air was sultry with held-over August heat and farm kids too recently reined in and washed up. I was tall for my age and sat toward the back, looking down a row of raw necks and homemade haircuts. The sound of a pickup on the county road lured us like a bird's song. When it shifted down for the corner, we went along with it, anticipating each rev and crank of gears—some neighbor going to town, checking cattle, returning a borrowed tool somewhere up the road. In the next second the familiar pattern broke and we came to full attention. Instead of swelling, then fading into distance, the noise grew steadily louder. Dust streamed through the open windows as a rust-colored pickup eased around the building to the eastern side and rattled to a stop by the front steps. The engine cut out, lugged a few times, and was still. Five heads lifted in the sudden quiet; five pairs of eyes fixed on our teacher's desk.

Mrs. Norby licked a gold foil star, tapped it into place, then squared the papers on her desk and rose to attend to this new business. I remember the tiny catch in her posture as she glanced out the window, not a motion or a movement exactly but a slight drawing in as she smoothed her skirt. At the time I interpreted her sudden freezing as fear, and today, four hundred miles and forty years away from that moment, I believe my instinct was accurate. There was no reading her face as she left the classroom. I can think of nothing that would have kept the five of us from the front window when the door closed behind her.

My older brother Kenny, myself, the twins Gary and Gail, and a neighbor boy made up the student population that year, filling three of the eight grades taught at our rural school. Standing in the shadow of the drapes, we could see outside without being seen. The battered pickup was not one of ours. The driver's door opened with a stiff pop and an old man eased slowly from behind the wheel. He stood with a red-and-black-plaid cap in one hand as Mrs. Norby walked down the steps toward him. The cab rocked slightly to the passenger side as a woman got out and made her way around the dented nose of the pickup. At the steps she turned and produced a little boy from the shadow of her skirts, prodding him forward until he stood in front of her.

Mrs. Norby had her back to us, and through the window we could hear her sweet modulated voice. The man spoke very politely in reply. His smile held as many gaps as teeth. The woman said nothing. Mrs. Norby spoke in her lecture voice, at ease now; there was nodding and smiling, a gentle laugh from the man. The boy turned to hide his face when our teacher bent over to talk to him, but when she straightened and held out her hand, he took it.

When the man raised his arm to put his cap back on, we flushed like grouse and were innocently at work by the time the second cloud of dust cleared and Mrs. Norby entered, towing a small dark-eyed boy with a mop of black hair. His name was Forest, and he was starting first grade. He lived with his grandparents, who were working for one of our neighbors. These things she told us. The rest we saw in the formal tilt of her head, the blank smile, the way her hands cupped together at waist level. Our company manners appeared on cue. That he was an outsider goes without saying. We had cut our first teeth on each other, and we had never seen him before. But Forest was different in another way. Forest was an Indian, and his presence in our world went beyond our experience, beyond our comprehension. We welcomed him to school politely, as we had been taught to welcome the children of outsiders. But we would have been no less bewildered had we glanced up from our math drills and seen a grove of seedling pine take root in the hardpan outside.

Forest. Even then I was struck by the irony. We paid attention to names, and there wasn't a forest of note for a hundred miles. Our community was identified by several layers of place names that signified ownership. The Plains tribes who hunted that prairie had left hammers and arrowheads, tepee rings and medicine stones, but no names. Trappers and immigrant homesteaders had labeled the land as they pushed the Indians west, and by the time of my childhood, those earliest names belonged to the land alone. Carberrey, Whitcombe, Krumweide, Cruikshank—to say them aloud was to conjure a place long separated from a face or a family.

The chunk of shortgrass prairie we called Regina had been named by French Canadians who drifted south out of Saskatchewan to trap beaver along the Missouri. The first homesteaders inherited a legacy of French place names that roll across the tongue like music, black-bottom draws and treacherous creeks and drainages identified by hisses and coos. The actual places seemed unrelated to the black letters and blue lines on the official Bureau of Land Management maps. We had little use for maps. Any rancher who wanted to see his land picked up a piece of it and rubbed it between his fingers. But the maps with their foreign spellings—Beauchamp and Fourchette—drew a solid line between insiders who knew the history of the land and outsiders who knew only maps and could not say the passwords. We all had our stories.

"Had a guy up here yesterday, asks me directions to Regina," a neighbor might say. We'd all grin and lean forward. The name "Regina" applied to a large community of farms and ranches, but on the maps it appeared as a little gray circle, just like a town. "I tell him he's looking at it, but he ain't buying any of that. So we get to jawing and pretty soon he goes for his map, and there she is." He'd pause and lift his eyebrows and hands in one gesture of innocence. "So, hell, I give him directions."

Strangers who were rude or adamant enough about the little gray circle on the map were sent there, to the Regina Post Office. The best part of the story was imagining the driver's face when he pulled into our mail carrier's barnyard. The official sign hung on the front of an old converted chicken house, where Joe and Ethel sorted the mail for Saturday delivery. The flag that waved over the Regina Post Office could have covered it like a pup tent.

We measured the wealth of our knowledge against the ignorance of outsiders and judged ourselves superior. We pulled cars out of potholes, fed lost hunters at our kitchen tables, sold gas from the big drums we bought in bulk, and for the most part we did so graciously. We could afford to be kind. But social or political upheaval going on outside seldom intruded, and families who managed to tuck themselves into a fold of flatland and hang on seldom went looking for something else to worry about. Their priorities were immediate— wind and heat and hoppers in summer, wind and snow and blizzards in winter. Our isolation was real. The nearest town was Malta, an hour's drive north when the roads were good. To the south, the land plunged into rugged breaks and badlands, then dropped abruptly into a mile-wide stretch of water the maps called Fort Peck Lake. We still called it the Missouri River. In later summer a double row of dead cottonwoods reared out of the water where the original channel had been, and we could point to the site of submerged homesteads, name the families flooded out when the dam went up in the thirties. Halfway between the river and town, my parents bullied a hundred acres of winter wheat away from the big sagebrush and prickly pear cactus, and grazed cattle on the rest.

Our fences marched straight down the section lines, regiments of cedar posts and barbed wire strung so tight it hummed in a strong wind. The corners were square and braced to meet the bordering fields of neighbors just like us. Our families had homesteaded, broken ground and survived into the third generation, and we shared a set of beliefs so basic that they were seldom spoken aloud. I remember them as commonsense adages: Hard work is the measure of a man. A barn will build a house, but a house won't build a barn. Good fences make good neighbors. That which belongs to everyone belongs to no one.

"This is no country for fools," my grandpa said, and these truths were what separated fools from survivors. They were the only explanation I was ever given for the way we lived.

To her credit, Mrs. Norby never gave up on Forest, although his lessons soon resembled a series of skirmishes. She always began cheerfully enough, settling us to work by ourselves, then calling him up to her big desk, where they would spend until recess working on the big alphabet cards. Our first-grade year, we all measured our progress and accomplishment by the lengthening row of cards, memorized and thumbtacked to the wall above the blackboard. We adored them. On each card the stout black lines of upper- and lowercase letters were incorporated into a picture and a story. The letter *C*, I remember, was a profile of a mouth lined with teeth; the sound of Mr. C coughing was the sound of the letter *C*. Lowercase *f* was the tail of a frightened cat. Mr. D was a soldier, and when he stood straight and beat his round drum, it went *duh-duh-duh*.

The first time Forest spoke aloud, Mrs. Norby killed our reaction with one remarkably vicious look, perhaps afraid that we would frighten him back into silence. But Forest loved the stories, and his soft, surprisingly deep voice became background music for our own lessons. He learned the cards quickly, repeating the sounds, grandly embellishing the stories unless Mrs. Norby stopped him, and she must have expected him to take the next leap as effortlessly as we had. But he did not. He saw nothing in the shapes and sounds on the phonics cards that connected to the words written in a book. Mrs. Norby persisted like a trainer with a jump-shy colt, putting him through his paces, around the cards faster and faster, gaining momentum, and then the book would appear and Forest would brace his feet and skid to a stop.

Against her decades of experience he had only endurance

and a calm, sad stare that he seldom directed at the words she pointed out. After a few days he would have the words of Dick's or Jane's or Sally's exploits memorized and matched to the pictures on each page. Mrs. Norby would open to a page, he would look at it closely for a few seconds and then begin reciting the story that went with the pictures, sometimes adding bits from previous pages and, often as not, reading with his eyes focused on his fingers as they twiddled with a paper clip or a bit of paper. When her voice grew clipped and brittle, he waited her out. Forest did not think in ABCs. For him, the story was all.

From my position as a third-row observer, I found Forest's academic difficulties neither surprising nor disappointing. Looking back, I can see it was his inability to read that kept him alive in my mind. From the first days I had attempted to find the mythical Red Man in Forest, and he had failed me on every front. We had studied Plains tribes in social studies. We had read the books, and when TV came to the county we were devoted to shows like *Wagon Train* and *Rawhide*. The Indians we admired had no use for reading; they wore buckskin leggings and medicine pouches on leather thongs around their necks. They had eagle feathers and long braids; they danced and hunted and collected scalps. Forest showed little promise of living up to this exciting potential.

Gail and I were more given to fantasy than the boys were, but all of us spent part of our childhood summers playing Indian. We made bows and arrows from green willow and cotton string and bounded barefoot through the creek bottoms, communicating with gestures and grunts like Tonto did on *The Lone Ranger*. We had horses and could ride like cowboys, but my sister and I rebelled at the discipline of saddles and rules. We rode naked to the waist, hell-bent through the meadows, on a palomino mare and a black half-Shetland pony. We had no bridge between make-believe and the reality of children like Forest. We knew our land and its people, every pore and every pothole of a close, contained world. From that knowledge came identity and security. But we had only the vaguest sense of our place in the larger world. The Fort Belknap Reservation that lies twenty-five overland miles from my parents' ranch is no more real in my memory than New York City is. What I knew about this place I learned indirectly— jokes overheard, fragments of conversation, phrases that slipped into dialogue sideways, in reference to other whites. *Shiftless as a reservation buck. Stank like an Indian camp. Wild as, lazy as, dirty as*—racial slurs we discounted as harmless because they were not directed toward Indians. They did not refer to anyone we knew. The Indian people we knew were ranchers, neighbors who lived like we did. The other kind were dark and dangerous and different. They got in bar fights and car wrecks; they hung around the Rez and took government handouts; they did not make good hired men. They were like the man behind the rodeo arena pouring his horse a big feed of commodity oatmeal, "U.S. Government" stamped right on the sack. There was, my father said through clenched teeth, no goddamned excuse for that, no goddamned excuse in the world.

Forest and his grandparents were gone before Christmas. I never knew where they went or why they left. I suppose the extra desk got retired to the storeroom, but I don't remember that either. What I do remember from that time is that, with all the inborn arrogance of a white child raised in a white man's world, I thought well of myself for being kind to him. I had a sense that we would not have been punished for picking on Forest, just as I felt sure that he had been temporary all

84

along, he and his grandparents, too. There were so many things I knew without knowing why, things I learned as a child listening with half an ear to all that was said, and most intently to all that was not said. I remember the silence most of all.

The trip to Havre is in my honor, my first visit to the dentist. He pulls four baby teeth to make room for the new ones sprouting through my gums at odd angles, and there is blood. When we leave the dentist's office I make it to the parking lot, then vomit everything I have swallowed and feel better. Breakfast happened before dawn, before dressing in our nicest clothes, before our three-hour drive. My father hands me a clean handkerchief to hold against my mouth and drives through downtown Havre in search of an inexpensive café. Afraid that misery is catching, my brothers and sisters crowd against the far side of the backseat. Under the stained hankie my cheeks feel heavy and pliant, like wet clay. My father swears softly at the traffic, a white-knuckle driver unaccustomed to stoplights, and I close my eyes to shut it out.

The café we pull up to is small but not crowded, and my stomach wakes to the perfume of hamburgers and french fries, a treat so rare that we could count their every appearance in our short lives, each event of "eating out." But when the food comes I am stunned to find a bowl of chicken soup set on the place mat in front of me, the kind my mother makes when she's too busy to cook. I stir noodles up from the bottom of the bowl and sulk, while the others take turns squeezing ketchup over hamburgers and fighting over split orders of fries. Even driven by hunger, I can't keep the soup from leaking through my numb lips, and when life becomes too unfair to stand, I slide to the floor under the table and begin to cry. My father drags me out by one arm and sends me to sit in the car until I can straighten up.

Outside, I lean against the bumper in pure defiance of direct orders. But my attention wanders to the bench just outside the café door, where an Indian woman sits holding a baby. I'm drawn to babies, and this one is a black-eyed beauty, her fat belly peeking out of a crocheted sweater. She's just big enough to sit upright on the old woman's knee. The woman sees me edging closer and smiles. "You like babies?" she asks, and I nod, my tongue still too thick to trust with words.

The woman is dressed in layers of color, wide skirts that brush the ground, a man's flannel shirt buttoned to the neck and a shawl that falls from her shoulders and drapes in folds around the baby. Thick gray braids coil at the nape of her neck. She bends her face near the baby's and clicks her tongue, tickling at the chubby brown chin, and the baby dissolves into giggles, her eyes fastened on the grandmother's face. The babies I have seen are next to bald, but this one has thick black hair standing up all over her head. I'm getting up the nerve to touch that hair when the café door opens and I leap back, scrambling toward our car, expecting my father. I turn, hand on the door handle, and an old man stands next to the woman and baby, regarding me with a puzzled look.

The man hands the woman a wrapped hamburger and a paper cup of milk and walks back into the café. She lets the baby suck on the edge of the cup while she chews the sandwich, her lips disappearing with the motion of her jaw. She sets the cup aside, and I freeze against the car in wonder as she dips into her mouth with two fingers and pops a bit of chewed food into the baby's open mouth. The little girl works over the mashed hamburger and they rock gently on the bench, each gumming her own bite until it's swallowed. After a sip of milk, the baby leans forward comically, eyebrows arched, mouth and eyes round, ready for more. My own stomach shivers, squeamish, thrilled, but the process is done so gently that I can't be horrified. I watch the wonderful shuffle of food from mouth to fingers to baby, the easy sway between bites, until I'm full to bursting with news.

Back inside the café, I ignore the cold soup and press against my mother's arm, conscious of slurring as I tell the story of what I've seen. Her forehead wrinkles and her voice comes out a whisper as she hushes me.

"Did she talk to you?" Her voice is too flat and even, a trap I can't quite read. I nod, ready to work my lips and tongue around an explanation, but her hand snakes out and grabs my ear before I can speak, twisting it, her knuckles hard against my swollen cheek. Her eyes lock mine into full attention.

"You were told to get in the car." She says nothing else, but continues to glare, giving my ear another jerk for emphasis. Something about the old woman has tricked me, but I don't know what. Stunned, I walk with underwater steps out the door, straight past the bench without looking, and to the car. I curl up in the backseat where I can't be seen from the outside.

It's a long ride home that night, late and dark, and the car is a crush of packages and sleeping children. My mouth has been awake for hours, throbbing. In the front seat my mother tells my story of the Indian woman feeding the baby. My father says, "Jesus Christ." I hear it in their voices, and my belly fills with anger and shame. On the outside, nothing is what it seems and I long for my own bed, the quilt my mother sewed from wool scraps and old coats, the comfort of a sure thing. My father drives automatically now, slowing for ruts and cattle guards, banking the gentle curves of the county road. Lonesome Coulee. Jackson's Corner. The Y. I press one cheek against the cool of the window and close my eyes, drifting with the motion of the car. Almost home. I can tell where we are by the feel.

Fighting Fire

When he finished his chores, Grandpa Blunt squatted down
beside me in a corner of his old barn. I settled back on my
heels so he could reach the new litter of kittens curled
together in a nest of empty feed sacks. He stroked their overlapping necks with a pinky finger, then gently pulled the jigsaw
of kittens apart. Turning to the manger window, he tipped
each one upside down in the light and studied its underside,
handing two to me to hold. The three females he set aside in
an empty five-gallon bucket. They scrabbled in the bottom,
and I reached in to nudge them together so they would comfort each other. "We don't need any more girl cats," he told me.

"How can you tell it's girl cats?" I asked him. He looked
startled for a second, then his eyes began to dance.

"You look at the bottoms of their feet." When he grinned,
his dentures clicked together. Still polite, I looked away from
him, down at the kittens in the bucket.

He repeated his punch line, *bottoms of their feet,* and
chuckled to himself, storing it up for later. When he told it
over the dinner table, eyebrows arched and knowing, most
likely those words would be mine, and everyone would laugh.

I knew how to sort boy kittens from girl kittens. I understood all the reasons for thinning out litters—too many cats around a place might starve, sleep with skunks and get rabies, start to eat eggs or even chickens. But no one would tell me why the limit was on girl cats. How could he tell when he had enough? Why were the girl cats the first ones to go?

"Wouldn't it work," I asked him, "to get rid of all the boy cats?" Grandpa's back and neck had fused over the years into the shape of a lowercase *f,* so when he swung a wary eye in my direction, his whole body turned. We seemed to be edging closer to the topic of how kittens came to be. I could have told him about that, too, but I knew better.

"Well," he said, clambering to his feet and reaching for the pail, "a person could do that, I suppose."

I knew this injustice wasn't limited to cats. Our ranching community applauded the birth of stud colts, bull calves and boy babies. We celebrated the manly man for doing the work of two men and the little woman for whipping up man-sized meals. And when television followed electricity to our community in the early sixties, the outside view it gave me confirmed my suspicions. I got from television names for what I already knew, an adult world divided neatly into Marshal Dillons and Miss Kittys. I reached for the role of the gunslinging marshal. If the twins and I played house after our baby days, we played wagon train, trekking cross-country to the stackyard and building a little soddy out of bales. We pretended to be mustangs, mountain lions and coyotes. When we played people, we played men at war: cowboys and Indians, cattle ranchers and sheepherders, sheriff and bad guys. We rescued womenfolk regularly, roles we saved for the battered baby dolls, but even a forked stick with a rag dress could wring its hands in a pinch. As we grew older and more daring, we tai-

90

lored our play to the precise role of Phillips County Man. We played Fire.

The twins and I formed a tripod out of sight and downwind from the buildings, our heads touching as we crouched to shelter the matches I struck, one after another, over the sun-cured grass. When the fire caught, we nursed it along, offering it tender bites of dried moss until the flame grew large enough to feed on its own heat. The game was on. The burlap sacks had been selected for size and heft from the pile in the shop, dipped deep in the water tank and held until they no longer tried to float. We stood back now, armed with the sacks, learning the creep of flames through blue grama grass, the jagged spread of fire picking its way over sod, around hardpan, the sudden dart upward at the taste of tall bunchgrass. Still we watched, stepping in only to steer it shy of hard fuel, woody sagebrush that burned hot enough to light the green leaves and raise smoke, waiting until a matter of seconds separated game from emergency.

The adrenaline rush that followed was real. Fanning out, we formed a line of attack, slapping out flames with two-fisted overhead swings, nailing the fire to the ground in a matter of seconds. Mop-up took longer for these play fires than it might have for a genuine lightning strike. We started at the point of ignition and scrubbed the prairie with our sacks, blending the black ash into dirt and stubble, until the fire site could pass for a patch of short-clipped grass.

In the aftermath, the twins and I sat in the shade of the old pull-style combine, puffing on contraband cigarettes and passing a bottle of rank booze we'd concocted from supplies on hand: equal jiggers of any real whiskey we could scrounge, chokecherry wine, lots of lemon and vanilla extracts, Listerine and Aqua Velva aftershave. The recipe amounts were guess-work, but the ingredients we knew from stories of the neighbors' hired men who came home off a week's drunk and chased the snakes and shakes with anything they could find in the boss lady's cupboards. The resulting brew was swill, but we didn't have to swallow it. For the purposes of the game, tipping the bottle and numbing a small spot on the tongue was real enough. The rest we acted out with staggering, slurring, backslapping abandon.

The only honest swigs of our home brew went down my father and a couple of neighbors, who discovered it while robbing scrap iron from the jumble of old machinery. They carried our bottle to the house. The twins and I formed a trio of round-eyed innocents, exchanging sly glances as the bottle went around, thrilling to the adjectives and expletives that graced the sniff test; each adult touched the bottle to his nose, then tipped it up. Dad brought it down with a shudder. "Christ!" he wheezed. The three of us beamed at each other. High praise, indeed! The bottle circled the table a second time, and Mom tried some, too, rolling it around in her mouth, sorting flavors. Lemon extract and aftershave. The work of old Marvin Rice, they agreed, although it was strange, out of character you might say, for old Marvin Rice to have abandoned such a bottle 99 percent full.

Marvin's stint in our hayfield one year had been brief, sober and uneventful, but legend held sway. Some years before, he had shambled into every bar on Main Street at the tail end of a monthlong binge, pleading with bartenders until one took pity and let him hock his false teeth for one last quart of Jim Beam. If the story was true, he never got them back. I had observed him at our table—a slow, polite eater, face collapsing around each bite, the toughest steak going down on nothing but gums. As speculation circled the kitchen, the twins and I ourselves came close to believing he was guilty. Legends make anything possible.

We never replaced the bottle—in fact, by the time Dad ran across it, we had nearly forgotten it was there. We had quit playing Fire by then, though not from any inborn burst of maturity or responsibility. It had taken a strong dose of reality to cure us. Our last fire was a camp for traveling cowpokes set in the duff of rotten hay by the corrals, a less-than-brilliant location, but perhaps we had become complacent. We were not ignorant of the consequences of fire. We could point virtu- ously to the many precautions we took, forgoing our games when range conditions were dangerously dry or windy, using a coffee can or a circle of rocks to contain the flames of a cook- fire, keeping water, a shovel, wet sacks within arm's reach. But the midsummer day was hot and windy enough for us to seek the shade and shelter of the windbreak and barn, a conve- nient setting for cowboy games. We imagined our story line through the first campfire without incident, smothering it and scattering the remains through our fingers to make sure the ashes were cold.

The story might have ended there, but for something that separated us, a squabble, perhaps, as Gail and I grew bored with the game, or maybe a voice cutting through the wind, calling us girls back to the house. Alone, Gary lit a second campfire. This one went underground.

I imagine his panic as the fire began to sink through the packed brown compost of ancient hay that we had all mis- taken for dirt, flames crawling into earth and springing up out of reach as he stomped and dug and tried to bury it deep enough to die. Whatever terror he may have felt, when the moment of decision came, that instant when both he and the fire crossed over and quit pretending, he was man enough to run for the house. Smoke roiled over the windbreak by the time we formed a human chain to the well, Mom and four of us children running water to my father, who stood on the smoldering hay and tossed it, bucketful by bucketful, against the east wall of the barn.

I remember that fire best by its sounds: wind whipping flames through the gaps in a board fence; milk pen calves bawling inside the barn; the rush of fire in hay, like static or wasps, and the snap where it hit dry wood. And like a roar in the background, I remember the absence of human voices. No one yelled or screamed. No one called the neighbors. And even when the fire was finally out and we gathered in the house, the enormity of this error, the obvious shame of the charred windbreak and blackened barn wall, made words superfluous.

"You understand what you did." My father's voice broke and drew thin over the last word. His huge shoulders stuck in mid-lunge just over Gary's head, his arms pulled straight on either side. At that point Gary could have folded and spread the blame. We wouldn't have faulted him. The rules of sibling loyalty were foolish in the face of this father whose legs still trembled from exertion. Had it been me, I would have confessed on the spot, every illicit match. Gail and I held our breath and waited. We could not volunteer, we would not deny. Gary never flinched. He owned up with one bloodless nod, so far beyond sorry that the beating we all expected would have been welcome. Instead, there was silence, a dismissal.

I think Dad could have forgiven Gail or me had one of us taken the blame for that fire, girls with too much time on their

hands, girls whose stupidity and carelessness were explain-
able, but there were no words to excuse any son of a cattleman
who would willfully, deliberately, betray his land. For months,
Gary followed Dad with his eyes, and for months, Dad focused
an identical blue gaze on a spot just above Gary's head.

By the time I hit twelve a couple of years later, I had given up
questioning why it was different to be a girl and fought to separate the biological fact of being female from the roles that
went with the plumbing. I had no quarrel with the God-given
facts. I was fascinated with babies and birth, curious about
sex, in love with James Arness and the young Clint Eastwood.
The roles went like this: Every rancher who stepped out the
door scratching a full belly through a clean shirt had a partner
who was willing to stay indoors and wash another load. "Someone to make the mess, and someone to clean it up," as my
mother put it.

Most of the women in my community were like my
mother—strong, capable women whose names were listed on
the ranch deeds alongside their husbands', but who accepted
second say in the business of it. On the fringe of their wifely
example lay stories spawned in days of the penny dreadful and
beyond, the Calamity Jane–type of mythology that held just
enough truth to be dangerous. In these stories, landowning
women were admired for their staunch independence and
toughness—the sort of women who hired cooks and ran their
own ranches. They were in books. They had their own TV
shows. And every ranch wife I knew crossed over just enough
to make the stories seem possible, if not practical. In a book,
when myth met reality and crashed, I simply skirted the
wreckage, taking what I wanted from the opening chapters

and flipping through marry-the-foreman-and-turn-over-the-reins scenes two pages at a time. To my great dissatisfaction as a young reader, these outwardly strong characters routinely made foolish decisions and took on more than they could handle, were taught a good lesson in "what's really important," and in the end fell in love with the patient, indulgent men who rescued them from themselves.

In my real-life, out-west community, the depressing sequel was being written as I watched, and the weak parts were harder to skip. I knew women savvy to the working of cattle and horses, women who rode the hay rake in June and took to the fields at harvest. But without exception, they picked up a thank-you and walked back to tackle the work that was theirs alone. Woman's work. If I learned nothing else in my early years, I learned the scorn that twisted those words into insults.

My mother despised the repetitious and thankless nature of housework and was an expert horsewoman, characteristics that brought her closer to my ideal than most. The downside was her unshakable sense of duty. I was a daughter, and must be pinned to my seat with threats until I learned to cook and sew and butcher chickens and can green beans. But it was also Mom who hazed for me the first time I left the corral on my green-broke bronc, Sunny, riding up to turn him from the barbed wire fence as we bolted across the pasture. "Stay with him!" she cheered, and I did, until the front cinch broke and Sunny bucked straight through the reservoir with her good saddle hanging upside down on his belly. I dusted off my pride while Mom rode after the colt, leaning sideways at a full gallop to jerk the buckle on the flank cinch and snub the hackamore rein to her saddle horn. Womanly arts be damned. I wanted the ease, the power, of my mother, horseback. I wanted the real myth, and I set out to get it.

Fighting Fire

That fall, as I turned twelve, the sole member of my peer group defected. My cousin Lois turned thirteen, and despite our blood-sister oath forbidding such things, she put on a bra, ratted her hair into haystacks and kissed the hired man. I worked on my own appearance with grim determination. I spit and crossed my legs like a field hand. I peeled my nails off with my teeth, and kept my hair bobbed away from my face. I preferred stacking bales and working cattle, and ducked house chores when I could. I climbed trees, rode the milk pen steers to a standstill and strung frogs ten-deep on a willow spear. Come winter, I read myself into the strongest characters of half the Malta library. I made it last a year. And when, in the inexorable process of time, my body betrayed me, my rage was terrible.

That spring I stood exposed to the cold draft of the bathroom, one ear tuned to the night sounds that crept through the locked door, my father's rumbling snore, the shifting squeak of the double bed my brothers shared. My sister slept just inches away through a thin partition. I steadied my hands against the sink and leaned forward, recording the changes I saw in the medicine chest mirror. Dark brown hair, sun-faded to the color of old hay, ear length and shaggy, needing a wash. A big, raw-boned girl, my mother said. Tall for twelve. A square, horsy face, I thought, eyes hidden by owlish glasses, chin jutting like a shoehorn, my father's chin and his wolfish teeth wrangling for space behind the tight lips.

Hands shaking, I shrugged into my pajama top, giving up, finally, on the buttons, then lowered the lid on the toilet with exaggerated care and sat down, waiting for the rubbery, queasy feeling to subside. The lump on my chest throbbed like a heartbeat, movable under my fingers but still firm, despite a

97

tiny trickle of blood. The rest of me felt numb with dread. I hadn't expected a permanent cure. I just wanted a little more time, a few months, maybe a year.

My idea was a product of bad pasture. With Kenny gone to Malta for high school, I'd been called on to help Dad work half a dozen cows with abscessed jaws. Sharp-pronged seeds of cheatgrass or foxtail barley had drilled through the lining of their mouths, infecting the flesh. We hazed each cow into the chute and caught her lopsided head in the squeeze gate. Some of the abscesses were fist-sized, others filled the jawline from chin to throat, tight and ripe as watermelons. Dipping the thin second blade of his jackknife in iodine, Dad slit each swelling, standing to one side so the first geyser of pus and blood would miss him. I worked the vaccine gun, pumping a dose of penicillin into the meaty part of each rump as it passed through the chute. Dad explained, as he cut along the bottom of a lump, how gravity kept the wound open and draining until it healed from the inside out; cut too high, and the abscess would form again.

In the months that followed, I thought about the sure jab of his knife, the slick sideways cut, the gritty sound of the blade slicing tough skin, the immediate release of pressure. I thought it through, modifying any steps that appeared unreasonable. I suspected the procedure was painful, though with cows you couldn't tell. That night I tiptoed to the bathroom, selected a clean sock from the laundry basket and gripped it in my teeth, just in case. After dabbing my bare chest with alcohol, I attempted to lance my breast buds with a darning needle.

My first bid to become sexless left no scars, aside from the mental anguish I suffered when the punctured breast actually swelled larger for a little while. But it marked my last quest for an easy answer.

Fighting Fire

≠

In late August the prairie hills rippled in the wind, bunchgrass grown tall in a late, wet spring, sun-cured by July, six weeks of heat with no rain. The excitement started before noon, the first call coming in as a dry lightning storm, all wind and no rain, still popped to the east and the phone bristled with static electricity. One bolt had hit the face of a dam on Bill Knight's reservoir, a few miles south of us, a small fire they had slapped out within minutes. Dad and Bill stood in the lee of a pickup cab for a while, trading gossip as they watched the dead burn for signs of resurrection. Later, the day would be told as a story, and it would start with this red-herring fire, a fire the size of a kitchen table, the ease with which two men soaked a gunnysack and smacked it out in an ocean of knee-high grass. "We were still congratulating each other," my dad would say, "when Bill looked over his shoulder." To the northwest, a knot of smoke hovered at the skyline.

The community fell together. Wives grabbed the phones, husbands and older boys jerk-started rickety fire trucks and aimed for the smoke, picking up speed on the fencing trails heading west. Younger kids stood out of the way, absorbed by one of the rarest scenes played out in our community: visible panic. Grown men ran. Rules were broken without pause— fences cut, gates pitched open and left. In the seconds before it pulled away, I stood beside our pickup, working the zipper on my fuzzy coat, trying without success to catch my father's eye as he topped off the gas tank. To distract him by begging to go along would be shameful in the heat of an emergency. Kenny threw an armload of burlap sacks over the tailgate, Dad jammed them into the water barrel and the two of them swung into the cab, a team working in tandem. A team. My chest

Breaking Clean

thickened with unspecified resentments. I hadn't expected to go, really, but I had changed my sneakers for boots and stuffed my leather gloves into my coat pockets, just in case.

After they left, I wandered back to the general uproar around the house. News was routed to our place as the fire closed in. Pickups bounded into the yard, pulled up and revved once while the screen door banged and Mom dashed into shouting distance, pointing, directing, watching as they pulled out in a spray of dust. On guard inside, I waited for the phone to ring, ready to fly through the same screen door and screech "Telephone!" then dart back in to watch the receiver until she got there. It was an important job, like keeping tabs on a snake until she fetched a hoe, but one that was quickly taken over. The house began to fill with neighbor women who rode along as far as the yard and leaped out with whatever they had grabbed from their own kitchens—a sack of cookies, a loaf of bread, a jug of Kool-Aid. Black plumes in the lighter-gray grass smoke were reported breathlessly upon arrival, and the kitchen conversation turned to tense speculation. Was it the Nesbits' garbage dump, or their house? Could corner posts treated with creosote burn that black, that big? Or perhaps a truck overtaken by the fire, cut off, someone's husband or son.

By three o'clock pickups began to break through the haze and roll toward our well to get water; boys too young for the fire line raced to string hoses and fill buckets from the stock tank. When our outfit pulled up and my mother emerged from the house for an update, I trotted behind her to the pump house. Dad's jeans were filthy with soot, and sweat traced clean stripes from his hat line down each cheek to the point of his jaw. A red rash dotted the vee of bare skin at his collar. Mom followed him with phone messages, while he pulled off his gloves, wet his bandanna and bent over the tank to rinse his face. I fidgeted and eyed the door of the pickup.

"The fire passed the Nesbit place," he said, voice muffled and urgent through the hankie, "came a stone's throw from the barn and corrals." I edged around the nose of the pickup. Wind held the driver's door open, dirt swirled along the floorboards.

"When the fire got close, Grace came out with a broom," Dad was saying, "a wet broom."

"I tried to call. I thought she'd gone," Mom said. "I wondered." Their voices closed in, talking fast. I slithered under the steering wheel to the far side of the bench seat, eased my gloves on and tried to breathe the fine dust quietly. The hose thumped against the back window.

"Hey!" Gary scrambled out of the back end, whining. "Why does she get to go?" The voices died away.

I settled deeper in the seat. Clenching my teeth, I called up the familiar shape of Gary's head and placed it in the center of my mind. Blond crew cut, crooked grin, wide blue eyes. Perfect. I squeezed my right fist and his face exploded in slow motion, pattering against the windshield. Behind me I could still hear his voice. I rewound the tape and played it again, depressing the plunger slowly, deliberately. *Ka-boom!*

"Dad, can I go? Why does she get to go?" The pickup rocked as the tailgate slammed. *Ka-blooey!* Dad slid into the cab, the smell of sweat and burnt grass. The engine roared up. I looked at him sideways. His eyes were bloodshot and watery, not unkind.

"Not this time, Sis."

Mom opened the door on my side. I was holding up the show. Gary stood at her hip, smug but wary, edging a prudent distance from the cab as I jumped out. The door shut with a

solid *chuff.* I pulled at the fingers of my gloves, casually remov-
ing the evidence of my folly as the grind of the motor dwindled
and dissolved into the clamor of wind in the cottonwoods.
Mom's arm lifted as if to circle my shoulders, and I ducked it
smoothly. There were sandwiches to be made. "God knows
we'll be feeding the Russian army when this is over," she said.
Her voice carried behind me halfway to the house, until it,
too, was lost in the roar.

Hours later, I stared out from the shelter of the tall windbreak
fence at the familiar outlines of the farmyard blurred by
smoke, willing myself not to blink, calming the hitch in my
chest. The weakness that came over me that spring had grown
worse as the weeks wore on. It started out gradually, like a
tightness in my chest, then moved up, swelling my throat until
I could no longer swallow. The cure was crying, gut-deep and
out of control, the sort of watery-eyed, lace-panties, town-girl
behavior I especially detested. I pushed up a sleeve of my coat
and ran a thumb along my inner arm. A faint pattern of yellow
and lavender stippled with fresher blue began at the tan line
on my wrist and disappeared under the coat cuff at my elbow.
I folded a patch of clear skin carefully between two knuckles
and began to twist.

The coat was a hand-me-down from my brother, charcoal-
gray fake fur bristled in a buzz cut, cool nylon lining against
my skin, baggy enough to hide the disfiguring lumps on my
chest. I'd worn it straight through the heat of summer, per-
fecting a mute and sullen shrug for adults, turning so savage
under teasing that my brothers and sisters left me alone. I
hated being looked at. I would not be touched. I relaxed my
fist and focused on the bright throb that bloomed on my inner

arm, a clean pain that calmed me and helped me focus, then opened my coat and rubbed my face against the inner lining.

Across the barnyard, house lights burned and women moved behind them, passing in shadow along the west window. All afternoon my mother and the neighboring wives had circled the cramped kitchen, sidestepping from sink to stove with the grace of square dancers. Chairs had been shuffled aside and the table shoved tight against the wall to make room. A two-gallon coffee urn burped and moaned, dripping progressively darker drops into the cup under its spout. The enamel dishpan of canned venison sandwiches and a half a dozen cakes were draped with flour sack towels to keep the flies off.

The fire had traveled the miles between ranches in a matter of a couple of hours, and in the time I spent indoors, smoke had closed in around the buildings. The wind was visible, streaming overhead until it ran out of sky. I took a deep breath and rested against the haystack. My arms and legs trembled, my throat still tender where the knot had unraveled. The fire had moved within sight of the windbreak, and I became conscious of distant shouts floating up whenever the wind eased. I sat up, burying the past hour with a fresh sense of purpose. Hay bales leaned against the windbreak like giant stairsteps. Where they left off, I jumped to grab the top and swing a leg over. A four-by-six brace ran along the top of the boards, a narrow bench I could straddle in relative comfort, fifteen feet in the air.

Clamping my heels to the rough boards, I swiveled away from the house, balancing the wind gusts by reflex, leaning to offset the steady push against me, rocking back so I didn't fall forward when they turned loose. My cheeks pulled taut in the heat. I held on with my legs and tongue-wet my jacket cuff, scrubbing at the salt crust around my eyes before I looked up. Squinting one eye shut, I held my hand at arm's length in front of my face and located the sun, a lighter-gray smudge in the sky two fingers above the Little Rockies. The wind churned smoke four fingers higher than the sun, then blew it straight east like chaff off a flat palm.

On the near horizon, flames topped a ridge and poured down the other side. A quarter mile closer, a slash of raw dirt opened slowly behind a rust-colored road grader. From the north, another neighbor stood over the steering wheel of his John Deere tractor, legs spread for balance as he careened toward the firebreak in high gear, a three-bottom plow bouncing along behind like a child's pull toy. The tractor slowed and veered to one side of the grader's path, and the driver dropped to the seat to shift down, reaching behind with the other hand to jerk the plow line and set the shovels to sod. The plow skipped once, twice, then it bit and the tractor squatted with a jerk, bellowing a thundercloud of diesel smoke. Behind it the prairie began to boil.

The fire ran low to the ground, rearing up on its haunches when the wind fell off, then dropping down to sprint on the next gust. Men with pitchforks fought to clear the fence line ahead of it. A stream of tumbleweeds raced for the firebreak, bouncing over each other as they neared the line and crossed the ribbon of dust without slowing. Heat devils rose from the flames and skipped through the grass a few feet ahead of the fire. A flatbed tank truck crawled by the fence, collecting the pitchfork crew, then jounced across the plowed strip and stopped. The figures tumbled off the truck with wet sacks and formed a line facing the fire, ready to slap out airborne sparks.

Another jagged stretch of men laced the south edge of the fire, arms lifting and falling, funneling the fire north toward the meadows. I studied the size of the silhouettes along the line. Boys were out there behind the lines, making things happen. I worked myself up and spit deliberately over the side of the windbreak. Kitchen duty had not been without satisfaction. Assigned to the sandwich team, I'd pushed up my sleeves so they didn't drag and set to work without back talk. A little nod of encouragement and Mom went about her own business. She was as immune to my coat as I was. Dot and Jane were not at all immune, and stared dumbfounded as I plunged a lightly rinsed hand cuff-deep into the pickle jar and began hacking homemade dills into chunks, absorbed by the growing ache in my throat and chest. My fellow sandwich makers drew up on either side of me.

"Aren't you hot in that jacket?" Jane asked sweetly. She smiled, eyes wide with effort, fanning her face with a potholder. A clue, perhaps, to the correct answer.

"Not at all." I smiled back at her. Sweetly. Dot seemed mesmerized by my sleeve, and I glanced down, gratified. Mine was truly a coat of many colors. In addition to hay and oat chaff, the clipped gray pile carried evidence of a palomino mare, a Black Angus steer and half a dozen cats. To me it smelled doggy and comfortable, but I wasn't stupid. From the corner of my eye, I saw Dot wrinkle her nose and look first toward Mom, on the phone with a finger stuck in her other ear, then at Jane. I breathed through my clenched teeth. I did not belong in this kitchen. I knew that. Everyone but my mother knew it. But their eyes measured me with, what—scorn? pity? disgust? I would make their job easier.

Baiting them, I set down the knife and scooped a drippy fistful of pickles into a huge bowl of ground venison and onions, squishing the mess together with plenty of arm action. Their mouths drew down, but they kept up an idle chatter, poised on either side of me. I paused in my venison mashing and held my slimy hands over the board, as if considering what to do next, and they moved in. Jane snatched up the paring knife, Dot went for the pickle jar, I took one easy step back and their elbows met midway in the space I left. Wiping my hands on my pants, I sidled out of the kitchen, easing the door shut in a thrill of restraint.

The new job description I worked out was a natural. The windbreak and some cottonwood trees around the yard screened the fire line from the house. In the next twenty minutes, the fire would reach the firebreak of raw dirt and either deflect toward the meadows or jump straight across and aim for our buildings. If the fire crossed, all hell would break loose, but somewhere a pickup waited, ready to carry a warning to the house. They would pass the very windbreak I perched on. My duty, as I saw it, was to beat the pickup and spread the alarm myself. I would be a Fire Scout.

I flexed my legs one at a time, feeling for pinpricks, staying limber, planning the steps. I would launch the second I read panic on the fire line, cut across the feedlot, fall and roll under the pole fences rather than waste time climbing. I would slow to an urgent stride by the house, calm, in control. The women would turn to look at me when I stepped into the kitchen, my shoulders filling the doorway. "Gather up," I'd say, "we're clearing out. The fire jumped the line." My mother would wheel around to the window and turn back slowly. I imagined the fear in her eyes, and shivered.

I modified the scene every five minutes for the next hour, but my dream died with the wind at sunset. Pickups that had raced through the farmyard for hours now lurched and rolled to a stop, as if hit by sudden waves of exhaustion. The men climbed out slowly and lined up at the basin set up on a bench by the front door next to a pile of ratty towels. They ate in shifts, new rigs rolling in as others pulled away. The breeze, when it reappeared, smelled damp. Lying hidden on top of a haystack, I fingered my collar, holding it snug around my neck, waiting for the yard to empty and the people to go home.

When the fire died and the smoke began to clear, I had worked my way along the tall fence to a power pole and stood for a better view of the mop-up. Fire rigs lumbered over the naked landscape, patrolling for live embers, gathering in groups of two or three on hilltops to watch for flare-ups. A raw black scar narrowed as it rounded the north end of the fire-break, flowed east for another mile, then dipped through the barrow pit and stopped in a neat line. Tank trucks stretched nose to tail along the county road. Pressing my arm against the pole, I turned, finally, to the wet and stood for a long time.

The glow of dusk seemed part of the air, a soft light that washed the gentle step of hills evenly, without direction or source. The grass had burned clean and fast, but wisps of smoke still rose from the range fuel, the cow chips and sage-brush. A row of stumps flared along the fence like candles, flames that bled out and disappeared against a blaze of sunset. Five thousand acres of grazing land and grain fields, once as comfortable and taken for granted as the coat I pulled around me, stretched to the horizon in black waves, stripped to meat and muscle. The soft contours were gone, coulees and draws naked of grass rose stark as bruised skin, every wrinkle and rock exposed to the air. I slid down and kicked a bed in the top of the hay, lying hidden as true darkness grew under a thin blanket of clouds.

There are moments of recognition that empty you, times when no amount of arm pinching can mask the who and what of you that stares back up from the hollow. Eventually I would come to understand that the rules and roles I fought were less about me than they were about my place, this piece of earth I came to identify with as clearly as I did my family. This lesson was inexplicably difficult for me, and I have no explanation other than to say my sisters appeared to step around the restrictions and freedoms of our family and our community, selecting what fit them and moving on with far more grace than I mustered. I suspect I wanted too much, but maybe I simply wanted more and grew bitter when it came clear what was, and what was not to be.

Some childhood games are played for real. My brother had learned that in one harsh lesson, standing in the ashes of a play fire gone wrong, the blackened boards of our barn an accusation that stood for years. It seemed to be taking me longer to get the message. Some things couldn't be taken back, and some games lived in consequence far beyond my precocious urge to be grown-up and powerful. I recalled the day two years before, when I tethered a half-grown kitten we called Tiger to the headboard of a hayrack, measuring the twine leash carefully so he couldn't jump off either side, tying him so he would be there when I came back to play after lunch. I left him some water, I studied the shade that the headboards cast, ladderlike, across the bed of the rack, made a nest for him in the coolest spot and walked away, confident of my own brilliance. Unable to escape off the sides, the kitten did the one obvious thing I hadn't seen. He crawled between the boards he was tied to and jumped for the wagon tongue. When I returned with my pockets full of lunch scraps, he was already cool, his eyes open to the wind that swung him gently, the tips of his hind toes brushing softly, back and forth, as if smoothing the faint scratches he had left in the silvery wood of the wagon tongue, or perhaps pointing out how close he had come to surviving, how unforgivably cruel his death had been.

Years later, pushing my son on a playground swing, I would catch our shadow at the corner of my eye, the sway of a baby seat with the stripe of bars overhead, and the memory would punch through the surface so fast I would plead aloud, *I didn't know I didn't know,* standing with one fist buried in my hair, mindless of the stares I drew, the way my two older children gathered close to my legs, watchful, protecting me for long seconds until it passed.

Mercy, I've discovered, is hard learned and slow to stick. A whiff of burning grass can still fill my head with color, the terrible bloom of sunset through smoke, the endless, aching stumble of hills over the land below. From this distance I can see myself squirming a bed in the top of a stack and know it was not disappointment that held me there, nor defiance that made me crouch lower when the dinner bell clanged and my father's whistle pierced the silence. It was failure, a shame so pure I absorbed it in tiny gusts, flinching when lights and voices drifted up from the house. Inside, they would be telling stories of the fire, a community of men and women pulled together by the work they had done for each other, and their pride in doing it well. Work had to do with the land, with people big enough to fight fire with a wet broom if that was what they had to work with. I had not set myself aside and pitched in. In the end, I had done the one thing worse than doing nothing. I had rooted for the fire.

Ajax

Like most farm kids, I can count the years of my childhood by the procession of animals, those born to the farm and those "rescued" from the wild, that I knew and cared for and claimed as my own. Early on, I came to see the animal kingdom as divided into three more or less distinct groups. The first were the protected species, like the horses, the dog and cats, that provided a service in exchange for their care. They were intentional animals, like the livestock, but they belonged to us in a way the cattle did not. These were animals designed to live out their natural life span in our care, barring accident or illness, and assuming they earned their keep. My passion might be safely spent here, stuffing kittens into doll clothes, harnessing our collie dog to the sled, galloping horseback through the creek bottoms.

The presence of animals in my life was as important as the presence of my siblings, and our interactions were no less weighted. The cats, especially, brought out a side of my mother I seldom evoked in my own right, a lovely gift of language and gentle wit, mock disgust and play anger, brief lapses in the strict, no-nonsense tone that guided our lives. My mother's parents were middle-aged when she was born, and in lieu of siblings, she had grown up surrounded by an expanse of empty prairie and a multitude of dogs and cats, horses and bantam hens. In the humorless grind of tending five children with few resources and less money, she found her imagination and her sense of play in the presence of her animals, bringing it all together in quiet moments. "Streak, you're a big platter-footed fool," she would begin in a conversational tone as the big white cat with tiger patches lumbered toward his dish. Something in his answer always sparked an argument. Back and forth they would go: "Don't you use that tone of voice with *me,* buster. I'll dust your pants. Well, quit blundering around underfoot if you don't want to be stepped on, you big goon. Go catch a mouse if you're hungry." All this as she strained the milk from morning chores into clean jars and poured the last cup or so into his dish.

We children worked to create those moments, greedy for the softness of eye and tone, thrilled by the cleverness of words, the roll and rhyme of language. Cats, we learned, did not simply rub against us—they polished our shins or stropped their whiskers on our pants legs. They purred like teakettles or thundered through the kitchen like a herd of wild elephants. If they got too rambunctious with their claws, one told them to haul in their toenails, that they had the manners of a warthog. Little Bits, Pantaloons, Beetle Tracks, Ginger and Cocoa. Friendly, a glossy black little mama cat with a milky moustache, belly and paws who was not especially friendly to anyone but Mom. In her litters of two or three huge kittens appeared an occasional solid chocolate or ginger-brown one with white markings. Her tail felt like a string of rosary beads, each bump another lesson in the behavior of teething toddlers. Her son, Streak, was a fat tom my sister and

I decked out in doll clothes and propped up on pillows in a clothes basket, where he lay for hours licking a doll bottle gripped in his front paws. In those days, it would have been unusual to spend money neutering farm cats or dogs, and no one I knew vaccinated, wormed or purchased special food for pets. Cats and dogs ate table scraps and hunted for themselves. Extras were shot. But the ones we claimed did not go without love.

There were limits, of course, practical guidelines to observe, places a cat didn't belong, behavior that earned dogs wholesale beating or horses a kick in the ribs. But these rules seemed sensible, the punishment little different than that accorded our own transgressions, and in neither case did I doubt my mother's authority.

The orphans we rescued or kidnapped from the prairie around us were animals I loved at my own peril, for they did not belong in a barnyard and those that lost their fear of humans generally signed their own death warrants. The wild ones—mallard ducklings, cottontails and jackrabbits, the white-tail fawn and the blind, hairless baby skunks—span a decade in the family photo albums. They pop up like seasonal flowers, small doomed creatures swaddled in rags, cradled in well-meaning hands and fed makeshift milk from makeshift bottles—part of the scenery for a snapshot or two, then gone.

Most were casualties of the hayfields, either orphaned or injured as the machines made their rounds in early June. The hay mower's seven-foot sickle bar did not follow directly behind the tractor, it jutted to one side, slicing through the tall alfalfa a few inches from the ground. A driver paying attention to the tractor's path also kept watch for obstacles hidden in the thick, uncut hay to the right. Pheasants leaving their nests ran low to the ground for a number of yards before breaking cover; ducks crouched over clutches of pale-green eggs until the last possible second. Skunks and porcupines might run from the sound of the tractor directly into the path of the cutting arm.

My father avoided the nests and the scurrying wildlife as best he could. A solid hit that resulted in an explosion of feathers or porcupine quills, or worse yet, the reek of skunk, not only ruined hay, it usually put the mower down for repairs. Though he was more likely to grumble about the inconvenience and expense, he would cut a wide path around a nesting bird if he saw it in time. He'd stop the tractor and walk ahead if he thought something was hiding in the uncut hay. In the process of keeping track of the meadows all spring, he'd know where the white-tail deer were hiding, their fawns dropped just as the alfalfa began to bud. Entering a new meadow, he watched the margins of the field for a nervous doe, her alert, tail-twitching, hoof-stamping dance a sign that the mower was entering the field where her fawns hid, hardwired to lie flat and still in the very teeth of danger. The fawns that broke rank early and ran, lived. Others held to instinct, trusting their spotted skin to make them invisible, and sadly, it often did.

I raised one of these to weaning size, a small doe fawn that jumped up too late and lost a hind foot to the sickle blades. Baby rabbits we captured in the woodpile or rescued from the cats and kept in little cages. The baby skunk crawled from beneath the chicken house, blind and hairless one day, hours after its mother was shot raiding the nests. I named the little creature Flower, after the Disney character from *Bambi,* though only her gender prevented a moniker of Pepe Le Pew. I warmed canned milk mixed with water and fed Flower every few hours, teaching her to suckle a squeeze bottle I'd salvaged from a Toni home permanent kit. I rose to feed her when she cried at night, stroked her stomach patiently to stimulate her little bowels and kept her box toasty warm with hot water bottles, seemingly oblivious to the fact that I was rearing what amounted to vermin in a community devoted and committed to killing vermin.

Perhaps the novelty of wild animals was enough to earn them asylum, or perhaps it was their baby features, the rounded ears and helpless mewling, that made grown-ups carry them home rather than brain them outright. They had to be allowed to grow up before one could honorably kill them, it seemed, or at least given a chance to refuse domestication. My mother tells the story of how, as a small child, she managed to capture a baby gopher. She found a box and made it a nest, offered up a variety of victuals a little gopher might enjoy. He was a cute little fellow, but when she scooped him up to play with him, the ungrateful thing bit her on the finger. So she fed him to her tomcat.

When the cute wore off the wild animals I raised, they had to find new homes. Flower left with my teacher Mae Bibeau when school was out that spring, and though never descented she made a nice pet until she was shot by a varmint-hunting neighbor. The fawn, given to a ranch near the highway, survived until hunting season the next fall, when even her missing foot and a red bow around her neck couldn't save her.

It seems strange to me now that just as I never questioned my motives in rearing these orphans, no one ever doubted our right to do as we wished with the creatures that shared our land. Imagine the life of little Jack the Rabbit—any one of a dozen we caught in the woodpile or rescued from a prowling cat who aimed to offer him up, frightened but alive, to her half-grown kittens for hunting practice. Bundled to the house, the new Jack is soon ensconced in an apple crate with a door of wire mesh that's a bare fraction too small to admit a cat's paw, though the owners of such paws give it a whirl whenever no one's watching. When they can, the cats terrorize him through the mesh and he huddles bug-eyed at the back of the crate until we shoo them away.

In spite of the lodgings, he manages to recover from his superficial injuries within a few days. We pull grass for him to eat and offer garden leavings, and keep a tin can of water weighted with rocks in a corner of the cage. He eats and drinks. He sits in his tiny cage in the porch watching the cats watching him. Jack is a good-sized bunny when we decide to set him free a few weeks later. Dad loads us all into the back of the pickup and we ride with Jack's cage to the wheat fields west of the house, rabbit paradise. We form a stately procession into the rows of green winter wheat and open the door of the cage. There's a pause.

"How will we know him from the other jackrabbits?" one of us asks. Dad thinks a moment, then slides out his pocketknife. Reaching down, he grabs Jack's right ear and with one swift movement cuts off the tip. The rabbit squeals once and bounds for freedom bearing the right crop earmark our cattle wear.

Looking back over the tailgate as we bounded the short road home, I remember feeling intensely proud to have rescued the jackrabbit, tended it and now returned it to the wild. At no time did I or anyone around me question how Jack might have fared in this reunion with nature—Jack, a half-grown rabbit with senses and reflexes dulled from his weeks in a cage, wounded, sprinkled with fresh blood, and loosed among the predators at sunset. I imagine Jack's fate was swift and sure, its onset merely delayed by the days spent on our porch.

Still, the novelty of caring for an injured fawn or hatching some orphaned duck eggs made a break from our routine chores, and while their eventual fates changed little, there was always room for hope. And in any case, it was better than getting attached to a member of that other group of animals that populated our life—the poultry, cattle and pigs that lived for the sole purpose of dying and becoming meat. Some things are not safe to love, and like most children raised around live-stock, I learned emotional detachment as a form of common sense. My first direct lesson, when I was nine or ten years old, concerned Pet, a young rooster. I had been given the chicken chores for the first time that spring, not just the feeding and egg gathering of the older hens, but the more challenging job of tending the baby chicks that arrived in the mail. In the days before their arrival, we scrubbed out the water founts, put down clean sand in the little brooder house, and then lit the gas brooder, checking the thermometer every few hours to make sure the temperature remained even: too cold, and the chicks would pile up under the brooder and suffocate; too hot, and they would wilt with dehydration. We waited for a call from the post office telling us when the chicks arrived. Some-times we drove to Malta to get them, and sometimes they caught the Regina mail as far as our local post office.

The chicks were shipped in flat cardboard crates with holes punched in the sides, one hundred freshly hatched chicks in each crate. In the brooder house, we lifted them out one at a time and gently dipped each beak in a water fount to teach them how to drink. The first couple of weeks, I spent hours watching and tending the little flock. A dusting of red-dish fluff had allowed me to pick Pet out of the swarm of plain yellow chicks early on. As the summer progressed and I spent more and more time with my band of gentle chickens, I continued to pick him out for special favors. By the time they were old enough to be turned outside, Pet was as domestic as a chicken can get. He ran to meet me when he saw me coming, and I swear he raised his wings like a small child lifts its arms to be picked up. In the heat of the afternoon, he climbed into my lap and dozed as I sat in the shade of the granary. I swiped food from the refrigerator to feed him, and he learned to pick my pockets.

Mom had told us stories of the little bantam hens she had kept as a child, and she seemed bemused when I wandered by with this large, obliging bird under my arm. Still, she was not unaware of the position I was taking. "You know what's going to happen," she warned, and of course in some part of my mind I did. Roosters were called fryers for a reason. I suppose I answered her with a tough-girl shrug.

That fall we waited until the last butchering to kill him, though he'd grown to roasting size by then. I carried his jerking, headless body from the chopping block to the steaming bucket under the cottonwoods. Wordlessly, Mom grabbed him by the feet and dunked him in the scalding water. Pet's destiny had never been in doubt from the moment he set foot under the brooder, and her business-as-usual actions bore this out. She rubbed a thumb up one drumstick, testing and dipping until the feathers slid easily from the skin, then she handed him back to me for plucking. I would not have had to do this, but I remember thinking it was necessary to perform these actions myself, the same way a man has to put down a faithful old dog or shoot his own horse if it breaks a leg. In this way, I saw Pet through. Naked and footless, his carcass stiffened into meat and merged with a dozen others bobbing in the washtub of cold water. When I turned away and looked back, I could no longer tell which body was his.

Late that afternoon, the butchering long over, I sorted through the pile of severed heads beside the huge cottonwood stump that served as our chopping block. Dozens of them littered the ground. The fresh ones looked nearly alive. The ones from previous days had dried to five-pointed stars—beaks open, comb and wattles dried stiff, feathers hardened to points at the neck. I turned over the heads of my flock, one at a time, until I spotted the familiar pattern of rust-colored feathers. I squatted for a moment without touching him, aware of a tingling in my belly, like electricity, that made my muscles feel weak. Finally, afraid of being caught, I spread a threadbare washcloth on the ground, placed Pet's head firmly in the center, and wrapped it up like I would wrap a doll in a blanket.

I palmed the flat, cold package and stood, glancing around to be sure I was not observed. It was certainly possible to get in trouble for taking the washcloth, but I believe my deepest fear was of being caught in the ludicrous act of mourning a chicken. I kept Pet's head tightly bound, unwilling or unable to meet the gaze of his half-lidded eyes, and held his quiet burial in our pet cemetery behind the woodpile. In the end, it was less a tough lesson than an embarrassing one. Any idiot knew better than to get attached to a chicken, for pity's sake! The only surprise was that I had not stopped myself.

In the years that followed, I picked feathers off a hundred chickens, said my good-byes to a dozen milk pen calves and nonchalantly carried the gut pail to the house at the butchering of Curly and Lacy, a pair of clever little weaner pigs Grandpa Blunt had given us kids to fatten. Even with horses and cats, there was no guarantee that illness or accident

Ajax

would not carry them off, and so I took deliberate measures to keep my tender feelings to myself. By the time I was twelve, I felt immune to sentimentality of any sort. But somehow between twelve and thirteen I stumbled; there was Ajax.

In the one photo I have of the two of us, it is a gray spring day, and I am zipped up in the winter coat I will wear straight through the summer and into eighth grade. Over that armor, my face is cocky, my chin tipped at a rakish, almost defiant angle. I am sitting astride a big yearling steer, proud of us both, because I no longer have to plow-rein him or pull his big head around by one rein to get him to turn around the arena. He's learning to neck-rein like a cutting horse, responding to the light touch of the reins along his neck and the nudge of my feet along his ribs. Ajax faces the camera with his head up and his ears flipped forward, reins slack on his neck. His Angus sire is revealed in his rich black coloring, his solid, shiny hide blending into the shadow of trees behind the feed-lot. The white star on his forehead, the long legs and gawky face are gifts from his Holstein mother. He's over a year old, a coming two-year-old, and by ranch definitions my butt is planted directly over his T-bone steaks. My heels dangle by his short ribs. My eyes are dangerously empty.

I began breaking Ajax to ride when he was a youngster, the ugly duckling of the milk pen calves. They all got a workout, but Ajax loomed head and shoulders taller than the orphaned range calves that shared his mother's milk, and by virtue of size and temperament, he won the largest share of my time. Had he not been half dairy stock, he would have disappeared in the fall and I would have thought no more about him. But purebred still ruled the market then. Stockmen raised Hereford or Angus, or they crossed the two breeds, using Angus bulls and Hereford cows to create Black Baldy calves.

When it came time to sell, stock growers were at the mercy of the open market, whose trends and mysteries were interpreted, predicted and explained by those middlemen known as cattle buyers. Three or four cattle buyers worked our community, drifting through to test the waters in late summer. Arriving in a mud-spattered Cadillac, a buyer moved first to the kitchen to talk weights and prices, weather and market trends, over coffee. Then rancher and buyer climbed into a pickup for the drive through the herd. Buyers developed a shrewd eye for livestock, and often could accurately predict the weaning weights of calves while they were still in the fields. The cattle buyers all had feedlot customers back in Iowa or Nebraska somewhere, and though they competed with each other for our calf crops, they all had the same goal: to purchase calves from many ranches and have them all look like siblings when they were sorted into feedlot-sized groups.

Nature being what it is, not every calf fit the load. On shipping day, the buyer himself often stood in the cutting alley with a stock whip giving the thumbs-up or thumbs-down to each calf as it came toward him. A side pen gradually filled with the cutbacks. There were practical reasons for some of the cuts—usually age and size were the determining factors. Calves born too late or too early in the season might not do as well in a feeding program designed for a particular stage of growth and development. But often cosmetic differences were enough to earn a thumbs-down. A calf with its ears or tail frozen round or one that had sprouted a stubby horn after a bad dehorning job likely found itself in the cull pen. There it might be joined by other perfectly normal, perfectly proportioned, perfectly healthy Hereford calves that were born with some variation of the standard Hereford markings: red necks, line-backs, white splashes above the knees. These purely aesthetic culls were argued endlessly, but the buyer had the last say.

In a market where buyers demanded uniform loads of identical calves, my dog-gentle, half-Holstein milk penner fit no one's idea of a feeder calf. True to his breeding, by weaning time Ajax stood a foot taller than his beefy pen mates. Against all reason or breeding, he retained a model temperament, despite the persistent human who fit him with harnesses and disturbed his drowsy afternoons with rodeo games. For years I had longed for a colt to train, and I suppose it was that passion and energy that I spent on Ajax. All summer, as I climbed into the corral he separated himself from his buddies and trotted happily to meet me, snaking his long black tongue out to hook the green grass I offered in one hand like a farmer's bouquet, ignoring the latest bridle or harness contraption I held in the other. He stood placidly, eyelids drooping over dark liquid eyes, tail swinging idly at the occasional fly, while I made adjustments to the rigging, for he was continually outgrowing his gear. When I swung aboard, he waited to be prodded into action. As I drummed my heels to counter his passive resistance, we circled the corral reining a lopsided figure eight in the soft dirt. Other times, I hooked his harness to an old tire and drove him like a cart pony.

When weaning was over that autumn, he and the other cutbacks were turned out to pasture for a couple of months and I turned to other interests. His baling twine bridles, halters and harnesses hung from nails in the rafters of the old pig house, forgotten.

The young replacement heifers, destined to become herd cows, and the culled steers, destined to become meat, spent the coldest months of the winter in the feedlot behind our house. Early that winter, I walked to the well house and turned on the water, waiting in the sunny shelter of the building as water rose to fill the feedlot tank. Ice rimmed the edges. An axe leaned against a support pole, and for something to do, I picked it up, stepped over the stile into the feedlot and began breaking ice loose from the wooden tank. I was leaning to reach the ice buildup under the tank cover when a blast of compressed air hit the back of my neck with a loud *chuff.* The axe hit the water with a splash and I wheeled around, automatically swinging one arm to fend off whatever beast had cornered me. Ajax fell backward a few steps and then stood blinking stupidly as I caught my breath. Again he extended his leathery black nose with bovine curiosity, another *sniff-sniff-CHUFF* confirming my scent. My heart was still thundering, my voice louder than necessary.

"You stupid sonofabitch!" He gazed at me expectantly, his tongue sliding over his muzzle to clean first one nostril, then the other. When I continued speaking, he stepped forward, head nodding. Submissive. Waiting for something to eat. What a memory he has, I thought, as I slipped my coat and gloves off and rolled up my sleeves. Turning my back to him again, I gritted my teeth, reached into the icy water and fished the axe out of the reeking muck at the bottom of the tank. I kept up the conversation, describing his parentage and personal faults, and when I turned around, he had moved within arm's reach, still licking his chops. If he had been a dog, he would have been wagging his tail and laughing. I used his broad back as a towel, wiping my arm dry on his thick black winter coat. He scratched against me, nearly knocking me over. My God, he had gotten big. My arm could barely reach over him. He shone with health, his back wavy with swaths of spit curls where he had been grooming himself, a sure sign of bovine well-being.

Ajax

At some point during the next few weeks I began carrying barley-cake, the cubes we fed to the range cows, in my pockets. When the weather allowed, I changed clothes after school and wandered over to the feedlot. If he wasn't bedded down staying warm, I'd yell, "Hey, 'Jax," and he'd lumber out of the group and come to meet me, licking his lips. At some point during the next few weeks, I dragged his old bridles out of storage and brought them over to the feedlot, grinning as I held them up to his huge head. I took two of the old halters apart and made one from the braided twine. I bent No. 9 wire into a snaffle bit. Toward spring, I led him out of sight behind the windbreak and swung astride. He looked back at me sitting on his back, puzzled perhaps, or remembering, and moved out, head nodding, when I touched my heels to his ribs. I think it was then, that very moment, that I gave up pretending to myself.

When spring came, he might have gone with a short load of culls and canner cows to the sale ring, but he did not. Ajax was destined for our table. The replacement heifers were put to pasture when the grass greened. Ajax and one other culled steer had the feedlot to themselves. The fatter he got, the less motivated he was, but I kept up his riding lessons until early summer. When the weather turned warm, I stopped rather than risk him dropping dead. A trot around the feed bunks left him drooling and heaving for air, jaw hanging open, tongue lolling. He had no way of cooling off once he got overheated. He was fat beef.

Not long after that, Dad called to arrange for the two steers to be butchered. The animals would be killed on the ranch in the cool of the evening, and transported in the butcher's truck to

Malta, where he had the facilities to chill and age the carcasses, cut and wrap them for the freezer. His pay would be a percentage of the meat, which he could sell to someone else. I listened with calm balanced on the surface of my skin, turning aside when Mom glanced over, shrugging her off. It was my own fault, my own business. If I didn't let on, then at least I would not have to listen to the lectures and "I told you so's." The butchering was scheduled for the following day; both steers would be taken off food and water and held in a small pen until the butcher arrived.

After supper that evening, I slipped the steer's halter over his head and worked to secure the ends; he had nearly outgrown it again. Leading him out of the catch pen, I stepped up on an empty feed bunk and jumped astride his broad back for the last time. I rode Ajax to the well, tied him to a post away from the tank and turned the hose on him. Although he hadn't been penned up for long, he already acted grateful for the water. His tongue curled around his nose to catch the rivulets as I worked the hose up his spine and over his forehead. I squeezed a thick strip of dish soap over his wet back, then started at his head, working every inch of him into lather with a scrub brush. He leaned into the bristles, grunting with pleasure, and stood patiently under the cold hose for the rinsing. I brushed him dry in the evening sun, turning up cowlicks along his neck and ears, curling the tassel of his tail around my finger until it hung in ringlets. When I turned him loose, he arched his back and bucked a few steps, his black hide glowing with a smell like flowers and leather.

He was clean. It seemed all I could do, and I didn't visit him again. In the course of the next couple of days, we ate the organ meats. I dished up my plate and chewed and swallowed, filling myself with everything except my meal. I concentrated on sounds and smells of the table, the dull click of silverware like fingernails drumming on glass, the pattern on the paper napkins, the texture of the bread, the vomitlike smell of raw butter gone rancid in the summer heat. I made it through meals of fresh liver, of sweetbreads. And heart. In the end, only once did I pull away, mute and nearly choking on the lump in my throat. I could not, I would not, eat his tongue.

The Year of the Horse

Late spring, late fifties, my mother lines three of us up by the front door, moving with tight jerks and tugs down the row of buttons and shoelaces. Tall, with dark eyes and hard, slim muscles, she's a horsewoman who has made the shift from corral to kitchen with quirt-popping efficiency. Taken by the hand or ear or lock of hair, we will lead to the gates of hell without pulling back. We turn to face her automatically when she speaks. The words "whoa up" will cause us to slide to a stop, even when escape seems a lucrative option. We stand very still as she works over us, arms held out to present our coat fronts with as little fuss as possible. Mine is itchy wool, material cut from an old dress coat and treadled back together on the Singer sewing machine, and although I'm four, the original buttons are too big for my hands and the new buttonholes too stiff for me to work. The twins are three. She need not tell us to stay in the yard, to stay out of the mud, to keep our clothes clean. Already the bulk of what we know is unspoken.

Our yard is a rough quarter acre shaded by Russian olive trees and a dozen sprawling cottonwoods. From the front step of the house, paths cut across the yard like spokes on a wheel, to the well, to the garden, to the front gate, to the light plant house that houses the generator that feeds power to the wet-cell batteries in our basement. The deepest path hurries due north for twenty yards, then ducks left behind a blowzy thicket of caraganas to the outhouse. Under a full moon, the shadowy path becomes a gauntlet of predators who shift their shapes and lick their lips just beyond the pale dance of the flashlight beam. The rattle of leaves, a rustle in the underbrush could cause an imaginative young girl to wet her shoes in full flight back to the house.

In the daylight, the woven sheep wire fence keeps us safe, circling us like a tired sentinel, pulling to attention at the posts and slouching along between them. It will still turn a cow, though a child drawn by dare might climb it like a ladder or squirm through any of a dozen sags and gaps without touching a strand. It's a boundary drawn like a line in the dirt, but as a colt learns respect for a rope, we have learned respect for the fence. Slow learners earn the smart end of a cotton-wood switch, and by now Mother trusts our memory. We are allowed outside under the sole supervision of Tippy, our ring-necked Border collie, who is a general-purpose snake and skunk dog.

From the front steps, Gary and I survey our territory, eyes automatically falling short at the wire and moving sideways along the boundary. We will stake out a play ranch where the sun hits and bunchgrass is greening, fence pastures with twigs and build windbreaks and barns with palm-sized chunks of cottonwood bark that litter the ground every spring. Beneath the bulk of knitted mittens, our side pockets bulge with plastic farm animals. The baby pigs and hens have been lost, swallowed up in the mud of previous ranches, and we are forbidden to take the survivors outdoors until the ground dries. We do it anyway. In our narrow range of possible bad deeds, we are in the medium-risk category called "asking for a good licking," which is tied to the facts that we "know better" and if we've been told once we've been "told a million times" not to take these particular toys outside in the mud. We are not terribly worried. Whippings don't result from misbehavior, even deliberate misbehavior, and already Gary and I know this. Whippings result from getting caught.

Gail's pockets are empty. No stiff trotting horses, no cows with heads bent for realistic grazing, for she is a poor accomplice. Tattling comes as easily to her as dimples. While Gary and I perfect the art of deceit to avoid capture, Gail trots guilelessly into enemy camp and disarms her captors, volunteering information to anyone willing to listen to her chatter. She even tells on herself, seeking out our mother to admit an episode of chocolate chip thievery or name-calling, drawn to the absolution of a good confession.

Outside, she tags along while Gary and I select some prime ranchland where the rope swing dangles between two trees. Our toes have scuffed a trough under the swing and it has filled in the runoff. Cattle need water. We tuck our chins and hook our thumbs in our pockets, voices dropping to manly levels to plan the grand system of creeks we will draw down from our natural lake. But the most valuable aspect of our land is the screen offered by the cottonwood trunks and a frostbitten lilac bush. The house stands to the west, a low-slung white clapboard affair with square windows set up under the eaves and a squat porch that faces us. Behind the lilac we can't be clearly seen from the kitchen window, and the older kids are away at school. Before we set the first corner post, Gary and I turn, shoulder to shoulder, and face Gail. Sometimes she's a coyote, a direct threat to our future calf crop, other times she's a rustler, out to steal our herd. Man or beast, she finds no shelter here, in this small hardpan clearing, and no protection. We are both bigger, and together we are more. She knows if she squalls we will pummel her.

Glancing south through the kitchen window that morning Mother would have seen a landscape limbering up for spring, the faint pastel of budding sage, gray-green over the paler bur of old cactus, a minty breath of willow tips ringing the reservoir. In the distance, three shaggy saddle horses wander the west corner of their pasture searching out the half-buried glacial boulders that draw the sun's warmth into the soil, rolling back their lips to crop the fringe of grass that greens in fairy rings around each stone. Closer in, the low-lying garden trickles full of snowmelt, the pale stubble of last year's sweet corn afloat in a gravy of dark loam. It will take weeks for the ground to hold a plow.

Snowbanks drawing back from the barn leave shadows on the boards. A short distance from there an Angus bull, a recent purchase and nearly full grown, lies on a knoll, forefeet tucked under his brisket. The way his features merge in the sunshine, black on black, he might have passed for a hole in the scenery. Only the silhouette gives him away: sloping face, neck humped a size wider than the head, one smooth line drawn tight around a ton of black bull. Still, a bull soaking up the sun, even a large one, was no novelty in our barnyard. What draws my mother's eyes to this one is Gail, three years old and all of thirty pounds, rolling on the ground in front of him.

Stunned, Mother reaches down and clicks off the burner under a kettle of soup just beginning to simmer. Steam clouds the bottom edge of the glass. In the next deliberate second she fumbles the latch on the window and pulls it wide. A breeze billows the curtains back and she stills them with one hand, listening. No crying. Nothing but the scratchy rant of redwing blackbirds in the cattail slough behind the house.

Easing the door shut, Mother pauses at the front steps, her eyes skipping to Gary and me, counting heads, even as her hand gropes for the hoe leaning against the house. Tippy falls in behind her as she walks rapidly toward the gate. The situation calls for a panic of caution. She cannot yell or run toward the bull, nor can she sic the dog on him. A bull lying down is a far smaller threat than one up stomping around fighting a dog. Slipping through, Mother raps the yard gate shut on the dog's nose and hisses "Go lay down," the only command Tippy knows besides "sic 'em." She slinks back to the front step and collapses.

Leaving the gate slightly ajar, Mother slows her pace and circles to approach on the downwind side. The scene defies logic. Gail has shed her jacket and cap, and her dark pigtails bob on either side of her face as she rocks on her hands and knees in front of the bull. Closer, Mother can hear the sounds of battle, Gail's high-pitched bellows mocking the bull fights we witness at branding time, tongue lolling from her mouth as she bends forward and charges. The bull answers with a slick ripple of hide, tilting his shaggy poll to meet Gail's forehead, butting her back on her heels, nodding as she pushes into him again. Lying with his feet tucked up, his nose brushes the ground in slow arcs as he twists his great head side to side. Then with swift cunning, the bull shifts. Tipping his head in a graceful loop, he hooks the wide bridge of his nose under Gail's chest and flips her like a dime. She shrieks with laughter and is scrambling to all fours for another sally when Mom speaks from a few feet away. "Get back to the house." Her voice is as flat as the head of a nail. She holds the hoe ready to swing.

At three and a half, Gail must have heard those words with the same sinking heart that Tippy had heard hers. They are training words, ones we recognize as a single sound, a single sequence of sound. That particular command is not one to beg questions. Mother poises for action, hoe balanced on one shoulder like a baseball bat. Gail's small coat is sprawled on the hardpan at her feet, one sleeve inside out, the knitted cap a careless ball beside it. Without moving her eyes from the bull, Mother pushes them together with one foot as Gail passes her, heading for the house.

The bull stares after the child for a ways, then his ears flip back and his loud breathing stills, as if he's been struck by a sudden thought. Mother tenses, her eyes unwavering. She listens for the clank of the yard gate. Seconds pass. The spring sun hums around them, drawing grass out of the ground, drying mud. A rumbling, ominous as distant thunder, launches from ground level and gurgles up the bull's throat, erupting in a deep belch. The hoe sags on Mother's arm. The bull settles back squinting with pleasure, his jaw grinding in easy rhythm around a cud of half-digested hay.

By nightfall, I knew the tone of the story by heart as it would be told winter evenings while pinochle cards flicked across the kitchen table and our guests drew long sips of after-supper coffee. *There she was, covered with straw, right where I by-God found her, no bigger than a grasshopper, butting heads with an Angus bull.* Here a pause for the response, the disbelief. *A bull, big as the south side of a barn, and her just as happy as if she had good sense.* This is the story the neighbors hear. The second part is family business.

The bull was still ruminating when Mom stomped back

into the yard, banging the gate behind her. We jump like thieves. If Gail was out of the yard, we should have come and told her. Why wasn't she playing with us? The illegal livestock on the ground at our feet is noted with a glance and dismissed. Later. Now it is Gail's turn. Mom takes her by one shoulder, heads her for the kitchen, punctuating every word with a shake. Gary and I trail a safe distance behind them, our ranch behind the lilac forgotten. Yes, Gail sobs contritely, she knows better than to go outside the fence. Yes, she knows better than to wander off. But on the last and most important issue, she refuses to budge. No one ever told her not to fight with bulls. She's sure of it.

Mom sets her face in a way that makes Gary and me back against the wall. "Anybody with the sense God gave a *goose* would know better!" These words are often punctuated with slaps, and my hands rise up to cover my ears. Gail settles back on her heels and her arms cross with a touch of defiance.

"Anyways, we weren't fighting," she sniffs. "Me and Bully Wooly were just *betending* to bump heads." She repeats her explanation, *just betending,* then gazes upward and gives a go at shrugging, judging the effect. My hands move to protect my cheeks, but the room is quiet. My mother is flummoxed. "Bully Wooly?" she says finally, her mind stuck on the ton of beef under all that winter hair. "Bully Wooly?"

Gail's eyes tear, but her voice steadies. Things are coming around. She drops her hands on her hips and wags her head back and forth. "You know, like Bully Wooly was a bear and Bully Wooly had no hair—" And then a giggle sneaks out around the hiccups that come from hard crying, a terribly wrong sound, like the wrench of violin strings. Who could stand it?

My little sister. The child caught between tears and laughter, a bubbly little girl somehow misborn into this family of sturdy, practical farmers. The summer she was two she drew a standing ovation at Lang's Café when the waitress, cooing and clucking, leaned over her to ask, "And what do you want, sweetie?" Gail looked up at her very primly, then closed her eyes, lifted her chin: "I—want—an—itsy-bitsy teeny-weenie yellow polka-dot bikini—" She belted out the first chorus before Mom got her hauled up and the foot-stomping, hat-waving cowboys sat down. Gail works like magic.

She finishes her bull song now, and all the air goes out of the room in a rush. Mom's mouth twitches at the corners. "Bully Wooly," she says in a wondering voice. "Great galloping gods of war, child. What gets into your head."

Where I grew up, no daily papers shifted our view of the world, and television didn't intrude until the mid-sixties. Radio broadcasts from Havre, Montana, bounced off the Little Rockies and gave all we desired of the outside—market reports, weather forecasts and a little Patsy Cline. When the roads were decent, come Saturday we had mail. Dry summer days I climbed the windbreak after noon to watch for a mare's tail of dust snaking south along the county road, a gray stream that hung for miles on a quiet day and at the last possible second exploded and rose like a mushroom as the mailman slid to a stop. Fuel drums mounted on railroad ties stood like short-barreled cannons wherever a private lane met the county road, mailboxes large enough to keep parcels dry, large enough to be landmarks, signposts, billboards announcing the name of a ranch and the brand stamped on its cattle.

Ours was one of twenty-some families scattered like islands on a hundred square miles of prairie, farm and ranch

folks loosely connected by crank telephones and narrow rib-
bons of gumbo road. Most of the neighbors I knew were the
sons and daughters of farmers, a second generation distilled
from turn-of-the-century homesteaders who stuck it out.
They say only one in ten made the first decade. In south
Phillips County, the high ratio of public to deeded land suggests an even poorer showing, but in our community, for every
claim abandoned or turned back to the government, another
never left the care of Uncle Sam. Wide swaths through the
breaks and hardpan sage were plotted out and passed over,
acres where the nearest water lay twenty miles overland or a
quarter mile under. Of those who stayed, some started out as
Russians, Germans, Norwegians or Swedes—first-generation
immigrants. Others came from some direction—up from the
south, down from Canada, all of them bearing the sound and
taste of other worlds.

The prairie they settled made marginal farmland, and with
extended families left behind, they were forced to depend on
community. No one worked a homestead alone. To stay
required common focus and collective effort, a sharing of
labor, machinery and knowledge. By the time their children
took over, expanding the original claims and jerking the plow
line from a tractor seat instead of behind a work team, families could no longer be sorted by nationality, religion or expectation. Parents still spoke with accents and told stories of city
life, of ocean crossings and foxhunts, of sleigh rides and
homemade skis, of the way dumplings were made in the Old
Country. But their children, my parents' generation, were
born on the land and to the land, and they all told the same
stories of schoolhouse dances and county fairs, or runaway
teams and 'hoppers and dry wells. Theirs was an intimacy
born of isolation, rather than blood relation. They told stories

on each other, but like a large family living in tight quarters, they obeyed strict rules of privacy, a polite turning of heads at the glimpse of naked skin.

Word from the outside, whether it arrived in a mail sack or a news report, seldom overshadowed the facts of our lives. We talked in facts—work and weather, the logistics of this fence, that field—but stories were how we spoke. A good story rose to the surface of conversation like heavy cream, a thing to be savored and served artfully. Stored in dry wit, wrapped in dark humor, tied together with strings of anecdotes, these stories told the chronology of a family, the history of a piece of land, the hardships of a certain year or a span of years, a series of events that led without pause to the present. If the stories were recent, they filtered through the door of my room late at night, voices hushed around the kitchen table as they sorted out this day and held it against others, their laughter sharp and sad and slow to come. Time was the key. Remember the time . . . and something in the air caught like a whisper. Back when. Back before a summer too fresh and real to talk about, a year's work stripped in a twenty-minute hailstorm; a man's right hand mangled in the belts of a combine, first day of harvest; an only son buried alive in a grain bin, suffocated in a red avalanche of wheat.

Only time softened these facts into stories. The boy's death became a tragic lesson. The doors to the wheat bins by our shop were never chained shut, but in the years that followed, my father never missed a chance to remind us how grain slopes up the sides, how just bumping the wall can cause wheat to shift and pour down around you, pinning your feet in seconds. My father's mangled hand became a story of a wild ride to town and a doctor who administered morphine, but not until he identified the exposed nerves by twanging each one with forceps. Storms came together like patchwork, neighbors joining their individual accounts to create one shared experience: The blizzard of '64; the ice storm of '74; the winter of '77–'78. How did you manage when the lights went out, when the lines went down, when the wind came up? How did you make it, what did you lose?

Stories are the lessons of a year or a decade or a life broken into chunks you can swallow. But the heart of a story lies in the act of telling, the passing on. Listening to stories, I learned what was worth saying and what need not be spoken aloud; I learned how we remember and whom we remembered and why; how facts are shaped or colored or forgotten. Few facts of my childhood remain. No one recalls my first words or when I spoke them. The patter of my first steps is lost in a blur of siblings who ran before or crawled after. What survives are the milestones, my family's oral history of near hits and close calls, stories of five children and our first steps into an adult landscape that made small allowance for age or ignorance.

The first story about me goes like this: The summer Judy was four she trotted into the kitchen, so full of importance you could have popped her with a pin. We had company, but she was holding something and I looked over to see what she'd dragged in. She had one of those big round cockleburs. She steps up to the table with it cupped in both hands. "A cactus just calved," she says, and holds up the baby to show it off. "I saw the whole thing."

It's hard telling what I have actually seen that day, perhaps a simple trick of wind and weeds, my childhood elements of weather and imagination. But by day's end I have seen the eyes around a table light up with genuine respect for wit, for the art of timing, the deadpan delivery. My parents look right at me and smile. That smile is not about innocence. By age four I had witnessed a wide range of barnyard conceptions and deliveries. Cats had cats and cows had cows, and I knew why. What do they see in my yarn about a cactus calving a cocklebur that makes it worth keeping and telling over and over?

I believe the truth is this: the summer I was four I spoke my first good story and was born into my community, into the collective memory of my family, into a mythology that grew more real to me than fact. For the balance of my childhood I danced and waved on the fringe of a world defined by its miracles and natural disasters, observing and imitating, trying to amount to a good story—or barring that, to tell one.

The real adventures of Gail and the bull were less dramatic than my telling, but still one of many that grew around her, breathless episodes she listened to again and again with little interest and no comment. My story required a skill that was slow in coming. I wrote dog-frog-log poems and penciled witty news reports onto tablet paper, folding the wide-lined pages into fourths and stapling them along one edge to create a newspaper I called the *Animal Farm News*. I read and listened, a storyteller's apprentice who came to envy the deeds of heroes more than the craft of speaking them. I was clearly no match for my little sister. I could roughhouse and yell, throw rocks and tell jokes; I was a regular force of nature. But I could not be dainty and perky. My voice never had that high range needed to giggle. Gail was the baby of the family, even though she and Gary were twins, for she had the fine distinction of being forever twenty minutes younger and about half his size. Even better than her dimples, she was born with a knack for falling deathly ill and surviving, a skill Gary and I envied but were far too robust to accomplish. We picked at our chicken pox or scratched our measles, resigned to the drama on the other side of our tiny bedroom—Gail nearly comatose or raving with fever, Gail honking and whooping at every breath, a swathe of old sheets and menthol steam rising over the crib she fit until she was five years old.

Whether Gail held a charmed position in our family is debatable, but I believed it true and my revenge was real. Her story took shape in a decade of sibling warfare, with Gary or me cast as Goliath to her brash and fearless David. Prodded into a rage, cornered into fighting, she screamed and swung blindly, she bit like a weasel, she drove us back with sheer ferocity. An hour later she'd be back in our game. She would not give up. And even as we grew older and I came to understand the shame of bullying and my own lack of honor, I could not make myself quit.

I was born in 1954, the Year of the Horse, and the calendar came full circle on my twelfth birthday. When we trade stories about that time in our lives, my sister and I, that's what we call it—the Year of the Horse—though we both know we spent more than that lone year horseback. We had ridden the family horses since babyhood, and nurtured wild dreams of owning our own horses, like Margaret did. She'd gotten her palomino mare, Cream Puff, as a weanling filly, had raised and trained her, but we would never be that lucky, we thought mournfully. Descended from bucking stock, Cream Puff had an iron will, a tough mouth and a crotch-killing trot. My mother called her a dithering idiot. Fresh from the barn, she could shy sideways in ten-foot leaps, triggered by the flap of a grain sack or a passing car, or often enough nothing at all. But she could outrun anything on the place, and I loved her completely. The pony Gail rode belonged to her in a different way.

The Year of the Horse

Like Gail, Feller was a born story, a gift from a neighbor named Frank Locke. One of the last old-time horsemen in the county, Frank raised cow horses, quarter horse with a touch of thoroughbred for speed. Like most of the old-time cowboys, he enjoyed good whiskey and a hot hand of poker. One winter a horse trader found himself on the hard-luck end of a game and tossed a bill of sale into the pot. Frank drew to an inside straight and won. When the game broke up, he drove to the stockyards to admire his new horse. No need to send for the truck. Home was seventy-five miles south, and Frank laughed all the way there with a full-grown Shetland stud hog-tied among the supplies in the back of his battered old station wagon.

Never keen on barn chores, Frank turned the pony out on open range, half expecting one of his big quarter-horse studs to kill it on sight, and no great loss at that. But Shetlands are nothing if not tough, and for the better part of a year this one kept pace with the real horses, pattering along behind the herd like a big shaggy dog. Frank found the sight amusing until the following spring, when not one but six of his rangy brood mares dropped button-sized black foals. Like any good businessman, he cut his losses. The stud hit the sale ring as a gelding. The foals he donated to a worthy cause. "Got me six little bastards that have to stand on a rock to suck," he bellowed into the phone, and by weaning time half a dozen farm families leaned against the corral admiring their free kid ponies. Our roly-poly new baby stood at the far end of the pen and watched us like a coyote. "Well, he's a cute little feller," Dad remarked halfheartedly, and we children nodded in unison. Feller it was.

Gifted with the speed and smarts of his mother, Feller had also inherited a black coat and a blacker heart from the Shetland side of his gene pool. He was built like a nail keg, short-coupled with no withers to speak of. A saddle cinched into place stuck for the first two jumps, then slipped and rolled onto his ribs. Mom started him early. Hat clamped over her hair to keep the dust down, her lips drawn to a grim line, she balanced her horse-sized saddle in the middle of his back and rode with her spurs nearly dragging the ground until he mastered the walk of a perfect gentleman, a veneer of civility. This battle of wills took not weeks but months. We met him halfway. About the time he grew wise, we grew large enough to take the beating. Mom dusted off her gloves, pronounced him a kid horse and turned us loose. The moment she left the corral, his ears slid back. He kicked, he bit, he scraped us off on fence posts and corral rails. He veered under low-hanging cottonwood limbs at a dead lope, clearing his back in one sweep. We knew about "one-way" horses, the kind that bolt when you step off to open a gate or rub their bridles off when you tie them. Feller combined all versions of the one-way horse into one compact package. "You might as well walk as ride him," Kenny would grumble. "Either way you'll come home afoot."

Feller tolerated Gail best, perhaps because she weighed the least. She returned a love that bordered on obsession, stubbornly defending his mischief even as she limped out of the barrow pit, victim of a hit-and-run with a cottonwood tree, and watched his dust streak toward the barn. She knew what it felt like, the pain of being littlest. She called it spirit.

"For God's sake, Gail, you don't show one glimmer of sense," Mom would snap, patching her up after one wreck or another. And for a year or more, that went for both of us. We took to the wild, losing ourselves on bareback gallops through the meadow, flying over the jumps with our eyes closed, drunk on speed and power. That was the year I nurtured my first tangible fears of growing up and developed an emotional range that began with passionate outbursts and ended with sullen silence. My body was bent on treason. I retreated, pulling the last of what passed for my childhood around me like a shroud.

That fall, Kenny left home for high school. That fall, my sister Margaret waited in the kitchen for Dad to finish putting gas in the car and Mom to finish dressing for town. She too was leaving, just as she had left home every fall, first to go to Malta High School, then to start college at sixteen. This leaving seemed no different. The bags and boxes piled by the door held everything she owned. The rest she held in her hand, a slip of paper with formal print and blank lines written over in ink. She offered it casually and I took it in my own hand, turned it around to read. A bill of sale: *Sold to Judy Blunt for the sum of one dollar, one (1) palomino mare.* My heart lurched. I owned Cream Puff, the one possession I had coveted for years. Margaret's face was impassive and I drew myself away, barely able to breathe through the collision of joy and grief. *My sister has given me her horse. She is never coming home again.*

And that long year, as I turned my back on the adult world I found myself face-to-face with the innocence still visible in my little sister. My attacks on her had grown more sophisticated over the years, a verbal sniping almost as savage and satisfying as fistfighting. She had no reason to trust me. Yet when I turned to her for companionship, she swung in beside me without hesitation, following my lead with a loyalty so unswerving and undeserved it was frightening. I needed her story, this child of fierce emotion and blind courage, for I could not find my own.

≠

Gail took Feller over the ditch flat out, her jeans barely lifting from his back as they lit and sawed to a stop on the opposite ridge. Cream Puff jigged sideways, dancing under me as they swung around to face us. Our hay meadow stood out against the backdrop of prairie like a fat green caterpillar on a bare branch, a field that curled and clung to the banks of Beaver Creek, rows of new haystacks dotting the arch of its back. Easing the reins, I grabbed a fistful of blond mane and leaned over the mare's neck. Her front feet left the ground and the irrigation ditch rose like a welt against the smooth contours of the meadow, a break in the dark alfalfa that greened over the stubs of the first cutting. Slicing through the heat, the mare's hooves pounded up a smell of damp soil, bruised alfalfa and horse sweat, a taste I carried on the back of my tongue. I clamped my knees, feeling her stride shorten to a sprint as we neared the lip of the ditch and the split-second connection— muscles drawn under us, bunched, pushing off in one stride—and the release of riding airborne.

Atop the ridge, Gail and I leaned over to rub the sweaty necks. Summer vacation stretched behind us, weeks we lived horseback and out of yelling distance from the house. Mornings were filled with chores, but after lunch Mom took a break, settling down with a book while Gail and I cleared the table. We left the front door slightly ajar when we slipped away, for the noise of it closing often broke the spell. Walking with forced casualness toward the barn, we marked the milestones by increasing our speed. Past the front gate, the clothesline, the chicken house, alert for the slam of the screen door and a voice rising in the heat behind us. Out of sight but still in yelling distance, we raced through the barn grabbing bridles and a bucket of oats, then out the wide rolling door to the horse pasture, to freedom. As the horses finished the grain we poured on the ground, Gail and I jackknifed our bodies over their necks, grabbing for mane and sliding into position as they flung up their heads. Saddles were for sissies.

I nudged Cream Puff with my bare heels, lengthening her stride until Feller's shorter legs had to jog to keep up. Gail didn't complain, though she knew I did it to be mean. She kept watch from the corner of one eye. I pretended to stare straight ahead. The summer showed on us all. Our horses were trim, ridden down to good manners. Our legs had grown so strong we no longer held on with our hands, even bareback at a full gallop. We were riding easy. The seat of my jeans had worn a bald spot on Cream Puff's back, a heart-shaped mark that winged out on either side of her backbone just behind the withers. I worried that it might not grow in. Winter was coming. I was restless and edgy.

The hottest part of the year held on, and Second Creek ambled through the meadow like a low, twisting road paved with tiles of parched gumbo that crunched underfoot. Dropping over the steep bank, we rode in the dry creek bed, ducking occasionally to avoid brush that grew along the lip of the creek at head level, aiming east toward the bridge and the fence. Knotting my reins, I fell back and closed my eyes, head rocking side to side on my mare's rump as she picked her way beneath the willows that draped the steep banks on either side. Behind me, Gail lay back on Feller, reins slack, guiding him with her feet. In the long stretch of linked potholes the willows grew thickly above us and the air was cool and green. Here the horses moved slowly, pausing to brush away flies, willing to stop if we'd let them. But in places the deep channel disappeared, ending in a deer trail that led the horses up and over a steep dike pierced by a culvert and irrigation head gate. Other detour trails plowed through the thick willows to avoid potholes still holding the green, mossy gruel that passed for late-summer water. We rode flat on our backs with our eyes closed and the reins knotted over the horses' necks, guessing from the movement, the feel of the muscles bunching and stretching, when we hit a detour in the creek bed. We had to lie still until the last possible second, the moment our horses settled on their haunches to lunge up the steep trail, before we sat up and took hold of the reins again. It was easy to get dumped riding this way, for the horses were full of tricks and wise to the opportunity we gave them, but we'd gotten too good at the game and I lost any real interest halfway across the meadow.

In the late August sun I was in long sleeves, with my coat zipped to my chin. The gray fake fur was matted with chaff and reeked of sweat, but as we lunged up the last trail and emerged into the meadow, my muscles clenched. Pain traced from my lower belly to my inner thighs like something tearing loose, slow moving, deeper inside than anything I inflicted on myself. I was bleeding again. The battle had shifted, a loss of ground, but I hadn't given up. The outhouse sat idle unless the electricity failed, and I kept my stockpile of toilet paper and clean rags there. I was still winning. No one knew except me, and I could choose not to know. It was the chill I couldn't shake, the feeling of legs grown too long and heavy, arms that lay like dead meat.

Lost in my own thoughts, I didn't turn until Gail's hand touched mine, then lifted again, pointing to a dark mound across the field. The porcupine waddled toward us with an air of purpose, dragging its tail through the hay stubble, making a beeline for the cottonwoods along the creek. I had read stories of men trapping the mountain streams who left them alone, even when they raided stores of bacon or chewed up saddles in the craving for salt. If stranded and starving a man could run down a porcupine and kill it for food. A porkie could save your life. But here where trees were more dear, they were not revered. The animals ate bark from saplings and older trees, often girdling the trunks and killing them. Whenever my father noticed new damage to trees along the creek or had to pull a beard of quills from a cow's face, he went cruising in the pickup after dark, shining his spotlight up the trees and along the branches, alert for the flash of eyes, the dark burl against the trunk, aiming his rifle as instinct turned the animal butt-first to the light.

This porcupine lumbered nearer as we watched, a tree creature, landlocked and graceless. Something in his awkward shuffle, his wrongness, ate at me. I slid from Cream Puff's back and tied her to the willow behind us. We did not speak, but at some level I heard Gail's feet touch down, the sound of branches shaking where she looped her reins, her footsteps dogging mine as I searched along the creek bank. The thick branch I pulled from the underbrush had bleached white and was cured hard as a baseball bat. The porcupine peered near-sightedly down his nose, tipping his head to gather sound and smell, then changed his angle of approach, aiming for trees to the right. He had twenty feet to go when I swung, bouncing the limb off his back. Instinctively, he tucked his head and curled around his soft underbelly, his quills bristling outward, his tail rigid and ready to lash at us. I raised my arms again, savoring the stretch of muscle coming to life, calmed by the power that drove the branch. Beside me, Gail lifted her own stick in an overhand swing.

We worked out a rhythm, rising and falling as the porcupine squatted lower, flat to the ground, unable to recover from one blow to the next. When he straightened suddenly and scuttled for the trees, we leaped back, then ran ahead and turned to block his way. We struck together now, Gail at his exposed head and I across the round of his back. Grunting on the downswing, panting between blows, the wet thud of wood hitting flesh—sound traveled nowhere in the heat of the meadow. But when his spine broke, I felt the pop of bones all the way up the branch to my fingers, and he began to squeal.

Any animal will scream when that's all it has left, a long note of terror or grief so pure it lifts the hair on a killer's back and spurs the final, merciful frenzy. His cry took breath after breath, a sound like ice, numbing my hands in midswing. Even when he stopped and began clawing his way forward, dragging dead weight toward the trees he would never climb, I could not end his suffering. It was Gail who bent to the kill, her face flushed and glittering, battering him as he pulled himself along. He quit moving a few feet from the trees, and she stood over his body, triumphant.

There were quills buried deep in the sticks we dropped back over the bank. A spray of blood along one sleeve of my coat. A small mouth opening around long orange teeth, a stubby tongue folded at the center like a heart cut from red paper. There was the look in my sister's eyes, something bloody and profane that was mine, and in me, a shame so swift and sure I still find it today in those memories marked by change. It was the moment I slid out of my soiled coat and stood in the meadow, bleeding. It was the moment childhood became no longer possible.

At thirteen I stood where the world I knew ended, imagining no future beyond my ordained leap into the abyss at my toe tips, vanishing into the station of woman, wife and mother—

storytellers with no story of their own. The things I feared were real to me. Some even came true. When the coat came off, a box of bras appeared on my pillow. I survived the mercifully brief confrontation when my mother turned up a stash of bloody pajamas I'd squirreled away under my bed. Supplies appeared in my closet. But another predetermined passage loomed for me as it did for a number of country kids, one that would require far more of me than acquiescence. I would leave home soon, to attend high school. I readied myself in a twist of dread and impatience. There was no ceremony for my eighth-grade graduation, and no other graduates; Mrs. Nesbit simply handed me my diploma on the last day of school. But at home that afternoon, the occasion was commemorated by the gift of a new suitcase, a family tradition as sensible as any other, though mine was an unlikely white with a dainty pink lining.

I packed the new suitcase and all my resolve, and headed to Malta that fall to begin ninth grade, thirteen going on thirty. I lived in a rented room with kitchen privileges, managed my own checking account, found my first job waiting tables at the Sugar Shack Café for thirty-five cents an hour and tips. I studied the town kids, took what I wanted from their catalogue of cool moves and social savvy, and returned to the ranch on weekends and vacations. I did not discover myself as much as I invented myself, as a woman. What I had not foreseen in my struggle to hold on to my girlhood and my safe piece of prairie was how easy it would be, in the end, to let it go.

Learning Curves

Blunt. The sound of my name fell like an axe on green wood, an abrupt thud of consonants that usually made me jump. This time I was ready. I slid out of my alphabetically ordained spot behind Jim Anderson and Alice Blundred and approached the makeshift podium as Mr. Miller, our English teacher and assistant football coach, walked to the back of the room and crunched his form into a desk that would have held a Z person, if we'd had one. Thirty fellow freshmen raised their eyes in wary attention, pleading to be entertained, prepared to be bored.

I had practiced my five-minute speech for a week, pacing myself with an egg timer, and the index cards rattling in my fingers held little more than cue words. The year I entered high school, 1968, was a year that began and ended in distant riots and social upheaval, and now, in the spring of '69, we'd been given free rein to select our topics from those social issues and current events. I'd never given a speech before, but I'd heard bits and pieces of them on the television news. Kennedy and King. Listening to the first few speeches the day before, others that morning, I felt a flicker of anxiety. Odds were I had screwed up again. How carefully my classmates approached their topics, how dutifully, numbly, I took notes on urban crime, desegregation of schools, the war in Vietnam, the first Apollo space missions—all of it in numbers, dates and statistics. No whys, no taking sides except where the road had been comfortably paved with stale slogans. Crime didn't pay. Only dopes used dope. All men are created equal.

My topic had filled my imagination since the first week in September, a Saturday night on the ranch. Mom had settled at the kitchen table to read while the rest of us gathered around our new color television set to watch the Miss America pageant, broadcast live from Atlantic City. As the contestants filed onto the stage, chests jutting, sashed and smiling, we analyzed their conformation with the same skills that won us awards in 4-H livestock-judging competitions, comparing features, inventing faults. The emcee gave measurements along with other pertinent information, like age, city of origin, hobbies; 36-24-36 was the accepted ideal. The contest was no more real to me than any other television show. I had never seen anyone who looked like those women, never heard anyone outside of TV talk in that gushy rush of accents and clichés. I thought the women vaguely embarrassing, the emcee who courted them with snide banter and sappy songs, altogether stupid. Still I watched, half asleep, as the outgoing Miss America launched her farewell address. She hesitated, there were shouts, the camera wobbled, and from a side balcony a group of protesters unfurled a banner reading WOMEN'S LIBERA- TION. Uniforms filled the balcony, and within seconds the first real-looking women I'd ever seen at a beauty pageant were pushed down, shut up and carried out. I was enchanted.

Back in Malta that Monday, I searched the papers in the school's library for more information. Montana papers were relatively mum, but national magazines reported a few tantalizing details. I discovered that while I watched Miss Illinois bounce and flip through her winning trampoline performance without dislodging a single platinum curl, a small fire had flickered into life outside the building. As she loped down the runway in the costume that won the bathing suit competition, a group of about a hundred women, some from as far away as Iowa, had continued to feed the flames of the Freedom Trash Can with symbols of American womanhood—bras and girdles, hair curlers and false eyelashes, fashion magazines and cosmetic goop. A bottle of dishwashing liquid. A pair of spiky high heels. As Miss Illinois burst into happy tears and Bert Parks launched into song, the protesters had ceremoniously centered a tinfoil tiara on the head of a sheep. A live sheep on a rope leash.

In study hall, I ignored algebra and daydreamed my way to Atlanta, Georgia, pondering which of a list of items I would have tossed in the fire. Nylons, I decided, and for sure the garter belt that was supposed to hold them up but in the stand-up-sit-down course of a school day tended to work its way down my rump until the stockings bagged like loose skin.

National news in the weeks that followed concentrated on the antiwar rioting that had nearly shut down the Democratic convention in Chicago, Nixon's landslide victory in November, Yippies, hippies and black freedom marches, but here and there I gleaned snippets of information about this new commotion called the women's liberation movement. Uppity women were uniting, though not in the streets of Malta, Montana. Still, I had a name now, a rallying cry for the anger that had smoldered behind my unplucked brows since puberty. The speech I offered in freshman English was not an objective view of women in American society. Women had not been "given" the right to vote, I announced; they had fought for it, a right that should have been guaranteed by citizenship in a democratic society. But that was only the first step. The fight for women's rights would not be over until we could cast our ballots for women candidates.

I quoted statistics gathered by the National Organization for Women, numbers proving discrimination in the workplace, males paid twice the wage of females for the same work. I countered the then-popular notion that women were somehow emotionally or mentally unsuited to high-stress or physically demanding work, too scatterbrained to manage a business, too unpredictable to trust in positions of power, by giving examples of strong women who were doing these very things. I went on and on, looking down at my cue cards rather than at my classmates as the first sniggers and snorts punctuated my radical claims. The ending I had worked on for a long time, trying to sum it up with a punch—I have a dream!—but my voice was faltering by the time I finished, and even to myself I sounded shrill. "We cannot call our country a democracy and continue to treat fifty-one percent of our population as second-class citizens."

I looked up at the class and braced myself for the final hurdle. In Mr. Miller's class, the audience earned extra credit for asking questions and the speaker could raise a mediocre grade by answering well. "Are there any questions?" I asked a second time. No one raised a hand. Mr. Miller's mouth turned up in a lazy smile as he shifted his gaze around the room, his pencil rap-tapping a drumroll on the grade book. "Well?" The silence seemed louder than his voice, a hiss of muffled breath, empty echoes. He turned to me again with the same slow swing of shoulders, and with a comic expression of fear widening his eyes he raised one hand to touch his eyebrow in a mock salute.

The tension broke on a wave of laughter. I laughed too, as I threaded my way like a drunken sailor down the aisle to my desk, my legs rubbery and nearly spent. The next speech passed in a blur as I shielded the tremors in my fingers by hunching over my notebook, trying to breathe slowly as my knees danced against the underside of the desk. That the topic was shoplifting I remember only because Jim Anderson ad-libbed his final line, drawing a second gust of hilarity. "Judy forgot to mention another area where women are proven superior—most shoplifters are women."

By the end of my high school years I had gone underground, though I never grew immune to jokes about women's liberation. The only thing rescued from the Freedom Trash Can, it seemed, was one label, a twisted and blackened fragment of ideology used to dismiss the larger issues. *Yeah, she burned her bra in the '60s and nobody noticed. Ah, she's one of those bra burners, all smoke and no fire.* Fighting the jokes was like sweeping feathers—the harder you worked, the higher they flew. All in fun, of course.

The saddest versions were those we told on ourselves. Called out to run the vaccine gun or help sort cattle, a ranch wife enters the kitchen at noon, the table bracketed by hungry men—a husband, a couple of neighbor men or hired hands—whose contribution to the noon meal is to tune in to Paul Harvey's radio news and wait with good-natured forbearance while she scrubs manure from her hands and jerks the roast from the oven, microwaves a few potatoes. By the time she sits down, the guys are done eating. They catch a thirty-minute nap while she bolts her food, clears the table, tosses a load of underwear in the washer, runs a broom over the floor, throws the hose on the tomato plants. Then they all go back out to "work." "They can stuff their women's lib," she snorts to a friend. "I've got about all the liberation I can handle."

At the root of the joke lies our most seductive mythology, one that suggests rural Montana women are a special land-tilling, snake-killing, rope-swinging breed for whom liberation is unnecessary, if not redundant. Women who work in the barns and corrals and fields are doing a man's work, this myth tells us, and by doing it have achieved equality. Strong-woman stories stem from the earliest days of white settlement, a time when Victorian standards demanded a way to justify the rustic conditions and "unladylike" activities required to scratch a living out of the dirt. But the fact remains that even as gender roles blurred and gave way to practicality, very few women either sought or found increased social status in the physical labor of farming. Women of my grandmothers' generation fought hard to maintain a veneer of gentility that belied hard work. They hid their chapped hands in white cotton gloves, attended social gatherings in starched shirtwaists, crossed their legs at the ankle and addressed each other by formal titles. Their daughters grew up learning the value of appearances, the knack of doing without seeming to do. When women's lib hit the headlines many of these second-generation ranchwomen sniffed around its edges and pitched it back like a dead carp. If equality meant doing a man's work, you could have it. That brand of equality had dug their mothers an early grave and was three feet down on their own. They'd come a long way, baby, and were on the road back to being real ladies—or so it appeared.

I grew up admiring a community of women whose strength and capacity for work I have yet to see equaled, true partners in the labor of farming and ranching. Where the occasional man fell short, whether drunken and reckless or merely self-ish and careless, his wife maneuvered carefully to make up the deficit. To be accused of "wearing the pants" remained the worst form of insult. In public she held steadfastly to the role of silent partner. I saw this quiet endurance as a choice women made, one that made them secretly superior. Men did not drop what they were doing to tend to women's work, nor did anyone imagine they might. Only women did it all.

As a young ranch wife, I wed my sixties-style feminism to a system of conflicting expectations and beliefs only slightly altered by a century of mute nobility. My brand of feminism celebrated strength through silence. A woman could do anything, so long as she did it quickly, quietly and efficiently. It never occurred to me then that silence looked passive from the outside, or that the two served the same purpose of not making waves, maintaining the status quo. It would take me ten years of doing it all to finally get it. The work we do isn't the issue. Work is the tool that wears us down, draws us in and keeps our eyes on the next two steps ahead. The issue is power. And it's the silence that kills us.

The sixties were slow getting to our little corner of the world, and even as the more visible social changes began to tiptoe across the city limits, small Montana Hi-Line towns like Malta tended to bustle about their own business, eyes averted in polite dismay. Our region boasted no goat-milking communes, no sit-ins or protests unless the theater showed a movie with sex, and few of the town's residents indulged in any pinko talk against the war in Vietnam. The majority voted conservative—Nixon in '68, citizenship, patriotism and family values right down the line. Still, by the end of the decade, town kids had picked up on the sixties signature rock music, mod bell-bottoms, groovy slang and assorted recreational chemicals. Beer was still the drug of choice and not hard to come by, but other options had arrived by 1968, and by the early seventies were not uncommon in high school circles. Even the doctrine of free love was becoming popular in theory, although for girls it remained anything but free. The birth control pill was available, but as in any small town, prescriptions were written by the doctor who had delivered you and filled by the pharmacist who went fishing with your dad. Only the few, the proud, the brave succeeded without sneaking out of town to anonymous clinics in Havre or Glasgow.

What the media called the generation gap seemed a less-than-serious affair in some ways, like a game of rebellion passed down from one generation to the next. "Never saw a teenager who wasn't revolting," one of the old geezers at the café used to cackle, slapping his knee and repeating the joke like a scratched record until everyone "got it." Friction between generations was a game that required a fair degree of hysteria on the part of our elders, like panic before a predicted storm, worry that it would get worse, great tearing of hair when it did, all the while knowing everyone was going to survive it just fine. The young rebel's role was easy. Being a badass takes little time and less effort in a place where everyone's paying attention. Why go to the trouble of bombing city hall when a pair of tight jeans or smoking in public got the same reaction?

Outsiders were another matter. Out there, the Antichrist prowled the country in a Volkswagen bus with flowers painted on the side. Stories linger on about this Long-Haired-Draft-Dodger or that Stinking-Barefooted-Hippie who pulled off Highway 2 and walked into the Mint Bar or the Stockman for a cold drink, stories of righteous head shearings and beatings delivered by local cowboys, but like most urban myths, the stories are impossible to pin down with facts, always the cousin of a neighbor's hired man who held the guy down while somebody's best friend's brother did the dirty work, a set of clippers mysteriously at hand. Where, I always wondered, did the deed take place? Surely not in one of the turn-of-the-century, false-fronted, brick-sided Main Street bars. One imagines two or three cowboys lugging their bewildered victim around the barroom a few times, then out the door and up the street looking for an electrical outlet.

So the sixties stormed on "out there" somewhere, while around town, talk of weather, crop prices and high school sports rose with the steam of morning coffee as it always had. And that was town. Fifty miles south, I'd grown up in a world yet another step removed from the mainstream. We dressed in our best clothes for a trip to Malta. Our parents often went alone while the four of us younger kids were in school, but every few weeks the trip was planned for a Saturday. Going to town was not all entertainment for youngsters, for there was endless shopping in mostly boring stores, but there were high spots like lunch in a restaurant or a visit to the library. And of course we had our own shopping. We earned a dime a week for doing chores, and with a month's wages jingling in pocket or purse, we were set loose after lunch to wander the aisles of the Ben Franklin store, deliberating over trinkets and candy, stretching out our purchases to last however many hours our parents were occupied with parts and hardware, banking and insurance business.

The clerks watched, squinty-eyed as we strolled from the bins of plastic cows to the racks of penny candy, touching and comparing, arguing the benefit of owning this toy or that in fierce whispers, and as the afternoon dragged by, often we'd be told to buy something or leave. We always obeyed politely, either making a dime purchase and resuming our shopping, much to the clerk's exasperation, or trotting up the street to read comics at the GN Hotel's newsstand until it felt safe to go back. It only took ten or fifteen minutes to get run out of there unless we laid out ten cents for the adventures of Uncle Scrooge or Superman.

I was a good-sized kid before it occurred to me that our shopping habits were odd by town standards. One afternoon a clerk grabbed my arm as I was leaving the store and demanded to look in my red patent-plastic purse. There was nothing in it that didn't belong there, but I'd earned a lecture punctuated by little shakes that made my head bob. I'd been in the store for a solid hour, picking things up, carrying them around, putting them back when something else caught my eye, clicking my purse open and shut to count pennies and nickels against the price tags. "You can't do that or people will think you're stealing," the clerk said. The fierce edge of her voice made customers turn and look, and I walked out with my face flaming. My mother was a force in her own right, and likely had I told her about the encounter she would have taken Ben Franklin's door off its hinges on her way in to straighten out the misunderstanding. But there was a chance, equally likely, I thought, that she would pierce me with her own suspicious look and side with the clerk. I kept quiet. It took me years to grow old enough and bold enough to try shoplifting, but eventually I got even with a pocketful of Bazooka bubble gum.

Town kids, especially teenagers, were mostly invisible during these daytime excursions. I had no sense of Malta outside the two-block-square business district, no sense of the world beyond Malta. The nearest cities of any size, Great Falls and Billings, lay an eight-hour round-trip from the ranch, and I would not visit these places until I was grown. Dad traveled alone to Havre or Glasgow for repairs or livestock sales, though Mom rode along more frequently as we grew older, but for the four of us still at home, venturing beyond the county line was an event that didn't happen every year.

My story would not happen in this age of VCRs and satellite dishes, computers and CD-ROMs. Self-contained ranch communities still exist out here, insulated by the same layers of prairie and miles of dirt road, but today the world comes to them. Their mail is delivered on the rural route three times a week instead of once, which makes a subscription to a daily newspaper more practical. An FM radio station gives the local news right out of Malta. Today it's hard to imagine any child growing up so ignorant of her own world.

The Sunday before my first day of high school, I sat on the edge of the double bed, testing the springs with slow bounces. At thirteen, I could add a year or two to my age without raising eyebrows. A big, rawboned kid, my mother would say, though she stopped short of words like "chubby." I had written my first check of sixty dollars for room and board and signed with a flourish, carefully deducting the amount and balancing the register as my mother had taught me to do. One hundred minus sixty equals forty was also the balance of my math skills, but that hardly mattered to me. I had ten dollars a week left over for school supplies and spending money, riches beyond belief. I had privacy for the first time in my life, and in a room that "went"—the carpet went with the curtains, the curtains went with the bedspread. The blond furniture all matched and glowed with polish under embroidered dresser scarves. The windows faced north and east, two quiet streets on the south end of town.

A few decades earlier, I might have stayed in a special boardinghouse kept for rural kids, a dormitory-type arrangement for rural families before there were school buses, paved roads and snowplows. High school students from the most isolated regions were on their own by my generation, and we joined a long tradition of country kids forced to "batch or board" to attend high school—students who batched set up bachelor housekeeping in rented shacks, while boarders rented rooms with meals. The nearest school buses ran along Highway 191, thirty hard, gumbo miles north of our place, an impractical commute. The school made no provision for the students outside its district aside from a minimal mileage payment for transportation, and each family made its own arrangement. Some moms moved to town with their children, some placed their high school kids with town relatives. In some enviable cases, parents with several kids attending rented whole houses for their kids to share. With no family resources to fall back on my first couple of years, we shopped the list of widowed ladies and struggling families who advertised for boarders.

My landlady, Mrs. Crowder, had cleared the linens from three drawers in the mirrored dresser, and in one I arranged a small stack of new underwear, a slip, a nightgown and a sweater. After-school clothes, the jeans and old shirts, filled another, leaving the top drawer for sundry treasures. Her winter coats had been pushed together in the closet to clear space, and there I hung the four new outfits my mother and I had sewn over the summer. Beneath them a pair of sensible "go with anything" shoes awaited my first steps into the halls of Malta High.

Mrs. Crowder had taken time to show me how to work our

shared bath before she left for her shift at the nursing home, and that evening I stood under the spray of my first shower feeling terribly worldly. The house rules were easy. I was not allowed in the basement, where my brother Kenny shared a room with another country boy, nor were they allowed in my room upstairs. I was in charge of making my own bed, cleaning the bathroom after I used it and fixing my own breakfast and lunch. My laundry would go with me to the ranch on weekends. Supper was at six.

I was far more prepared to enter the adult community at that point than I was to join the freshman class of '68. I'd gone eight years to a one-room school with no other child my age since second grade. Most years that I attended rural school, I saw only siblings and a familiar handful of neighbor kids— never more than ten students in first through eighth grades. Now I took my place at the tail end of the baby boom with nearly seventy classmates gathered from all over Phillips County. The whole process beggared my imagination. How did school work when you had more than one teacher, more than one classroom, all those kids? Bells rang, I knew that much, but did everyone just know where to go? Did they move from class to class in groups or alone? Wouldn't it be more logical if the students stayed put and the teachers simply changed rooms? "You'll figure it out," Kenny said. "Everybody figures it out." And he was right. That was the easy part.

The suit I smoothed out on the bedside chair that evening featured a gray knit A-line skirt, shaped more like an H than an A in deference to my waistline, and hemmed to modestly cap my knees. With this went a tailored western-style vest of the same gray knit and a white long-sleeved blouse with flat-felled seams and a round Peter Pan collar. A three-piecer, I thought, dressy enough for the first day but not too showy if I left off the rhinestone pendant. I didn't want to call attention to myself. A pair of white knee socks completed the ensemble, but I wondered if I should wear my lone pair of suntan-colored nylons instead. I studied my freshly showered legs for a long moment, trying to decide.

I'd spent the end of the summer stacking bales in the mosquito-ridden hayfields, and with the frequent exception of bruises and scratches, my legs were bone white. Knee socks it was, I thought. I pulled the new socks from their drawer and tugged them on, folding down the tops neatly to study the effect. The effect was startling. The flat grayish whorls of my knees stood out above the snowy cuffs, the skin as dry as a weathered board, untouched by lotion since babyhood. Spots of thickened red callus puffed my inner knees where they had rubbed against the saddle. A tickle of fear raced through my stomach. I couldn't believe I hadn't noticed them before.

I stepped into the skirt, slid it over my hips with panicky little jerks and studied the gap between sock and hem. Horrors. Half-lidded by the skirt, my knees peered out with the dull glare of a bored rhinoceros. With sudden inspiration I unfolded the top cuff and pulled it snugly over my kneecaps, stretching the socks up under my skirt as high as they would go. Standing on the bed, I pivoted back and forth in front of the dresser mirror, looking at my fuzzy white legs from all angles. Not a speck of skin showed. Perfect. There was nothing I couldn't figure out.

That night as I laid out my clothes and prepared for the next day, I imagined myself as a character in a novel, the young woman who leaves home to start a new life. I had closed the door on my ranch self, embarrassed now for that sullen, angry child, and wanted nothing more than to join the middle of the pack. For one night I allowed myself the luxury of imagining the students and teachers I would meet, what they might say to me, how I might answer. I drew on scenes from 4-H camp, the three days I spent each summer in the Bear Paw Mountains, where adult leaders taught us to "mix" with other bashful country kids. The rest I gleaned from books. In novels, pretending to be something you weren't was a red flag for trouble, causing no end of grief for the hero or heroine. No matter what, I vowed solemnly, I'll just be myself.

My parents had left for home in the late afternoon, and I watched with interest the way evening came on in this new place, the sun falling behind big elm trees a block away instead of behind mountains a hundred miles distant. Shadows streaked across the pale sidewalks and merged in a jumble of shapes, houses overlapping trees bleeding into fences. I absorbed it all with a thrill of excitement. Town had always been a destination, a place at the other end of the road. Now I was part of it. The distance felt different from this end, like a cushion of fresh air between me and the community that had watched me grow up. I was free, out from under and accountable to no one. The last part was a secret. Our parents hadn't driven away without exacting my big brother's promise to take care of me and show me the ropes.

Standing in Mrs. Crowder's kitchen, Kenny had punctuated Mom's orders with stoic little nods. I grinned, enjoying his show of composure, the warning glances he flicked in my direction. He had fought his way to acceptance like most ranch boys, first with his fists and later with hard work. At the start of his junior year he was looking forward to reclaiming a steady girlfriend and the circle of friends he left behind during summer vacations. He'd made himself clear. If I got into real trouble he'd listen, but I would not be walking to school with him or collaring him in the hallways to ask questions. In fact, I was to avoid him as much as it was humanly possible to do and still live in the same house. Same goes, I told him archly, and the deal was struck.

That Sunday he ushered our parents out onto the stoop, but Mom hadn't finished yet. She leveled at him, stepping closer, her eyes intense under the dark brows. A no-bullshit face. The act fell away, and Kenny braced, no doubt imagining the worst—trailing this pudgy, graceless sister by the hand from class to class the first few days, or, God forbid, escorting her to a social event. The directive, when it came, seemed to relieve him as much as it surprised me. Kenny's head wagged a stern "no way." He would not, he agreed, for any reason, under any circumstances, call me Hog Jowls, a name he'd gleaned from an episode of *The Beverly Hillbillies* and bestowed upon me a year previous, nor its derivative, Jog Howls, which he'd made up himself when the buzz wore off the first.

Huh, I thought as I baled my pin curl perm into haphazard rows with snap-together pink rollers and practiced making a mouth with the slick ruby lipstick I'd lifted from my mother's collection of Avon samples. *What's the big deal about a nick-name?*

I found my way to school the next morning, found my way to the auditorium for the first-day assembly, found my way to my first classes and by midmorning had found my way to the rest room. Girls bubbled and squealed around the short row of sinks, pivoting on one heel to catch the swirl of pleated miniskirt over jutting hipbone, pouting white frosted lips toward the mirror for touch-up. Wide-toothed combs floated down streams of silky hair. I crouched against the door of one gunmetal-gray stall like a cat on strange ground and took quick inventory of the odd-looking fixtures—a toilet with no tank, the flush handle jutting from a pipe on the back wall, nowhere to set my books. A chrome box with a lock hung from the stall at waist height, and sliding my hand to the bottom I found not a roll of paper but a slot that begrudged a few tiny squares of tissue. With these I scrubbed at my mouth, dropping the obscene scarlet smear into the bowl, then sat on the seat and shifted my books to my lap so I could tug up my wilting knee socks. They drooped down my shins when I stood, the elastic panel at the top stretched too far out of shape to spring back. I took a deep breath that threatened to catch and never come out. Next time I would know. *Next time, next time, next time.* I followed my heartbeat out the door, looking neither left nor right, and into the march of the hallway, shouts of greeting capped by the tin-slam-crash of locker doors, and the steady drumroll of feet pounding up and down the stairs to class. It was not quite noon, and I was exhausted.

If I opened a book the first two weeks of school, I don't remember, for it took me that long to learn to filter out noise and shield myself from the distraction of people, bodies pressing around me, movement always at the corner of my eye. I'd grown up learning to listen, straining to measure sound against the silence of open space. There, where the landscape repeated itself for miles in all directions, even everyday sounds meant something. A bull's high-pitched challenge drifting in from the wrong direction told us a fence was down; the honk of a car horn meant trouble, a call to come. We knew the sound of a rig turning off the main road, the pitch of a strange motor, the growl of our own pickup pulling in for dinner. When our dog barked at night, Dad got his rifle and followed the ruckus to the skunk in the chicken house.

Town seemed bursting with noise for the sake of noise. There was no stillness, no quiet place to sit and hear the wind sifting through dry grass, and it was this more than the odd taste of bleach in the tap water, more than the stuffy smell of too many cars in the air, that left me raw and shaky at the end of the day. The first few weeks I slept at the edge of my bed, waking instantly at the murmur of voices on the sidewalk outside, the whir of passing cars, and a veritable torment of bored dogs that yapped at the moon or each other or nothing at all.

During school hours, I studied the town kids with an eye to becoming one. Boys were no surprise, I thought, just like boys everywhere, loud, strutty fellows who wrestled and ran and punched arms. But the girls who caught my envy were nothing like the stolid little citizens at 4-H camp. These were giggle-at-boys, squeal-at-anything girls who leaped in pointy-toed circles and clapped their hands to show excitement. They sashayed. They screamed in fear of all God's creatures smaller than a cat, swooping birds included. Where I came from, running from anything as stupid as a bug would have inspired weeks of sibling ridicule, months of having the same or a similar species dropped down your shirt. Fear was a weakness to be overcome, or at least hidden behind a calm gaze. Even a grown man could admit that salamanders, what we called mud puppies, gave him the willies, but he surely wouldn't jump when he saw one. He could be "leery" of things like lightning, especially if he'd been struck before, and folks would accept his caution. But the word "fear" was seldom heard except in its benign form, the way you'd say, "I'm afraid the 'hoppers got the wheat at the Picotte place."

My father couldn't abide a snake, but he did not teach us to run from rattlesnakes we encountered in the hayfields or along the road when we were walking home from school. Instead of fear, he had something called "a healthy respect," and that was what we learned. This was not a live-and-let-live respect for the snake as a fellow creature but the nod of recognition one gives a potentially dangerous adversary. From observing the deed a hundred times, we learned to kill rattlers without risking our own skin. Outside and afoot, we watched and listened automatically, alert when turning new bales of hay to check the twine a second before our hands descended. Snakes tunneled under the windrows after mice and were sometimes baled up in the hay, their thick coils held fast by the twine, still alive and squirming days later.

Being kids, we crossed over the line a few times, erring toward that lack of healthy respect called "being stupid" or "not having a lick of sense." Gathering cattle one afternoon, Dad spotted Gary and me off our horses and rode over to see what had happened. The two of us squatted amid the sagebrush at the entrance to a badger's den, a burrow nearly a foot wide dug between two half-buried boulders, holding our reins in one hand. We were deciding which of us would grab the buzzing tail protruding from the hole, the only part of the snake we could see, and which would stand ready with a few rocks to kill it when it came free. We had already agreed to share the rattles, a trophy displayed button-down in the hatband. Our eyes were on the prize. We didn't think about where the head might be in that wide, dark hole until our father skidded up and bailed off his horse to grab us and pull us back. We thought about nothing else for a long while after.

I discovered in those first weeks of high school that town-style fear was the one reaction I could not fake. On weekends I practiced as I reined my new colt, Sunny, along trails farthest from the buildings. The face I could do, big eyes and a wide O mouth, but any clear, piercing scream I launched fought its way past three generations of constraint and emerged with the caution of a June rabbit. The best I could muster was a frantic, low-pitched groaning that made my green horse bunch up and walk flat-eared and stiff-legged until I ran out of wind. No good at being scared, I had to go with fearless. In biology class, I sliced into the corpses of earthworms and crayfish with exaggerated gusto, while real girls dropped their scalpels and cringed. Boys competed for the privilege of being their lab partners.

"How can you *do* that?" A voice on the tinny edge of hysteria would pierce my concentration as I sawed around in the smelly innards of a perch. "Gawd, I'd just *die* first." Like the screams, this language of exaggerated postures and eye rolls, flirting and tiny foot stamping compared to nothing I knew. Not letting on, that's what I knew, not showing your insides on the outside. But here, the emotions stepped on each other getting out, lavish with arm-flinging excess. The very melodrama of my peers fascinated me. I watched and listened, learning to read this new language with speed and accuracy, though in my heart I knew I would never speak it.

Surface changes came more easily. I basted up the hems on my skirts to fashionable heights, careful to pull the threads each Friday before I took them home for washing. From articles in teen magazines I gleaned some ground rules for being a teenage girl and learned what I was supposed to look like. I gave up my mirror and studied the pictures instead. Within days of paying my rent, I made my first offering to the cosmetic gods.

Following the makeover charts in the back of one magazine, I painted my face by the numbers, sinking my eyes in a slurry of black liner and sapphire eye shadow, coating my face with beige grease, white powder, rose blush and pale lipstick. Because I wore glasses with heavy black plastic frames, everything went on a little more thickly, as per instructions. What looked back at me was magically different. I looked very, very *something,* I concluded, narrowing my eyes and pursing my lips to catch the full effect, though whether very good or very bad I had no clue. It felt right, or perhaps "safe" is a better word to describe it. The world seemed safer with my skin covered. The next morning I rose early to prepare and entered the halls of Malta High with new confidence, my face several shades lighter than the sun-browned neck it perched on, fever spots on my cheeks and black-on-blue eyes that might have been the result of a fistfight rather than a cosmetic makeover.

In retrospect, my first sharp lesson was a mercy, delivered a few weeks later in the privacy of the girls' bathroom as I leaned over the sink adding another layer of black to my very black eyelashes. Two cheerleaders bounced into the room, their pleated blue-and-white skirts flipping at the bottom of their rumps with every step. I moved over to make room at the mirror as they sleeked and preened for the pep assembly. One of them caught my eye as I capped the mascara, her little fists settled pertly on her hipbones, her head cocked to one side like a sparrow at the edge of a grain trough. She spoke in a wondering tone, every word a question.

"You put your makeup on by yourself?"

The other girl snorted back a laugh and hissed at her, "God, Mary!"

I didn't know how to answer. Mary flipped her hair back and tipped her chin to the other side.

"Well, Jeez. Looks like a two-man job to me." A true punch line. Her friend shrieked and folded in the middle like a rag doll. Bent double, they staggered toward the door, helpless, howling, slapping at each other as they made their escape. In the mirror, my girl mask peered back with solemn eyes and deadly calm. So. In a half an hour I could go home for the day and wash. The toilet stalls chattered with the energy of two hundred shoving, shouting students as they spilled into the auditorium across the hall. I could feel them on my fingertips where I held the door shut, tremors damping down to a hum of expectation, then the explosion as they surged to their feet and roared out the fight song of the Mighty Malta Mustangs.

The same magazines that gave me a face promised me success at dating, and when my first call came early that winter I dug through the stacks for a quick refresher course. Advice columns lent tips on how to keep the conversation up and the sweater down, while stories portrayed a variety of wholesome sock-hop, hayride-type outings. The letters from readers were my favorite. Did nice girls kiss on the first date? I tried to imagine someone's wet mouth on mine, smooching around the way they did in the movies, and a vee of goose bumps rippled up my arms. I couldn't get past the idea of warm spit—some boy's slobber on my mouth. Jeez, Louise! Yuck. I bent my thoughts in another direction. First things first. Permission to go out with a boy required the courtesy of a long-distance call to the ranch, but the most difficult ordeal would be to refrain from boasting. Though he was three years older than I was, by anyone's criteria Dennis was a real catch—a star of the debate team, active in student council, member of a very respected and well-liked family.

With my mother's blessings secured, I had one remaining obstacle. I waited until the last minute, supper on Wednesday night, to announce that I was going to the movie. Kenny shrugged. It was Take a Chance Night at the Villa Theatre, a popular midweek attraction that offered newsreel, cartoon and an unannounced B movie for fifty cents a head. The rest I added casually as I rose to clear the table, stacking plates and cups as if blind to the fact that my bombshell lit smack in the middle of forbidden territory. I wouldn't be going alone. Dennis had asked me out. He'd be picking me up in half an hour. Dennis was Kenny's age, one of his sacred circle of friends. I braced myself, expecting him to puff up and rattle his spurs to warn me away from his territory. Instead, he wheeled toward me like a whip crack and his whole body seemed to tighten down. "You're not going out with him." I drew back, startled by the intensity of his voice. This was no bluff. At the same time, I felt the heat rising in my chest.

Since early childhood, the twins and I had accepted Kenny's authority as an extension of our parents'. He'd been groomed to follow in Dad's footsteps, and in the absence of hired men, he'd been expected to do a man's work at a very young age. He learned to drive a stick shift as soon as he could perch on the edge of the seat and reach the foot pedals. As young as ten he'd been left in charge of us when Mom and Dad were gone to town, directing us in our chores and taking charge of the ranch work that had to be done in their absence. By the time he was in high school, his directorate as Dad's right-hand man was absolute. Kenny was the crown prince of the ranch, responsible and honest to a fault, handsome, confident and smart. He was what we were supposed to be like, we knew, though not one of us quite measured up. He was only two years older than I was, but his approval had the power to make me happy. I hadn't expected him to like me dating. But forbid me?

Kenny had kept himself aloof from my town school struggles, either ignorant of, or indifferent to, my painful first few weeks. I accepted that, and thought little of it. We had an agreement, after all, and I did not bother him with questions about school. But now that I'd been given a chance to join in, a shot at being somebody, here he stood with his orders, ready to take away what I'd worked so hard to obtain.

But I held the upper hand for a change, and I let him know it. Mom had given me permission and there wasn't a damned thing he could do about it. I finished with my arms crossed. Kenny's lips clamped shut on what he'd started to say and his head wagged, as if in wonder at my stupidity. I waited him out. Again he started to speak, searching for a way in, then dropped his gaze. This was all too strange. My stomach felt taut and queasy, the way it always did when I lost.

"God, it's only a date." The words came out as a question. His hands rose from waist level, palms out, one wave of surrender and dismissal. He spun on his heel and disappeared down the basement stairs, retreating to where I could not follow.

The whole encounter had taken only seconds, yet rang so far out of proportion I stood uneasily in the kitchen staring at the basement door. Why the big deal? What did he know that I didn't? His eyes kept coming back to me like an echo, deep brown gone black in the center. The way his jaw clenched, the way his hands hung at his sides half curled into fists, that was anger. But his eyes held something else.

Whatever it was, it was his problem. I grabbed my coat and slipped outside to wait on the front stoop. I pulled off my gloves in the bitter night air and dug eagerly for the open pack of cigarettes in my purse. The smoking games that I had played since childhood had taken a serious turn since my move to Malta. While I was slowly finding my way through the first months of high school, my budding tobacco habit had zipped from zero to half a pack a day. Junipers bracketed the doorway. I glanced around, then stepped back into their shadow, cupping the match flare, palming the red coal as I drew deeply, calming myself. I made less effort to hide the smoke, partly because at ten below zero everyone exhaled white clouds, partly out of pure defiance. My first days in town I had imagined a future of boundless freedom. As it turned out, I'd been sorely mistaken. My new life was beginning to feel a great deal like the old one. A week seldom passed that I didn't experience the creepy feeling of being watched and turn to find some unidentified adult studying me intently, fingers *pop-pop-popping* until Eureka, she had it! "You're a Blunt girl, aren't you? I knew it! I've known your folks since when. Look at you, just the spitting image of your father!" Or mother or grandmother or brother. It didn't matter. The town was growing eyes around me.

Most recently those eyes threatened to reach all the way to the south country. Mrs. Crowder had discovered my stash of cigarettes in a dresser drawer. I had my suspicions when the pack began to migrate during my absence every weekend— not disappearing, just shifting from a nest under a stack of clean dresser scarves to a perch on the pillowcases, from one side of the drawer to another. I made them disappear, but the rumors were already launched, little nuggets of information skipping from ear to ear like flat stones on a still pond. So far, quite miraculously, they had missed my parents. Just a matter of time, I thought bitterly, before half the county had its nose in my business. Even my brother had shown disturbing signs of looking out for me. It was all so hopelessly unfair.

I doused the cigarette in a skiff of snow and pulled on my gloves, settling into the shelter to wait. Seconds later, a set of headlights appeared around the corner and pulled up in front of the house. Dennis was punctual, I noted with some satisfaction, yet another touchstone mentioned in my teen bible. He leaped out to open the passenger door, and I slid into the front seat as if accustomed to courtly displays. As we sped toward the main drag, Dennis filled the silence easily with talk about his car, his classes, the farm he remembered from childhood. He was a nice-looking boy, I thought, with a shock of blond hair that fell over his forehead and a toothy smile. I sat up tall in the passenger seat, laughing and nodding in all the right places, seeing and being seen.

As it turned out, I need not have pored over the pages-long discussion about whether to kiss on the first date. The answer was yes, though I had no part in the decision. By the end of the first month, our routine was firmly established. He picked me up in his car. We drove to the movie or more often, to Joe's In and Out, a drive-through restaurant, for a soft drink, then cruised the drag. After half an hour of circling, the car would begin to break from the predictable pattern, darting down a side street, overshooting the turnaround spot, and my stomach would clench. Asking to go home triggered instant obedience, a careening ride that ended in a sliding stop in front of Mrs. Crowder's house, engine revving as I got out, the door jerked from my fingers as he squealed away. Obviously that was the wrong thing to do. As our relationship progressed, the little test runs became shorter and soon were dispensed with altogether. Coke in hand, he looped the main drag once or twice, then veered east, steering in silence past the cemetery, past the cement plant to the wide dirt lot overlooking the city dump.

I dressed carefully for my dates by then, high necks, long sleeves, and under that, one of my brother's T-shirts tucked securely into a pair of jeans. I looked at Dennis quietly whenever he suggested I "dress up" for our next date, staring until he turned away, a flush darkening the fair skin of his cheeks. My role was difficult enough in tight jeans with a safety pin across the zipper tab so it couldn't be pushed down—this last my own invention. A dress, indeed. Once parked with the lights off, he had the first move, an arm stealing across the back of the seat as we talked about school and music, his activities and his car. I countered just as casually, leaning forward to adjust the radio to escape capture, and the game was on. When he kissed me, my hand rose automatically to his cheek, bracing to shove him back, for I'd learned how easily the force of his lips could pin my head to the back of the seat, a move that freed both of his hands.

Conversation generally dwindled away as he became more insistent. "Stop that" and "don't" pretty well covered my contributions, while his ranged from outright denial—he wasn't doing anything, I was imagining things—to accusations—I was cold, unnatural, a cock tease. "What's your problem, anyway?" he would shout, pounding his fists against the steering wheel in frustration as my ten o'clock curfew drew near. I won by acting calm and in control, but after he dropped me off, I would flop across my bed and wait for the shaky feeling to subside, conscious of the reek of my own sweat. Secretly, I too wondered what was wrong with me. I had felt my first sexual stirrings at eleven, sharing raunchy paperback novels with my cousin Lois. I knew I was supposed to want him to touch me, that it was supposed to be hard to say no. But it wasn't. I felt no physical desire for him and I did not enjoy having him touch me. What I loved was the idea of having a boyfriend. I tolerated his attentions dutifully, willing to trade some degree of affection for status, and it drove him crazy. I couldn't figure out what I was doing wrong.

By all the measures I'd been given to use, Dennis was a

nice boy from a nice family, and I was lucky to have him inter-
ested in me. I knew that what he was after fell short of "going
all the way," for he reassured me frequently that he knew
when to stop. He wanted something called "the next best
thing," which involved my hands on him in ways I refused to
imagine, and his all over me in ways I refused to permit. He
wheedled and reasoned and coaxed, and when I remained
unmoved, he raged. Clearly, as a female it was my job to keep
a checkrein on these forays and to enforce a proper standard
of decency, whatever that was. Were his demands really as
reasonable as he claimed they were? For all I knew, all boys
acted like Dennis, all dates were staged like contests in a dark
alley—the girl and boy faced off, one maneuvering toward
safety while the other tried to block her way and push her
back into the darkness.

My physical resistance seemed to surprise him. I suppose I
was stronger than he expected, but I had also been raised in a
tribe of fighters, which freed me of any ladylike hesitation or
caution. The rougher he got, the harder I pushed back. I had
no sense of the escalation taking place, his methods gradually
growing more insistent, his anger more easily triggered, or
what the culmination of this might be. And for the hours I
spent replaying events in my mind, deciphering his moods,
trying to figure a way through this maze of conflicting pres-
sures, it never crossed my mind to confide in someone else.

Our last date, I pulled myself out of the car by sheer determination and slammed the passenger door in his face as he
lay across the front seat. Lining out along the plowed shoulder
of the road, I tucked my chin into my coat collar and aimed for
town. The bitterly still night carried sound on a knife's edge,
and I tracked his progress by ear as he pulled out to follow me,
gravel popping like sparks under the frozen tires, his voice

ringing through the open window, pleading, apologizing, arguing. My hands and feet throbbed with cold when I finally relented and let him drive me the rest of the way to Mrs. Crowder's house. I was already late, an hour past curfew, and my brother simmered at the bottom of the stairs, waiting. I remember nothing of what he said, only my own inability to speak. I was afraid that I couldn't explain without making everything worse. By remaining silent, I made a choice. A sentence from me, a few words, one tear falling down one frost-bitten cheek and my brother would have been pounding on Dennis until someone pulled him off. Perhaps it was fear that stopped me, fear that this night would not end but continue to spread outward in ever larger ripples—from Kenny to our parents, Dennis's parents, the whole town. Perhaps it was pride. I had thought myself grown up enough to handle my own decisions, and I wasn't about to ask for help now.

That last date was not our final meeting, although it took a week of phone calls before Dennis persuaded me that we could not break up without a face-to-face talk. He picked me up at the house and with more resignation than outrage I endured his nervous chatter as we traced the familiar dirt road to the dump and pulled up in the usual spot. He shut off the lights but left the engine idling, the heater blowing a warm fan of air over our feet. His face was earnest and eager as he leaned toward me, one arm falling along the top of the seat. I turned sideways to face him, my back firmly against my own door. He had a surprise for me, he said. He'd been going to mention it last time, but after the way I'd acted, he'd decided to make me wait. His hand stretched toward me as he made his announcement, displaying the prize circling his third finger. He had decided to let me wear his class ring. We would be going steady!

Learning Curves

I shook my head slowly, baffled by his offer. Had he gone goofy? Had I somehow not made myself clear over the phone? Crossing my arms, I stared at him a second, then spoke with every ounce of disdain I could muster. "I wouldn't wear your ring if you gave it to me." I left the words dripping in midair and turned to the view out my window, the lance of starlight pooled below in the spread of the little town, the night achingly clear. I steeled myself for his anger, my muscles slack with forced nonchalance, arms folded across my chest, unprepared for the swiftness of his move. One hand closed over my crossed wrists, and with a strength he'd been reserving all this time, he pulled me forward, then bent me back across the seat. There were no more games then. We fought in dead silence until I freed an arm and began slapping the side of his head. He reared back out of reach, leaning his weight on the arm across my chest. The air left my lungs in a rush. I felt his other hand push beneath the waistband of my pants. He spoke then, his words grunted and muffled so only the last bit stuck: *whether you like it or not.* Words that held the firm resolve of someone doing something for my own good, doing what had to be done. At the precise moment I realized I could not keep his fingers from invading me, a piercing whoop echoed through the car and the front seat seemed to explode around us. Above me, Dennis's head jerked upward and froze in the red and blue strobe of police lights.

On slow nights our city cops cruised for parked cars, stalking passionate teens with the singular stealth and patience of the truly bored. If two heads were visible over the front seat, the patrol car generally moved on with only a blink of the headlights. An idling car with no heads in sight got a burp of the siren and the full bubble-gum light show. I sucked my first deep breath past the ache in my chest as Dennis lurched upward and fumbled for his glasses, then scrambled out, leaving his door wide open. I leaned across the seat to jerk it shut. The dome light winked out and I sat up, fighting a wash of dizziness. I could hear them talking behind the car, the teasing rumble of a man's voice, the rapid squeak of the boy's going high and low, rhyming the pulse of color around us. Then footsteps approached my door. A white glare lit up the backseat, as the officer drew a beam over the floorboards looking for beer. The light danced over the seat, shafting past the tip of my nose to the driver's side, then slowly back toward my feet. I watched the light climb my leg, slowing each breath as the flare oozed over my lap, crawled up my arm and along my neck. Heat bloomed against the side of my face and paused, wavering. I didn't make a sound.

The patrol car followed us back down the hill, passing as we pulled to the curb in front of Mrs. Crowder's. As if from a great distance, I watched myself slide out and swing the door shut evenly, taking care not to slam it. Then I was walking away, measuring each step to the entry, through the hall to my room. Six words survived as the epitaph, and even now they can summon a ghost, the flicker of disbelief I felt as the air left my chest and I could not pull it back, the shock of panic, roaring, electric, when I finally understood that I was powerless. *Whether you like it or not.* We never spoke again.

In the telling, stories appear to unfold one event at a time. We master them like songs, listening for keys and common themes, learning the clear notes that best connect beginning to end. Stories are contrived. In real time, life is less a song than a competition of sounds—new days spliced to the dying strains of days past, events within them merging without pause or explanation. I can say I entered my room that evening and emerged the next morning as if called to battle. Better yet, I can put my finger on that moment when my knees gave way and I sat facing my own reflection, and say there, right there I began coming to peace with what was real in myself. But only in retrospect do I imagine this clarity. And at the time, I felt only weariness.

Close to twenty pounds of me had disappeared since autumn, but what remained were the permanent gifts of four farming generations, a legacy of wide shoulders, strong arms and broad, square hands. I would never be cute or giggly. I also fell short of those pleasant virtues by which plain girls are forgiven, that sweet and gentle interior that redeems beauty. I'd been tailored to fit one particular family in one isolated community. Outside it, my ground-covering stride became ungainly, my brand of strength unnecessary, or even worse, I discovered, inadequate. Outside my community, only one cause made allowances for this puzzle of androgynous traits, and that was women's liberation. In the course of the next four years, I allowed the movement toward feminism to adopt me. But still, like my mother, like the ranchwomen who peopled my childhood, I would not spout ideology or argue theory. Strong women roared in silence. We roared by doing.

In the second half of my freshman year, I settled into a cruising pattern that kept me just below adult radar. I got decent grades. I gradually stopped hanging around with Lois, as her exploits grew more reckless; she began drinking, cutting school to ride around with wild boys in their loud cars. I was done dating, I thought. Thrown together by alphabetical seating charts, Alice Blundred and I became best friends, and gradually I grew to know her circle of childhood pals. Alice had money for clothes and movies, money for Cokes and french fries. Alice and her brother and sisters all worked in their mom and dad's restaurant downtown. A full malt shop menu and a selection of rock 'n' roll tunes on the jukebox made the Sugar Shack Café the closest thing to a teen hangout in town, a great place to see and be seen. At Alice's urging, I applied for a job as waitress.

I circled the block twice before I gathered my courage and entered the café, prepared to lie about my age if fourteen was too young. The topic never came up. An hour later I traded on my surname for the first time as I signed a rubber check and walked out of Anthony's clothing store with a white nylon uniform, trusting the bank to cover the default from my parents' account. When school let out the next day, I reported for duty. Stretched carefully, thirty-five cents an hour bought me obscurity—a beauty-shop haircut, a few ready-made clothes, a new item called pantyhose that rendered garter belts mercifully obsolete. Then through some sort of governmental mandate our wages jumped to seventy-five cents an hour and I felt rich. I bought wide bell-bottomed, hip-hugging Levi's, tore out the hem and carefully frayed the edge. I wore fringed moccasins and peasant blouses. The Beatles' "Hey Jude" was still the slow dance of choice, and I answered that greeting ten times a day as I served coffee and hamburgers, or layered ice cream and flavored syrups into fluted confectionery glasses. Three or four afternoons a week I stepped behind that counter, coming home to a place of clear rules, expectations and rewards. As slick as shifting gears, school faded into the background and work became the center of my town life.

From the first, my new boss seemed familiar to me. Elsie

ran her business with both hands and a quiet, tireless grace, still perfectly groomed at the end of a sixteen-hour day. As the second shift wound toward closing, only her eyes showed fatigue, a darkening that made her look gentle and hurt. The café quieted after the supper rush, and every evening she settled into a far booth to do the accounts, a quiet hiss marking the moment she sat down. I kept one eye on her coffee cup as I cleaned counters and filled the salt and pepper shakers, drifting over to top it off when the level fell below the red lipstick bites on the rim.

When she called me over at the end of my shift one evening, I was more puzzled than anxious. I slid onto the bench seat across from her, feeling the tightness in my calves and thighs from six hours of steady walking. In the privacy of my room that night, and for days after, I fed on our conversation, replaying her words in my mind, remembering exactly how she spoke, the soft laugh, the way she looked at me, shaking her head. *I've never had a kid work the way you do.* With the praise came a fifteen-cent raise in pay. In her voice, her simple words, I heard honesty and respect, a quiet nod for a job well done. The feeling that swelled up in me was not pride, but gratitude that bordered on worship. She had found me. Had I been capable, I would have thrown myself across the table and sobbed on her neck. Instead, I rubbed my thumb over a scar in the Formica tabletop, scrambling for the right thing to say. My town face felt nearly familiar by now, a careful face that had no connection to Maybelline or Revlon. It was calm and confident, watchful in new situations, ready to move. When in doubt, I remained neutral, a careful nonchalance I could shift to whatever seemed expected of me—a laugh, a frown, a shake of the head.

"Wow," I said at last. "Cool." But I couldn't stop the grin.

I ran home that night.

I ran with my head back, indifferent to the hooting and tooting cars full of high school kids cruising the drag as they did every night, endlessly. I ran, even though in town girls were not supposed to run, especially girls in skirts. Mistakes I'd made the first weeks of school were easy enough to shake off. Ignorance was not stupidity, I told myself, and I'd proven that by erring once and learning fast. Life went on. But my gut still shrank at the memory of one fall afternoon soon after school began. I was running downtown to the Ben Franklin store, mentally picking through the candy section as I galloped down the sidewalk. School supplies came first, but surely a few bars of chocolate wouldn't break the parental bank. As I neared Main Street, I was greeted by cars full of high school kids honking as they passed me. Some of them sped ahead and circled the block to pass me again, tooting and cheering. I smiled and waved as I would have on the county road, tickled by their friendliness. A block from the store, one of the cars finally slowed to a roll beside me, and a boy leaned from the passenger window, his shout nearly drowned by a squeal of tires as the car swerved away. "Hey, Speedy! Where's the fire?" Laughing, all of them.

Tonight it didn't matter. In the country, girls ran. We ran to get places, to cover ground. We ran because we by-God wanted to. Looping my purse around my neck, I zipped my jacket over it and set off, feeling a strange shortness tugging in my thigh muscles, reined in for so many months, then warmth as my legs stretched out, searching for a rhythm that had once been automatic. Blocks passed before I had a smooth stride and my knees began to lift and flex and fall without prompting. The winter dropped away, and what rose in its place felt endless. For a little while in the darkness that night I was simply fourteen, dodging from streetlamp to streetlamp, connecting pools of light like the dots on a puzzle page. If no one saw the picture, so what? It was enough to hear the applause of my own feet, to feel the power stealing back, sharp as the spring air that fed it.

The Reckoning

My sophomore year, the twins started high school too, and my parents faced the logistical nightmare of boarding four kids in Malta. One problem was solved when Grandma Pansy moved from her old homestead to town and purchased a small house near downtown. We were welcome to live with her. However, she was in her eighties at the time, and could not be expected to cook and look after us all, or to bear the expense of this, so Mom moved to town and took a job to offset the cost of running this second household. Dad joined the ranks of lonely bachelors during the week, learning to fend for himself. The rest of us shared Grandma's house, my sister, mother and I jammed into a spare bedroom with one double bed and a cot, assorted boy cousins and brothers crammed dormitory-style into the cement basement, all of us living out of suitcases and battling for the single bathroom.

Work remained the focus of my town life as long as I lived there, and by my second year I had molded an exterior that could slip through the halls of Malta High without a ripple. My hair finally grew long, my belly flat, my jeans tight, and eventually I saved enough money from my job to replace the thick glasses I hated with contact lenses. A few months after my dating debut, I replaced Dennis with Alice's brother Marty, a quiet, nervous senior on his way to the Army. We met on my first and last double date arranged by Lois, just the four of us and a backseat full of beer. A couple of hours into our drive, I added a new dimension by throwing up all over the car—a hardtop with no rear doors and tiny little triangle-shaped windows. I am spared much of the memory of that rapid drive home.

I stopped by his locker the next day to apologize and offer to wash his car, and he was shy and forgiving. For more than a year I would wear his class ring like a shield, writing letters on airmail tissue first to Germany, then to Vietnam. It was a time of healing, a withdrawal from the playing fields made respectable, even honorable, by hometown rules of war. Good women remained faithful to their soldier men. When that began to pall, I discovered that men in their early twenties treated me with all the respect due my tender years. I joked that the initials of my name, J.B., stood for "jail bait." If my mother, now close at hand, took an extraordinarily dim view of my hanging around with older guys, it followed that after a year of total independence, I took an equally dim view of her interference. And the battle was on.

One young man in particular bore the brunt of my teen rebellion, and that was Guy, a good-looking charmer of twenty-two with a fast car and a bachelor lifestyle. I was far more the kid sister than the girlfriend, but he would buy a Coke and let me flirt with him over the counter of the Sugar Shack when I was working. Lois was dating his roommate, Bill, perhaps the only reason I found myself at a house party that fall. It was Election Day Tuesday, a rare weekday of freedom since Mom had gone to preside over the polling place and collect the ballots for our rural precinct. Past experience told me the counting wouldn't be done until after 10 p.m., and I felt confident she would spend the night at the ranch rather than drive to Malta. Sometime in the rowdy, post-midnight leg of the party, I began to get sleepy. Thinking ahead to school the next day and work, I began wading through the noise and smoke looking for my cousin. On my second pass through a maze of legs and loud music, Guy rode to my rescue with an offer to drive me home.

We cruised the vacant streets of Malta for half an hour, talking about nothing in particular. With just enough beer under my skin to feel dreamy and tired, I kicked off my shoes and leaned back, savoring the quiet. Another car passed by. Guy drew a breath between clenched teeth. Swiveling, I caught the flare of brakes as the patrol car spun a U-turn and roared up behind us. Cop lights pulsed on. *What time is it?* I glanced at my watch. It was 1:30 a.m. Four hours earlier, the old civil defense siren had wailed its 9:30 curfew, a nightly reminder to underage citizens that when the last echo faded the city cops needed no other excuse to pull over a car or question the activity of kids on the street. Though seldom enforced, the curfew statute created the perfect cover for routine beer confiscation and general harassment. I could be hauled to the station and held until a parent retrieved me. I made a wild scramble for my shoes, combing my brain for a believable story. I'll say I was baby-sitting, I thought, just getting a ride home, something straightforward and simple. All I had to do was chew mints, act calm. I could talk my way out of this. Laces tied, coat snug to my chin, I drew a deep breath.

Guy slowed the car gradually, waiting for me to finish before he pulled to the curb. In the eerie light his skin shone a bruised red, his hair electric blue. He looked at me a second, eyes impossibly dark, hands loose on the wheel, then turned off the key and slowly rolled down his window. I had turned sideways to watch as the patrol car stopped under the street-light behind us. Squinting against the glare, I searched for clues to which cop we were dealing with, reading the profile as he stepped out and closed his door. He slid both thumbs under his wide belt, adjusting the regulation issue of clubs and cannons that dangled from his hips, not dawdling but purposeful, determined. In that sliver of time before he walked toward us, I could breathe again. Ray Cummings, a former neighbor from the country south of town. I knew his kids from 4-H. If anyone would give me a chance to pull out of this, Ray would. Good old Ray. The next bare second held such a maze of information that most of it arrived un-assembled.

Imagine a mouse daring to cross the snow under a full moon, streaking along, every hair alive to danger, and its relief as the refuge it seeks appears just ahead; imagine then, that second when everything changes and all comes clear, that blind instant when it feels the downbeat of wings overhead. In the final beat before the brain shuts down there is no room for thinking. Only knowing, a flash of simple fact that what might be a harmless breeze overhead is not, what seemed worth the risk at the outset was not and whatever comes next will be painful. It was like that. One form emerging from a car became a parting of shadows and two doors closing, *chuff-ka-chuff,* so close together that the sound came joined in the mid-dle with wings on either side. Of course I knew. And in the moment of knowing I would have struck a bargain with the devil to be dead in a ditch or to be someone else's child. Ours was no random stop, no routine grab for one of a dozen under-age teens flitting through intersections after curfew. I was the subject of an official hunt. For as surely as good old Ray sat in the driver's seat of that patrol car, it was my mother who rode shotgun and by the slant of her shoulders, the lean ridge of lip and jaw, she was loaded for bear.

They approached on either side. Guy sat bug-eyed as my mother hurled hellfire through his open window, a blistering catalogue of insults skillfully spliced to strings of dire predictions and one aspiring charge of statutory rape. On the other side, Ray dressed me down for my shameful behavior, disrespect for my mother's feelings and my father's good name. Then they switched sides. I remember almost none of what was said, but the tone was clear. Such was my shock that I recall neither how I got home nor what we said once we arrived. Probably nothing. I do remember working through the puzzle of why she had appeared, and feeling stupid not to have anticipated it. Someone had to carry the election ballots to Malta after the polls closed.

"If she wants to believe I'm a slut," I raged to Alice at work the next day, "far be it for me to talk her out of it." All my friends felt sorry for me, but then they knew my relationship with Guy was so benign as to be nearly nonexistent. I had taken no pains to share this fact with Mom prior to the big bust and felt no compunction to ease her mind after. Let her worry. I knew I was innocent. No doubt, I expected the usual punishment, a few weeks of frozen disapproval met by my own equally silent martyrdom. But it was not to be. The next afternoon Dad drove in from the ranch, and for the second time in as many days, I found myself darting, dodging, doomed. The two of them were ensconced at Grandma's table, waiting for me when I got off work. Their voices fell away as I entered.

Dad nudged a chair with his foot. I sat, slouching as far as the hard back would allow, and picked at a fringe of hangnail, waiting for Mom to tell me to sit up straight. Discipline had always been her job. Dad seldom intruded on our upbringing, partly because he was seldom around the house to observe it, but partly because raising kids simply wasn't his job. In our earliest years, he was the dusty giant we ran to greet when he came in from the field, clinging, two monkeys to a leg, for a ride through the kitchen to the bathroom to wash up. I fought for my share of his love, sinking tooth and nail into equally greedy siblings, but when we grew beyond the lap-climbing stage, when we no longer ran to meet him, nothing bridged that gap. He did not seek us out to chat about our changing interests. By my teen years, his undivided attention had long become a kind of currency, meaningful conversation weighing like gold coins, praise like hundred-dollar bills, and all changing hands just as infrequently. Facing him across the supper table on my weekends home, I would feel his gaze drift over me and away, ready to notice what wasn't there but never quite seeing what was, unless something made him look. Or someone.

I concentrated on the word "venom," shading my bland expression with thin lips, narrowing eyes. When the other kids came home late, Mom dealt with them as a matter of course. Bringing Dad into this particular case was an act of pure malice, I thought, a move with no purpose other than to raise my already staggering level of humiliation. Her eyebrows raised once and settled back, cool and steady, a trifle squinty. *You asked for it, Sweetie Pie.*

If Mom held the big guns in making law and maintaining order, Dad was the parental version of a loose cannon, given to unpredictable explosions of great force and random fancy. He had not the first clue about town life or about high school, I fumed, having neither lived in the one nor attended the other.

He'd gone to work on his father's ranch right out of eighth grade, and regardless of his success at raising grain and cattle, he remained sensitive about his lack of formal schooling. Having no experience in these matters did not mean he was without strong opinions, however. Quite the contrary. But I considered them ill informed and somewhat irritating. "Going to school is a privilege," he would begin, waving one of our less than perfect report cards—usually Gary's or mine. His voice would rise and deepen at the same time, hard as wire and strung with barbs of righteous conviction as he nailed home points, one thick finger thumping the other palm.

The complexity of what we actually had to accomplish our first few months of high school escaped him. We all started young, beginning with Margaret, who was only twelve when she boarded with a very kind, very old, profoundly deaf widow for the first year of high school. And all of us entered the city limits with only those skills acquired at the ranch. We all coped differently—Kenny with the confidence of a firstborn son, Gail with indomitable optimism—and with differing degrees of success. Gail's leap into the social whirl eventually paved the way for her more backward twin, but Gary's early grades, like mine, were those of a thirteen-year-old struggling to find balance on unfamiliar terrain. In those days, a country boy's initiation to town life included fistfights, and those unwilling to swing back were hazed and prodded until they did. Too young not to cry in his rage and frustration, Gary would eventually muster the grit to walk the four blocks home pantless and dry-eyed, pull on his spare jeans, and wade back to school to fight for his good pair. Of course he learned quickly, as all of us did, but it took a multitude of lessons that had nothing to do with books.

Today's lecture was no different. Getting an education was the most important thing a person could do in this life, and lest I forget—a pause here, for emphasis—that was the *only* reason I was in town. The *only* thing of any concern to me in Malta was schoolwork. My days of running wild were over. I was to go to school and work the way I'd been taught to work. Then I was to come home where I belonged. I sat through the lecture, stifling the backwash of bitterness. My punishment pretty much described my life, anyway. Go to school, go to work, come home. Compared with my little sister, I had no social life.

I saw Guy one more time. I remember the song that was playing on the car radio, "Gypsy Woman," and the way it seemed to stay on the charts for months after, and how my white uniform smelled of hamburgers and fried onions, the nylon skirt speckled with a history of grease spots. I remember the interior of his car, the air freshener dangling, maroon paint, yellow-tinted windows. I remember concentrating on one tiny detail at a time, unable to take in the whole picture.

A week or more had passed since I'd last seen Guy, palms up, talking with Ray Cummings. He'd stopped at the café for supper, but instead of the usual booth, he picked a stool at the crowded counter, ignoring my overtures as I took his order and filled his coffee cup. My shift ended before he finished his meal. I lingered until he paid, then followed him out the door to his car. I wanted to apologize for getting him in trouble, I reasoned, though my motives were far more self-centered than that. Who better to sympathize with my sad plight, my persecution by such rigid, unfeeling parents, than a fellow victim? We stood with the car between us, his hand poised over the door handle, my mind scrambling for the right thing to say. "Can we talk for a minute?" I blurted.

Seconds passed, cars passed, people walked by, glancing our way.

His lips tightened. "Well, are you going to get in?" Without another word, I opened the door and we backed away from the curb. My first mention of the big bust dropped like a stone, disappearing with nary a ripple. Guy never shifted his eyes from the street as we circled the block. He didn't want to talk about it, had no intention of wading any deeper into my situation than bare politeness demanded. Embarrassed, I fell silent, saving face on our second and final pass down the main drag, a loop I expected to end with him pulling up to drop me off at the café. We were two blocks away when the DJ announced the song, one of his favorites. He must have glanced in the rearview mirror at the same time he reached to turn up the volume because his hand remained frozen to the knob, then withdrew in slow motion. As he sat back, his wide shoulders seemed to shrink toward his spine.

"Shit," he said. Then, "You've got to be kidding," his voice so hushed and dead that I felt my scalp prickle before I even swiveled around to look. The grill of my father's pickup filled the rear window like the teeth of a great chrome shark.

Somewhere out there, a gypsy woman danced in the firelight. Sparks danced in my brain. Everything roared. Engines. Fires. Silence. With effort I cleared my throat.

"Can you outrun him?"

Guy shook his head once as if clearing his ears, a wry smile twisting one corner of his mouth. "I ain't even going to try."

Instead of turning the corner toward the café, we floated evenly up Central Avenue, dipped beneath the railroad overpass and turned left on Highway 2 with Dad's pickup stuck to our bumper like roadkill. Where the houses and businesses ended, a graveled lot marked the city limits, a place where kids in cars turned around or pulled up window to window for private conversations before cruising back the way they had come. Tires crunched. The radio crooned. Guy stopped the car and started to open his door. Dad got a hand on the front of his shirt and helped him out. I felt the car rock, once, twice, Dad's voice low, Guy's back slamming against the side like punctuation, then a spray of words against my cheek. Dog orders: "Get in the pickup."

We had all arrived at a point far beyond lectures, though we pulled our chairs to the same table. Mom spoke first. I was forbidden to ever see Guy again. "It's not like that—," I started. They leaned into their anger, Mom's voice rising to override me. If I gave my word, if I swore I would never see him again, they had agreed not to press charges against him. A bolt of fear left the long muscles of my arms and legs quivering in their effort to be still. Charges?

"Charges for what?" I choked out. "We . . . he didn't *do* anything!" I think I had assumed at some level that my mother would simply know this because it was true. She might use suspicion, accusation even, to regain the upper hand, but did she really believe it? Her face was unreadable. Charges for statutory rape, contributing to the delinquency of a minor. I was flabbergasted. How could they think that? Mom sat back, impassive, as I defended my innocence, Guy's innocence, agreeing to whatever punishment they thought up as long as they left him out of it. When Dad finally spoke, his face was chiseled steel. They'd raised me better than to run with trash. Maybe what I needed was time off from high school, say a year at the ranch to think things over.

I shook my head and swallowed. "No." I flushed at the sound of my own voice, the word spoken too quickly, their eyes registering the creak of panic with grim satisfaction. The threat was not an idle one. They never were. "No," I whispered again, lowering my gaze to my clenched hands. The trump card lay on the table between us—my call, play or fold. We left it at that.

I had a lot of time to think in the days that followed.

Christmas vacation drew near. I made good grades, worked my shifts and came home, a full-blown revolt contained only by the tension of my skin. The smallest shake—a teacher's question, my mother's voice, a brother's teasing—set me trembling. In spare moments, I daydreamed of revenge. If older guys were a problem, I decided, the next would blow parental head gaskets. I didn't have far to look for the perfect candidate. Better yet, he had had his eyes on me for some time.

His dad's ranch sprawled along the northern edge of the Missouri River Breaks fifteen miles south of ours, a place we seldom visited except to dig for fossils or hunt a Christmas tree in the stand of scrub pine. He was an only son, an ROTC college graduate back from the war, and the year before my family had been one of several invited to his slide show of Vietnam. The war was a distant event to most of us, as were the protests against it. But the county shared a long history of sons called to military service, and no matter where they served, there was no lack of patriotic support for those who returned. That evening John had stood at the end of a narrow room punching the button on his slide reel, narrating each scene as it flashed on the screen—water buffalo wading through rice paddies, women squatting along the riverbanks, villages of straw-capped huts—none of it more foreign to our eyes than the backdrop of dense, vibrant green. I had leaned against a doorway that opened to the kitchen, watching him.

Poised and confident, John played the officer and gentleman, suffering naive questions and the forced camaraderie of old war veterans with easy humor. I started the game of eye tag. He glanced my way, I shifted to the screen. He turned to the screen, I looked at him, a dance of tiny movements, barely restrained smiles. When the lights came on, our eyes met for a long moment. He lifted his chin, a high sign lobbed over the heads of a dozen oblivious neighbors. Being coy, I paused a second before I lifted my chin in return. I was fifteen, though he would always say I seemed older. He was twenty-seven.

John was a novelty to me, a man both familiar and new. He was a son we always knew existed but had never seen, raised by his mother in another county. Nearing retirement age, his father had set about luring John to Phillips County, offering him a place on the ranch. That winter, John divided his time between Bozeman and the ranch as he finished his industrial arts degree and considered his father's offer. We met again in the summer when I hired out to a ranch bordering their land, and our flirtation continued despite the difference in our ages. I had received a card in the mail, a phone call or two. Whispers stirred the benches at the First Creek Community Hall when we took the floor at a Saturday-night dance. The stage was set long before that November day in 1970 when Guy and I took our last ride to the strains of "Gypsy Woman."

John called me during Christmas vacation, and this time I was ready. Bored by what passed for social life in a country winter, he had decided to host another slide show, this one a chronicle of the first Milk River Wagon Train. This time I narrowed the distance, taking a place behind him, facing the screen. When he stepped back to change slide reels, he remained in the narrow doorway beside me, working the remote control, narrating the rodeos and runaways. I did not step away. The last were a series of night shots around the campfire. He eased closer in the near dark and slipped an arm around my waist, his touch surprising, soft as the stroke of a feather. I shot a glance toward my father, the back of his head almost indistinguishable in a row of heads. My mother sat in profile on the couch. I raised my arm in an answering squeeze. We stood touching, hip to shoulder, until the last cowboy sang, until the final scene shuffled to a new slot and the screen burst into white light.

We dated country style. On winter weekends, he'd pick me up in the battered four-wheel-drive and we'd spotlight for rabbits, driving for hours over the rough frozen prairie with a flask of whiskey between us. In summer, we took the shale ridge road overlooking the Missouri River, edging the truck around washouts and through creek crossings, stopping to explore long-abandoned homesteads. We went to the community dances at the First Creek Community Hall, rode together to neighborhood baseball games and brandings. On rare occasions he came to Malta during the school week. I pushed every limit of curfew and behavior to the very edge, making little secret of my fondness for cigarettes and sloe gin. But the battle I expected never arrived. Instead, I found myself basking in something close to approval, with resulting adult privileges, as if attracting this sensible, practical man caused my parents to look at me with newfound respect. Often I spent the first hour of our date drumming my fingers as John and my father swapped stories and talked cattle. My parents swapped supper invitations with his father and stepmother for the first time in my memory. A year after we began dating, John dug through a box of memorabilia and came up with his old class ring. We exchanged '61 for '72, a difference of age most succinctly measured by the music we listened to—his Kingston Trio and Hank Snow, my Rolling Stones and Three Dog Night.

By the week of my graduation from high school, I'd found a roommate old enough to sign for phone and utility service and together we rented a narrow, two-bedroom mobile home. I bought a used car with my savings, and as I stepped forward to receive my diploma it sat outside the gymnasium loaded to the roof with all my belongings. As the principal worked his way down the alphabet of names, I watched with a sense of detachment. I fancied myself older than my classmates, now, in all the ways that counted. An old seventeen. For the past two years I had divided my life into three neat and distinct compartments: work, school and John. I'd managed a succession of jobs, shoehorning a work schedule around classes and weekend travel back and forth to the ranch. I'd waited tables, cooked, pressed clothes at the dry cleaners and operated the switchboard and night desk at the local hospital. Friday night, I shifted gears on the way back to the ranch, looking ahead to a weekend of passionate, though chaste, embraces. Sunday, I left John without a backward glance, plotting the week's schedule to keep each part of me in safe, separate and secure orbit. Hard work paid off better on the job than it ever had at school. I'd drawn my circle of friends from the ranks of fellow employees, most of them older than I was. That last year, I spent four hours a day in class, then worked a full shift, double-shifting whenever the opportunity arose and banking every second paycheck.

I worked the afternoon they held the awards ceremony. I'd been a mostly honor roll student, excelling in English classes when I cared to, passing algebra because I had to, graduating in the top third of my class. But I was not scholarship material. At my senior interview, Mr. Moran, our guidance counselor, spoke vaguely of the careers most women chose because they worked best around a family life—secretarial, teaching, nursing, home economics—things you could drop for a while and pick up again when the kids were grown. Swiveled sideways in his chair, one argyle ankle resting on a knee, hands clasped behind his head, he fixed his eyes on the wall and spoke as if reciting some difficult passage from memory. These skills benefited a lot of women because they had a practical application as well as a professional one. You could work as a secretary, say, then keep books for your husband's business, or apply your home economics field directly to your general homemaking and child rearing. Teacher, nurse, secretary. We did not discuss aptitude, entrance exams, application deadlines or financial aid. All that hinged on an if and a shrug. If I decided to go on to college. Shrug. Margaret had managed to get her degree and was teaching elementary school. Kenny was wrapping up his second year of a range management program at Montana State University. College just happened for them, but how it got started, I hadn't a clue. My parents and I still circled each other like strangers, wary and polite, avoiding confrontation. I did not ask them for money, advice or approval, and they volunteered nothing.

A disciplined group, the Class of '72 queued up by height to march back through the double doors of the gymnasium, step-sliding as we'd been taught in order to create an oceanic illusion, waves of us pulled by the grand tide of "Pomp and Circumstance." The audience rose to its feet. John stood beside my parents in a row of family, all of them smiling. John remained the last enduring link to my old community, a man who'd been willing to wait for me through three years of high school, but who waited with less and less patience as my emancipation day drew near. In his pocket lay a flawless diamond solitaire in a web of tiny stars, a ring I refused to wear until after graduation. Pressed to set a wedding date, I had picked one more than a year distant.

Ahead of me the line began exploding by pairs as it passed through the doorway, like a string of firecrackers feeding itself to an open flame. Royal blue caps flew up with a roar. Boys pounded shoulders, shouting. Girls clung to each other and cried. I threw my hat as high as anyone and pushed toward the front doors of Malta High, returning a backslap here, a handclasp there, grinning at their excitement, laughing all the way to my car. I remember pausing on the dark street and deliberately looking around, intent on remembering the feel of these first steps as a free woman. Behind me, two stories of red brick seemed to squat and extrude people, squeezing them through lighted doorways in long, slow streams. The air was drenched with the smell of late spring, the musk of damp earth, of lilacs and new grass, the first whisper of heat still rising from the pavement. My wedding day barely glimmered on the horizon, but it was a secure feeling, knowing I had a man waiting on the land in case—in case what? I pushed away the thought. I had gotten the first two jobs I'd applied for, and was already working them both. The summer opened before me like a gift. John was comfortable and familiar, and I loved him dearly. Still, anything could happen in a year's time. Anything.

Humans are born with the fear of falling, the instinct to fling our arms wide when we lose our footing and claw the air for some solid purchase. Through that long, sweet summer I never once doubted the foundation I had built for myself. I held in my hands the ability to do for myself, the key to independence, and I neither looked to the past nor imagined a future beyond it. When the props gave way on September 16, 1972, I was sitting on a case of peaches in the back room of Ken's Thriftway, a mom-and-pop grocery store where I earned my major paycheck. When the owner called me back for a conference, I was more irritated by the interruption than concerned. Over the years, I'd gotten used to being a star employee, and as I perched on the stack of canned goods listening to the man ramble on about the grocery business and serving customers, it took me several minutes to understand that I was being fired. Me? The girl who hefted fifty-pound bags of flour and dog food off the truck? Who candled the farm eggs because everyone else hated that job? Who fearlessly dispatched the huge fuzzy-legged beasts in the banana crates when the produce woman came bawling through the swinging doors of the cooler? Me.

I sat back, barely able to catch my breath. The owner gazed at a pile of loose boxes as he explained his reasons for letting me go. I was a good worker, a hard worker, but the summer season was ending and, he added with a long-suffering sigh, there had been complaints. My head swiveled toward him with a level of impertinence I had never shown before, and I snapped, "From who? Complaints about what?"

Rocking back, he sharpened his voice to match mine. "From customers," he snapped. Seems I did my job fine. I stocked, checked and bagged groceries, doubled sacks without being prompted, packed boxes of even weight and no wasted space. What I sometimes forgot to do was smile. Over the summer, two patrons had called him—their duty as friends of the family and longtime customers—to report that my sullen attitude was hurting business. I felt stricken by something close to horror. For years I had assumed my public face appeared to others the way I intended. Neutral. Pleasant. A nothing face arranged to neither cause offense nor draw attention. I had been wrong. From the outside, my neutral facade appeared disinterested, aloof, even angry. When I wasn't smiling, the speed I took pride in came across as reckless impatience. I was all job and no people, the owner summed up. Like the fabled emperor, I stood naked the moment he pointed his finger.

The Reckoning

That night I paced the length of our shotgun trailer sharing my misery with the Grassroots and nursing a fifth of sloe gin. By the time my roommate came home I'd switched to Three Dog Night, playing "Mama Told Me Not to Come" again and again, and the bottle was half empty. My two-week notice was up on September 1, and my second, part-time summer job would end about the same time. I never looked for another. Still a month shy of my eighteenth birthday and less than four months after I had packed my car and left the ranch, I wedged my belongings back into the tiny room off the ranch kitchen that I had shared with Gail since our infancy. Mom had moved the twins to town for their final year of high school, and they were gone during the week. Kenny would do a few more months of college before coming home for good. Dad charged in and out of sight, preoccupied with a dozen projects in addition to the fall work of weaning and shipping. A week passed, maybe two. I wandered in a daze, cooking meals, trudging through barn chores, taking long rides through the meadows and fields, searching for comfort in the familiar childhood landscapes. It was not there. Cross fences jerked the land into new, taut dimensions, the posts still pale and raw. Huge squares of grazing land lay freshly broken, a mare's nest of old roots and rocks, yellowed grass still clinging to sod. The world I had grown up in was gone.

The changes had not occurred overnight, and in some corner of my mind I had made casual note of them. But four years had passed since I had truly paid any attention to the cycle of life on the ranch, and in that brief span more than landscape had shifted. About the time I started high school, a boom in land values had made small family farms suddenly worth more on paper than ever before, riches that had little to do with cash flow or real income but gave operators like my parents the borrowing power to enter the twentieth century.

In terms of technology the modernization that followed was as revolutionary as the leap from horse to tractor begun by my grandfather and completed by my father. In the same decade, a third generation of sons came of age, boys like my brother who not only had been raised on the land but had studied modern agribusiness in college. Now that the draft had ended, they were coming back to the land.

In my absence, the whole community seemed to have shifted gears and found overdrive. New steel granaries jutted up from cement pads centered in the ashes of the old wooden grain bins. Four-wheel-drive tractors sporting headlights for night farming, cabs with windshields, radios and padded seats, squatted in the lee of new construction. The steel arc of Butler buildings rose over dark, oily squares of ground where tiny, dirt-floored shops had been, and fifty years of farming filled the coulees: old forges and anvils, foot-pedal grinding stones, wagon springs and hand pumps, brittle leather harness dried into swags from decades of hanging on a wall.

In the four years I spent traveling back and forth to Malta High School, the population of our community had dwindled by a third as the smaller, more marginal places were absorbed by their larger neighbors. The few remaining homesteaders were in their eighties and ready to retire. Couples with no children sold out to those who had sons waiting in the wings. Neighbor observed neighbor in an undercurrent of expectation, noting which heads came together in private conversation, who was visiting whom, listening for news of this one selling, that one buying. At the beginning of the boom, John, his father and stepmother had added another large ranch to their holdings in the Breaks and formed a ranching corporation. The year of my graduation, my parents, too, bought a second place from a retiring homesteader and became Blunt

Ranches, Incorporated, a move that included Kenny as partner. Overnight, it seemed, the place I grew up on had fallen under the wheels of big business—big land, big lease, big machines. Big debt.

In the years when Dad had lived alone during the week, he had acquired the habit of calling neighbors to visit and discuss business as he fixed his solitary meal or drank coffee in the break between chores. I had no place in the new dealings. Our mealtimes together were silent aside from the jangle of the phone. One-sided conversations filled the kitchen at noon hour and took up again at dark. When Mom arrived on weekends, I slid further into silence, making sly but steady progress on the cache of sloe gin in my underwear drawer. Sundays when the house emptied I stepped back into place, clearing away supper dishes and straightening the rooms with a boozy attention to detail. One area of my life remained safe and familiar, and that was John.

The first evening call was often from John, and he regularly followed up with a thirty-mile round-trip to visit. As my father and I drifted through the week of empty evenings, anticipation of John's visits became our one shared experience. I cleared away the supper dishes while Dad watched the evening news, both of us alert for the muffled woof our dog gave when lights turned off the county road onto our lane. At the signal, Dad rose from his chair and turned off the television, then stepped into the porch to click the yard light on and hail him in. Pulling up a chair at the kitchen table, John would risk an eyebrow cha-cha in my direction while Dad wasn't looking, grinning as I turned to hide my smile in the task of making coffee.

I filled cups and served wedges of pie, ready for the tease of backhanded praise as John finished and pushed his plate forward. "I can't decide if that pie's any good or not—might have to have another piece to make up my mind." Not to be outdone, Dad would lean back in his chair and suggest I might improve my pie-making if I just practiced a little more, say a pie a day until I got it right. Beyond that, I had little to offer as they shuffled news and gossip across the cracked linoleum. I listened carefully to their talk of breeding programs, feed grains and land swaps, hungry for the feeling that comes of knowing every story, yet coming up empty. I felt suddenly rootless, invisible in a way I had never known. Grown beyond my child's role in the community, I did not yet fit in the adult world. I held no place of value on my family's ranch and was not yet a part of John's. My options were as frightening as they were simple. I could marry, or I could leave.

October. From the road, the prairie looks barren, all the grass thinned to stalk and stem, empty of seeds. At that distance, only the sagebrush stands out, big sage, silver sage. In a dry year, hunters and visitors to the region drive the trails in search of game, shaking their heads at the sleeping prairie, believing it dead. It's all there, though, if they thought to squat down and part the brittle guard hairs. Below is the short grass grazed by buffalo for centuries, blue grama and wooly plantain cured low to the ground, the last of its strength drained into the roots for safekeeping. It will come back with the rain. It can wait for years.

Since childhood I had believed that the plants and the people who live here were alike in that respect. If they survived for long, they knew one of two things. Some of them were landed, immovable—men like my father, plants like big sage. Sage drops a taproot like an anchor and settles against

the wind, drawing what it needs from deep below. Those without size find another kind of strength. They must ride the surface, bowing to the uncertainty of seasons. The ones that live
happily here are flexible, adaptable, willing to lie dormant
when the rains don't come, able to move quickly on the
strength of one good storm.

I rode out in the teeth of the west wind, the grumpy, half-
flat cant of Sunny's ears offering his opinion of late-autumn
rides. A plush layer of winter hair had begun shading out
his palomino tan, giving him the pale wheat color he would
wear until spring. Nerve sweat bloomed along his neck. I
hunched and straightened my spine, pulling at the knot of
muscles between my shoulders. We were both on edge. Like
most horses, Sunny hated facing into a hard wind. For me,
it was the noise of the wind that did it, a hiss and rush like
static on a radio tuned to nowhere. We might have grown
immune to a steady blow, but the volume of prairie wind
shifts constantly. Unpredictable bursts of silence broke through
between gusts, snippets of still air that carried the jingle of
snaffle rings, the squeak of saddle leather, and we'd have
one or two calm breaths before the next gust snatched them
away.

I guided Sunny gently toward the summer fallow, trying to
loosen his stiff-legged walk, alert for the bunchy feel he got a
second before he bogged his head. Riding a green horse is
work—no gazing at scenery, no searching the dried pan for
arrowheads or agates—but in Sunny's case we were edging
beyond "green" into the territory of "spoiled." He had mastered only a basic primer of skills before high school began
carving months-long gaps into his training. Our sporadic
weekend reunions did little more than reopen the skirmish.
Half the time he bucked me off, the other half I rode him to a

standstill. Although neither of us was learning much in this process, we were both getting craftier. I had discovered that a thirty-minute workout in soft dirt generally took his mind off of bucking. He tried every evasive action outside of actual balking to avoid the long grain fields west of the corrals, working himself into lathers of frustration as I countered one sly shift of direction after another, each move plotted to end at the barn door.

When I finally gave him his head, he lined out like a greyhound up the center of a plowed field, his feet sinking fetlock-deep with every stride. The intended runaway soon became a labored gallop, and by midway across he had thrown in the towel. I walked him out to cool him, then let him stand, tail to the wind, to blow. On the field before us lay the lopsided figure-eight pattern we'd worked over the past weeks, reining work done at a steady lope, turn after turn, no beginning, no end. Not today. I turned and rode east, leaving the tilled fields for the firm spring of grassland, preoccupied and restless. The early-summer wedding that had once loomed too near now seemed suddenly very far away. My head throbbed with a need for something I could not name—somewhere to belong, some way to be important.

The dry prairie that passed beneath my horse's feet felt cold and unfamiliar to me, even as I rode past landmarks and called up the stories that created them. Why didn't I belong here? Didn't the contours of this land fall under my gaze like a quilt under a smoothing hand, my eyes counting every knot of silver sage on the patchwork of cactus and hardpan? Not unless I was the eldest son it didn't. Nursing a wave of bitterness, I pulled Sunny to a stop and swung down, leading him along the trail toward the road. We stopped at Lupe's Rock, a broad slab of granite dragged to the edge of a wheat field by

Lupe Luna and his big Caterpillar bulldozer more than a decade before. I squatted in the lee of the boulder to smoke, cupping the coal carefully in one hand and reins in the other. The rock had been nearly as tall as we were, still raw and pink as an uprooted tooth, when the twins and I claimed it. It became our destination the morning we announced we were running away from home for the first time. Mother had brightened perceptibly at our news, and set about packing lunch into a red kerchief while we scrounged up a suitable stick for our hobo pack.

"Wear your shoes. Watch for snakes." She waved from the doorway, so unconcerned at our leaving that little fires of self-pity fueled the first leg of our journey.

It seemed a long hike to Lupe's rock then, out of sight of any house, any road other than the trail that bordered the fields. We spent half an hour rolling smaller rocks to the base so we could climb on top, all of us fitting easily, with room for the picnic spread between us. Later the three of us stood on the rock and shaded our eyes against the sun, telling stories about how far and what all we saw in the wavery line where the heat met the earth at the edge of our world. Stretching my arms east and west, I claimed my legacy of land, shouting that this part would be mine—my land, my cattle grazing the green lip of the reservoir there, my meadowlarks, my grasshoppers. It seemed impossible to have grown any larger than I had been that afternoon.

I stubbed out my cigarette and buried the butt, aware of a twinge of loss as I left the big boulder and remounted. Gail and I once borrowed luck by swinging from one stirrup to slap the rock as we galloped past, but that was impossible now. For years, dirt blown from the fields had drifted against it, and grass had seeded and regenerated around its base. Sod had filled in around the smaller rocks we once used for steps, forming a low mound with only the top stone exposed, like a bald spot in a head of curly hair. Lupe's Rock seemed bent on drawing itself back into the earth.

Perhaps the wind lifted the edge of the saddle blanket and it popped against Sunny's back, or maybe a tumbleweed bounced at the corner of his vision. More likely he sensed my mind's wander from the task at hand as I stepped down to open the gate on the way back to the barn. Instead of leading through the gate, he reared suddenly and sat back on his haunches, jerking the reins from my hand, then wheeled toward home at a dead run. It was not a long walk in the sense of distance, less than a mile to the buildings. I had plenty of time to wonder whether he would hit the fence between him and the barn or would slow down enough to find the open gate. Time to watch as he bogged his head and crow-hopped until the empty stirrups banged against his ribs and he took off again. Plenty of time to wish he would step on a rein and break his fool neck.

He was waiting at the barn door, eyes rolling white, nostrils flared, greeting my approach as he would have greeted a pack of wolves. I stopped a few yards from him, calling him filthy names in a soothing tone, calming him until he stood to let me gather the reins. I led him forward to show him we were attached again, and he followed anxiously, his legs trembling when we stopped, head slightly turned to keep track of the door. Barn sour, we called them, horses whose one focused thought from the time they left the corral was not turning the cow in front of them or watching the trail beneath their feet but finding some devious way of getting home. I could hear my mother's voice in the back of my head telling me what I had to do. He had shown the worst possible manners for a

range horse and I couldn't let him get away with it. Climb back
on. Ride him half a mile from home. Ride back to the barn
and get off, then get back on and ride him away. Again and
again and again. And again tomorrow. And the next day. He
associated the barn with comfort and freedom, and I would
have to break that connection, ride him until he forgot what
barns were for. No more combing or brushing or unsaddling
him indoors. He'd be eating his oats out of a bag far from
home.

He stamped his feet against the chill as the sweat dried in
stiff streaks along his neck, tugging the reins as he sidled
closer to shelter. To turn him loose now would be rewarding
his crime, the first leg of a short journey to the sale ring.
Standing in the cold wind I watched his ears flick, his eyes
shift from me to the barn. I'd made a bad job of him too, pure
and simple. The thought settled quietly around my shoulders.
A bad job it was, then. We turned toward the barn. He stepped
on my heels going through the door, urging me forward, and
took his place near the rail, standing quietly, almost poised as
I worked the cinches loose. Stripped of tack, he arched his
neck and trotted smartly across the big corral, straight to a
closed gate that led to the horse pasture, and stood there,
worthless and wise. I could muster no feeling, one way or the
other, no energy to cross the corral and turn him out.

The house was mercifully silent except for the muted
whistle of wind in the eaves. I loaded kindling and crumpled
paper into the black belly of the kitchen stove, wincing at the
ache in my left wrist. I'd been holding the reins tightly when
the horse jerked away. I massaged the tender joint with the
other hand while I scanned the cupboard for matches. Dry
cereal, syrup, rice, whiskey. Whiskey. Setting two measuring
cups on the counter, I poured one full of whiskey and the

other full of water. The whiskey went into a glass. The water went back into the whiskey bottle. I moved into the living room where the oil heater kept the chill off, and set Sandy Posey spinning on the turntable, jacking up the volume until the cheap speakers buzzed. I paced the length of the room, letting the music and the drink wash over me. Struck by the words of the first song, I stopped in the middle of the room and closed my eyes, as though hearing them for the first time.

Round, like a circle in a spiral, like a wheel within a wheel, never ending or beginning . . . When the song ended, I lifted the needle and set it back in the first groove. I danced a slow figure eight through the room. And again. When the whiskey ended, I poured some from a different bottle.

Memories of my grandfather's death were tied to another small death, the day I discovered that as a girl, I would never own my childhood ranch. In retrospect, it seemed I should have always known this, but I didn't. Grandpa Blunt's funeral was held in the same small nondenominational church where I planned to be married. The building dated back to the first years of the town's history, a steepled square with a foyer, dressed in spotless white clapboard except for the wide double doors in the front, and aptly named the Little White Church. Capable of seating perhaps fifty people in its double row of pews, the church had been too small to hold the county full of friends and neighbors who attended Grandpa's funeral. Mourners spilled into the adjoining funeral hall to listen to the service via a loudspeaker. I remember a thick damp in the hall, the muggy crush of bodies, the extra folding chairs set up between the rows. Uncle Junior, the eldest son who had worked Grandpa's ranch since returning from the Korean War—I remember him crying. And I remember Aunt Marie scolding a pack of us same-sized cousins for being too noisy at the potluck that followed. But more clearly than all that, more clearly than the sunken, icy face of my grandfather in its unlikely nest of tucked satin, I remember the talk my parents had with us children a few weeks later. We were lined up on the smooth red-vinyl benches built into the walls on two sides of our kitchen table. After the death of her husband, Grandma Pansy had elected to sell the ranch to the boys, my dad and Junior. In a family of seven remaining children, this decision left the five sisters high and dry, and apparently some of them had complained and threatened to challenge her. Dad had stubbed the table with one thick finger, emphasizing there would be no such fight when it came our turn to bury him. In our family the sons would follow the father; Kenny, the elder, would have first refusal. We girls would be left something of value, but we should know at the outset that we would never inherit the land.

At some point in the next half hour, I rinsed my glass and placed it on the drainboard, then stepped into the porch and locked the porch door, jamming the hook firmly into the eye. Hardly a cold-weather door, it was held shut by a long spring instead of a doorknob latch. Wind sucking around the corners of the house set it tap-tap-tapping against the jamb, a sound as irritating as a leaky faucet. I stood looking east through the storm window, toward the county road. The wind had dropped and steadied, rippling evenly through the dried weeds along our lane. Dad had left early, hadn't said when or if he'd be home for supper, or maybe he had and I'd forgotten. Working cattle somewhere. They were weaning calves down at John's place, too. He'd be tied up for days. I leaned against the door, testing the strength of the hook-and-eye latch, the tenderness of my swollen wrist. A pain rose in my chest, a familiar tightness in my throat that threatened to choke me. I stared down at my hands, the broad heft of them. How coarse my left hand looked, how out of place the arc of diamonds that graced the third finger. Sturdy, powerful hands. The fist seemed to form itself. In one smooth move, I stepped back and sent it smashing through the glass.

I made a good job of the window. I swung until only jagged shards stuck up from the glazing, then pounded at those with the side of my hand to knock them out. Once it was started, I saw it through, every punch a jolt of electricity that charged the next blow and the next. When it was over I stood still for a while, trying to sort one version of reality from another, as though I had turned a corner and come upon a terrible wreck only to recognize myself amid the blood and broken glass. Shattered glass covered the concrete step outside the door, the sash beaten clean except for a few smeared nubs stuck in the glazing. Trails and streams of blood ran down the white painted wood on both sides. My left hand bore a maze of shallow crisscross cuts that spoke of not one but many trips through the window, the side of my fist minced by repeated blows against the frame. In the jumble of superficial slices and gouges, only two or three deep gashes bled freely. My palm was virtually untouched, the ring undamaged. In the end, I felt a surprising sense of calm, almost relief. There would be no hiding this one.

Holding my hand open and flat had slowed the bleeding considerably, but when I flexed it rapidly into a fist, thin jets of blood shot from the two deepest cuts. Using my hand as a spray gun, I painted the door, inside and out. I made little puddles on the concrete. Inside the house, I marked territory like a tomcat, this doorway, that wall, the mirror over the sink, my elbow dripping a trail of red drops as I ran from room to room, giddy with my absolute badness and the feeling of being

212

intently, acutely alive. To say I felt no pain would be misleading in one sense, for while I felt no actual pain in my hand, I also didn't feel the slightest bit drunk. So intent was I on this job of losing blood that when the dog gave a short bark to announce a strange vehicle, I literally leaped into the air with a stifled scream.

By the time I'd grabbed a towel to wrap my hand, a young man stood on the sidewalk halfway to the door, one arm frozen in the act of taking his hat off, his face hanging like a bleached bedsheet on a still day. His wide eyes riveted on the mess in front of the door, then moved slowly up the looping river of red that appeared to pour over the edge of the sash. When he reached the still-intact upper pane and saw my face peering out, his reaction was no less intense than mine had been a minute before. He jumped like he'd been goosed. Gripping his hat in both hands, he opened his mouth twice before he got words to come out.

"Is everything okay here?" God knows what he thought had happened, but he didn't move any closer to the door. He still hadn't blinked that I could see.

I pushed the door open and stepped partway out, keeping my "bad" hand hidden, and gave him what I hoped was a reassuring smile. Had the visitor been one of our neighbors, he or she would have walked straight in and taken over. But this young cowboy worked as a laborer for a distant ranch and was obviously uncertain of what was expected of him. I could buffalo him into believing everything was under control, and he'd be on his way.

I assured him that I was just fine, had a little accident, nothing too bad. He asked if I needed a ride to town, and I smiled some more. No, no. Someone's on the way to get me now, no big deal. I remained blocking the doorway, made no effort to extend the conversation or invite him in, and in the language of the country he was effectively dismissed. He understood, but he hesitated, unwilling to take my word in the face of all that blood. *Oh, God, a real cowboy.* My mind raced, searching for some gesture that would allow him to feel useful.

"There is one thing you might do, if you would," I offered, pausing as if afraid to ask such a favor of a mere acquaintance. "I left my colt in the lot beside the barn. Could you turn him out so he can get to water?"

He drew himself up and slapped the wide hat onto his head, absolutely no problem, he would see to the horse, horses were something he knew. His pickup churned dirt all the way to the barn. As soon as he was safely out of sight, I grabbed the phone and called John's place, sending his stepmother on a dithering run to get him out of the corral where the men were sorting cattle. The visiting cowboy was only a few minutes up the road when John's big blue four-wheel-drive slid to a stop in front of the house. He said little as he handed me over the pile of broken glass and into the pickup for the ride to town. He said less as we drove. I flexed my hand once, spraying the dashboard with a dainty mist of blood, but he was not amused.

In Malta, he dropped me off at the doctor's office. My mother arrived in time to watch as the doctor peered down his bifocals and ran his thumb over the crosshatch of cuts, deciding on five that needed sewing. Her eyes were flat and unmoving, a dark gaze that held me pinned to the chair as the doctor tugged stitches into place. She smelled booze on me, I was sure. The story I prepared for the ride home made no mention of whiskey, nor did it explain the evidence written on my hand and on the walls of our home. I told her I had stumbled on my way through the porch. The dog flopped on the step and leaning against the door had kept it from pushing open when my hand hit the window.

I suppose it was she who cleaned up the glass and washed away the blood from the doors and floors and walls. I know I didn't. Dad offered no comment one way or the other, though he would have the chore of replacing the glass before snow flew. I slid into bed that night craving sleep. In the end, I found my own violence that day less strange than the silence it met. The story I told was one of the most transparent lies I've ever passed. Yet it stands today, unchallenged, never mentioned.

Late that spring I stood at the altar of the Little White Church and spoke the vows of silent partnership. The groom was nearly thirty, tall and slim, his solemn, sun-darkened face circled by the pale stripe of a recent haircut. He stood frozen by all those eyes, like a deer chased into a clearing, and I found the tremor in his fingertips oddly comforting as he turned to face me. We joined hands, callus to callus, in the presence of friends and neighbors, the sun through the stained-glass windows linking us all in a slow kaleidoscope of color, emerald-green softening to amber, purple bleeding out from red and royal blue.

In the vestibule, waiting for the march to begin, my father had looked at me, straight into my face for what I felt to be the first time in years. "Are you sure about this, Sis?" he asked, his voice cracking, his chin going soft with emotion. Any butterflies I felt died in the punch of heat that rose and spread outward through my chest, a heat so pure it numbed where it touched. I was conscious of my lips lifting in a stiff smile, my scarred fist gripping the wad of Tropicana roses and baby's breath, the way words and images battered at my skull like swallows trapped in an attic. There had never been questions. No questions for the fifteen-year-old daughter dating a twenty-seven-year-old man, no comment when we became engaged a year and a half later. He spoke as the man I had promised to marry moved to the right of the altar braced by trios of groomsmen and bridesmaids. Was I sure about this? In the pews, all eyes shifted to the doorway searching a four-beat pause for the first long strains of the wedding march, their signal to rise, our signal to walk.

I wonder now how I sounded as I answered, my whisper rising to be heard over the opening chords. "Don't you think it's a little late to worry about that?" His gaze faltered and drew inward. We turned together and stepped through the archway on a path of strewn petals. I had learned to waltz balanced on the tops of his boots, clinging to a belt loop with one hand, the other stretched impossibly high to meet his own. There would be no stumbling now. On the walk down the aisle, our feet moved easily in time with the music.

Learning the Ropes

Judy—we don't buy frozen juice and vegetables.
Too expensive. Rose.

I read the note twice, then propped it back on the saltshaker and looked around the kitchen. The floor had been swept, the dishes put away, the counters wiped. The rug I kept in the kitchen doorway had been spread on the floor in front of the sink. I tracked across the worn tile to retrieve it, then pulled off my boots and drew a shallow, steady breath. I'd left to go riding shortly after lunch. Probably ten minutes out the door when she showed up, I thought. I knew when she left. I'd seen the tail of dust rising behind her old car as I eased my horse down the ridge toward the barn. Peeling off my sweaty socks, I draped them over my boots and padded barefoot through the gloom, snapping up window shades, jerking back curtains to let in the late-afternoon light. The curtain rule had been one of my first: *We keep the shades pulled so the sun won't fade the carpet, ruin the furniture, heat up the house.* . . . I wandered back to the kitchen to see what "we" were fixing for supper. The stove gleamed from a recent scrubbing, and beside it a roll of round steak defrosted into a pie plate. I tested it with one finger, pressing until blood wicked through the seams of the butcher paper, then wiped my finger across the range top. A jagged streak of mud and meat juice rose against the white enamel then flash-dried to a dull brown in the August heat.

The stove had been warm to the touch, the air still perfumed with garlic, when I moved to the Loving U Ranch the first week in June. John's stepmother, Rose, and his father, Frank, had surprised us the week we married with their decision to turn over the main ranch buildings to us, while they set up housekeeping ten miles from headquarters. It was time, Frank reasoned, for them to get away from the grind of chores and hired men. A newer ranch house, vacant since they acquired more land in 1970, took little preparation to ready for occupation, and they had moved the bulk of their belongings over while John and I were on our honeymoon. The main ranch house, which John and I took over, stood at the base of one steep hill facing south to another, with the bunkhouse, outbuildings and corrals taking up the flat ground at the bottom of the pocket. Driving down the lane toward our ranch felt like aiming at the ends of the earth—nothing but hardpan and the suggestion of pines in the distance—when suddenly you popped over a steep hill and the ranch buildings spread out below, cradled in a bend of Fourchette Creek.

Recently removed from this hub of activity, Rose fought the boredom of her new, quiet life by gradually relinquishing her house, her kitchen and her role in bits and pieces. Within days of our return, I would discover that in all these thousands of acres, there existed one oasis, one room that my in-laws and the hired men could not enter with a perfunctory rap, and that was our bedroom. Even Rose drew the line at that threshold.

I changed out of my riding clothes, then sat on the edge of the unmade bed, groping in the dusky light for a cleaner pair of jeans. One low east window faced the bunkhouse, the other looked out to the road, right where vehicles popped over the hill on their way to the barnyard. I raised the bedroom shades only when I was cleaning the room, changing sheets. The rest of the time they were pulled tight to the sill. The room stayed cool in the muted light, the muzzy outlines of bed and dresser, lamp and mirror soft as welcoming arms.

Flopping back on the bed, I zipped my jeans and rested a moment, the muscles in my back and neck softening against the loose blankets. So much easier to think my way through supper than get up and start it. What would it be tonight? Frank went home to Rose around six, so the evening meal was as close to private as John and I ever got. Just two hired men and us. If John came in first, I would get a hug, maybe a quick kiss before the hired men trailed in to wash up. If they all came in together, it would be business as usual. John would ask the men what they'd seen that day, what they'd gotten done, any trouble with machinery. Fried meat. Boiled potatoes. Canned beans. I worked my way down the list, counting with slow blinks. I could make Jell-O, set it up with ice cubes. Maybe biscuits. My eyelids shot open and I sat up so fast a gray fog roared through my head. Bent over my knees, I waited as flashes of color gradually gave way to vision, then peered at my watch. *Half an hour lost.* I worked my neck and shoulders, driving off the last of the dizziness. Forcing myself to rise, I stretched against the ache in my hips and knees.

Our honeymoon had ended just as haying season began, and John arrived home to a relentless grind of fourteen-hour days and seven-day weeks. The men left for the hayfields at dawn, returning for lunch and again for the evening meal. After supper, after the cows were milked and the barn chores done, John started on the shop work, tuning and tinkering and welding on one of the fleet of hard-used balers, swathers and tractors. Something was always breaking down, it seemed. On my own, I walked the rooms, planning furniture and decorations, filled with a sense of adventure. The house had been hauled to its site decades before, the original structure still visible under a layer of tacked-on additions. In the kitchen, I looked through two sets of windows to see outside, the old ones separated from more recent ones by the width of a porch to the south, a washroom to the east. A wide metal floor grate lay in the doorway between the kitchen and the tiny living room, and the propane gas furnace beneath it provided heat for the entire house. Narrow stairs led to a pair of barely insulated upstairs rooms whose only nod to electrical power was lone bare bulbs with pull strings that swung from the ceiling.

If my contribution to the household had been small—an old black-and-white television, end tables, a few dishes and some cleaning supplies—John's was nonexistent. Moving from home to college to Army, he had acquired little in the way of household goods. We were starting out new. I unpacked wedding gifts and arranged them in cupboards and closets, towels and linens here, mixing bowls there, then sketched out meals for the first day. I felt scared, not a bad sort of scared but the kind that makes you alert, challenged. At eighteen, I was neither stupid nor totally naive. I had a lot to learn. The first few days, I elbowed through the unfurnished space of my new house, learning as I went along.

In the kitchen only the table had survived the moving purge—too large for Rose's new house and necessary for feeding the crew. From an outbuilding, Frank called up half a dozen chairs from retirement. I scrubbed away a decade of bird droppings and polished the chrome frames. The backs were original yellow, the seats covered with thick brown vinyl. I replaced the layers of peeling tape that held the stuffing inside. Since his move to the ranch, John had slept in a small spare bedroom rather than share the bunkhouse, and they left behind his double bed, a forties-era masterpiece of blond veneer complete with original wire springs and packed-cotton mattress.

At six feet four inches, John had to sleep crosswise or his feet hung over the end, and our nights passed fitfully until we gradually grew accustomed to the toss and turn of a bedmate, the bedsprings announcing the most innocent shift of weight with bawdy shrieks and groans. Still, the bed was the softest piece of furniture in the house and the only place to sit, aside from the kitchen chairs. John emptied half the matching four-dresser and vanity and I fit about half my things into the cleared space. The leftover items we stacked on the floor of the closet or stowed in boxes against the wall. Arranging the living room went more quickly. I set my end table in one corner, balanced my third-hand television on top, and that was that.

Within a few days of settling I managed to break the bed all by myself. I had spent the morning in a whirlwind of activity, had lunch on the table at noon sharp and cleaned the kitchen until it shone. With hours to fill until supper, I grabbed a novel and like a small child let out to play, I dashed to our room to read. I had changed linens that morning, pulling the gold velour spread taut over the crisp fragrance of sun-dried sheets, and with mindless exuberance I launched into the air over the bed and dropped straight down onto my stomach.

The result sounded like a two-car collision, a screech as the frame separated, then a crash as the mattress and springs hit the floor in a litter of broken slats. Horrified, I stripped off the bedding and assessed the damage. The slats were just boards spaced under the springs to keep them from sagging to the floor; those were easily replaced. But the angle iron frame that held it all up had broken at the corner welds.

After lunch the next day, John waited for his father and the hired men to leave for the fields, then slipped the broken bed frame out the door to the shop. A bashful and private man by nature, he dreaded the off-color comments that would surely follow if he were caught. Any other day it would have worked. This particular afternoon, John raised his welding mask to find his father smirking in the doorway, old Leonard peering around his elbow with a sly grin. Within twenty-four hours, the story would spread to the ends of the county. John hauled the mended pieces to the house with his face crimson and his jaw set. We propped the old bed back together. "This is bullshit," he said. We made plans to go shopping.

The next week, a rain shower lent just enough moisture to drive John out of the field for a day. We hauled a load of canner cows to the Glasgow market and brought the old cattle truck home filled to the top rack. John signed ranch checks for a queen-sized bedroom set, eight kitchen chairs, a plush couch and swivel rocker, and a big recliner chair that stretched to fit his lanky frame. We ordered them delivered, and headed for the grocery warehouse. I worked from a two-page list of items I needed to stock my pantry. Spices and canned goods, staples such as flour, sugar, salt and coffee. We carried out five hundred dollars' worth of groceries to fill the larder emptied when Rose had relocated to her new kitchen. When the delivery truck arrived, Frank's gaze flitted over our new purchases with idle attention, one couch as good as another to him, while John gathered up the checkbook and receipts and handed them over for bookkeeping. As I watched, Frank thumbed to the check register and read the amounts. His face went stiff, eyes widening, then going narrow. He lurched to his feet and left without a word.

The next morning, Frank came in for coffee alone. Humpfing and hawing, he dropped into his chair at the head of the table and waited for me to serve him. To the neighbors, Frank's moving away from ranch headquarters could be seen as turning over the business, a generous and wholly unexpected move for a man so involved with the daily operation of the ranch. In public Frank made great show of it, raising his arms in surrender to a question, grinning widely as he jerked his head from side to side. "Ask the boy. Hell, I don't know what's going on." The "boy" was thirty years old, and the facade was dropped at the front gate. Here, the ranch was Frank's and no one pretended differently. The lights of his pickup roared down our hill before dawn every morning, and when he slid to a stop in front of the shop, John and the hired men were on the front stoop picking their teeth and pulling on their gloves or he came storming in to get them. He lit out from the pickup at a stiff-legged gallop, throwing himself into each day's work like it might be his last. A huge man, Frank had heavyweight semi-pro titles to his name before being called to serve in World War II, and despite the onset of painful arthritis he still moved with the speed and aggression of a boxer. The stories I knew of him as a young man were violent stories, tales of fistfights at country dances, another of him evicting his second wife's daughter and her husband by physically kicking them down the steps of the house. I didn't know if they were true; even the rumors were ancient history now. But I did sense an edge to the man, something unpredictable.

He began telling stories, speaking between slurps of coffee as I nervously wiped down counters and tidied the kitchen. How young folks in his day started out with nothing and made do, acquiring as they went along. How his mother and father walked from Lewistown to the banks of the Missouri River with everything they owned in a wheelbarrow. He shook his head, abrupt jerks from side to side. Young people these days seemed to expect everything at once—big house, nice things, everything new. Didn't want to wait for a thing. He let this soak in for a moment, then rose to leave, his smile like bared teeth. If I was going to get along here, he added, I'd better figure out we were raising calves, not minting money. Stunned into silence, I watched him clump out the door. Heat rose in my cheeks. John drew a wage of one hundred dollars per month, a fourth of which went to pay for his life insurance policy. The rest had to stretch carefully to cover personal luxuries, such as clothing, birth control pills and shampoo. How could we possibly save for furniture on that?

Lunch passed as though nothing had happened, the men stomping in together, steam wafting through the washroom as they scrubbed their hands. Frank took his place at the head of the table, reaching for the serving bowls as I set them down. The hired men were allowed a full hour off in midday, and as they finished eating and left for the bunkhouse, Frank moved into the living room and stretched out in the new recliner. John flopped down on the new couch. I studied the two men for signs of trouble and found nothing. Puzzled, I finished the dishes and watched them stroll outside at the stroke of one. Had I imagined Frank's pointed comments?

An hour later, I watched uneasily as Rose's old car pulled up in front of our gate. She tapped at the door with her foot until I opened it, then bustled through, her hands full of empty boxes. Weeks after leaving, she was still emptying closets in the upstairs rooms and gathering pictures off the walls, finishing the move in small loads that fit the ancient Studebaker sedan. Rose was Frank's third wife, a plump Polish woman already middle-aged when she traded a populated area of Wisconsin for this ranch seventy miles from town. With no children of her own, Rose had lived a lonely and solitary life for several years, surrounded by men, a relative newcomer to the circle of ranchwomen and the business of ranching. She had no experience and little aptitude for the outside work, but she knitted and crocheted beautifully and in a community of standard meat-and-potatoes cooks, she earned her reputation in the kitchen. Her everyday meals surpassed company fare in most homes. Still, she remained at the edge of the circle, connected to community neither by family name nor by place name, but by marriage alone. She came with no set of expectations based on family or personal history, and if she behaved in strange or surprising ways, there followed a general lifting of hands—what could one expect, after all?

I had known little about her until I began dating John. Then, having the keen ears of a child just recently come to sit among adults, I tallied the hushed stories that passed among gossips and the sort of edgy silence preferred by the other half of the room, combined these with John's hilarious—and, I assumed, exaggerated—stories of life in Frank and Rose's household, and felt myself equal to the task before me. True, though I visited at their ranch fairly often in the year before the wedding, I still panicked if left alone with Rose for long—I could feign an interest in needlework and crafts only so long before our conversations stumbled and ground to a halt. But most of what the community knew of her seemed fairly benign, by my teenage standards.

One aspect of urban civilization that she had brought west

set her ranch kitchen apart from any other I knew, and that was the institution of Happy Hour. When the workday was done and the hired men slouched off to the bunkhouse to clean up and await the clang of our big dinner bell, Frank and John entered to the sound and smell of supper on the way, no different than most men in the community. But unlike their counterparts, their meal was not dished up and waiting. Their meal was timed to hold. While they washed, Rose hauled out mix and makings, and then joined them for a couple of stout whiskeys. If company was present, Happy Hour included hors d'oeuvres and lasted into the evening, as the hired hands waited patiently on their bunks for the bell to summon them for the meal. On a typical winter evening, she might garner half an hour of conversation before the taciturn Frank demanded his dinner.

As John wryly noted, Rose's personal approach to the cocktail hour was less rigidly scheduled. She frequently got a jump start on the drinks during dinner preparations. Perspiring from the heat of the kitchen, her round cheeks flushed a cheery red, she would greet the men's arrival with a jovial wave of the spoon as she orchestrated the finishing touches to the meal. Frank and Rose were always careful not to drink in front of the help. A measure of hilarity and her somewhat uncertain gait between table and stove as she served the meal were the only evidences of Happy Hour that remained by the time John pulled the bell rope to summon the crew for supper.

I laughed at John's stories and waved the rumors aside. What she did in her own home was her own business, I figured. In the months before John and I were married, only one episode gave me pause. I arrived at the ranch house as her guest the autumn day she hosted a meeting of the Near and Far Club, a group we more commonly referred to as Ladies

Club. There was only one, and though my mother did not regularly attend, I had been dragged along to the occasional meeting since early childhood. Many of the older members of the community arranged their social lives around the monthly meetings. Members paid dues, donated to worthy projects and gave craft lessons to one another—needlework, crocheted tissue covers, egg carton art, pinecone wreaths for Christmas. They brought along their current projects to share with the only audience able to honestly appreciate the procession of intricate fancywork that kept their fingers busy on rainy days, hot afternoons and after supper, that lull between dishes and bedtime.

The social atmosphere and the familiar homes of my neighbors changed when it was their turn to host Ladies Club. Even as a small child, I recognized the formal atmosphere of the meetings as something out of the ordinary. Whereas a typical drop-in visit was spent at the kitchen table with a pot of coffee and the stuff of neighborhood news, at Ladies Club the same women sat on parlor chairs in starched dresses and good shoes and shared news of distant relatives, old neighbors, new grandchildren, and all seasonal work in progress. Children were threatened into passable behavior. Young girls were encouraged to "sit in" on the program, though as a youngster I spent my rare afternoons of Ladies Club running outside with the other tomboys. The only lure for me was the luncheon. After the business meeting and the presentation, they stood adjourned and the mood relaxed a bit as women traded in eggs and cream, swapped plant cuttings and tomato starts, returned borrowed patterns and visited. Children would begin to sift in from outdoors and join the short food line while the hostess dished up the luncheon on her best china, perhaps a savory salad or tea sandwiches, some nuts and mints, and always, always a dessert whose calories measured in the quadruple digits.

I sat among the neighbor ladies as Rose's guest that day, comfortable among the familiar faces. My engagement was the news of the moment, but early conversation died as the meeting was called to order. I no longer remember the program offered at the meeting, but I do remember Rose mysteriously disappearing into the kitchen every so often, and wondering what breed of outlandish dessert could account for so much last-minute attention. By the midpoint of the meeting, Rose's cheeks were in bloom and her interruptions and additions to the president's message had taken on a raucous note. Judging by the grim circle of women in the parlor, this had happened before. I watched with rapt attention as the eyebrows lifted over a flurry of knowing looks and narrow-eyed glares. These did not pass over my head, as they might have the year before, but met my eyes before moving on. Soon I would be a daughter-in-law here, privy to the secrets kept by the family, but more than that, as an adult I had a place in this stiffly posed, silent circle of women; it would be as close as I ever came to an initiation.

As next of kin, it fell to Rose's sister, Irene, and me to assume the duties of hostess as the formal meeting ground to a close and Rose staggered to her bedroom and passed out on her bed. Irene and her husband had driven from Wisconsin to hunt deer, and though she had never met the women in her sister's parlor, she seemed to know a disaster when she saw one in the making. Irene eased the door to Rose's bedroom tightly shut, and the two of us made bright conversation to cover the moans and snores that crept beneath the door and into the kitchen. I understood the disapproval emanating from the older women in the group, though I didn't necessarily subscribe to it. They were teetotalers, and in the terms of their era, gentlemen might have a drink, common men might drink to excess, but nice women didn't drink beyond the occasional glass of Christmas wine. Only the coarsest women would be seen drunk in public.

My mother's generation had made inroads into that Victorian statute, and my generation had modified it yet further, but I still couldn't shake the embarrassment I felt for Rose. At my age, I would not have been as roundly condemned by my peers for drunkenness. At her age, with no excuse of youth or immaturity, she could not avoid it. Irene and I spread cheese crackers, set out the mints, scooped Mississippi Mud Pie onto china plates and brewed tea for twelve, doing our duty as best we could in an unfamiliar kitchen, the flurry of desperation shared in our maddening search for the silver dessert spoons, the sugar and cream service, whatever it took to advance this day to completion. No one left without a nod or a word of thanks, admiring a good job of saving face in the same way they would have admired any nicely turned piece of fancywork.

Though irked at her sister, Irene spoke of her with generosity in the hour we spent alone, the menfolk studiously sticking to shop or field until the last car left the yard, lest they arrive like a band of ruffians in the midst of our genteel company. As the door closed on the last look of pity and word of condolence, Irene turned, and with an uncanny instinct, stepped to the shelf over the washing machine and spooked Rose's bottle of vodka out of hiding. The two of us killed it as we sat waiting for the lady of the house to get up, the men to come in, someone to take over the sweaty reins of this kitchen. One of the few women who reached out to offer advice before I was married, Irene unfolded a frank twenty-minute diatribe that left me speechless. She shared an uncompromising tale of alcoholic parents, the lives she and her sister had known during the Depression. In an effort of will that I was to relive for fourteen years, I worked to interpret Rose's response to pressure, her craving for praise and attention, her sometimes bewildering demands upon me, as those of a needy child. But nothing is ever that simple.

At sixty-three, my mother-in-law-apparent could not have been more pleased with the growth of her immediate family, and having a potential crop of grandbabies to show off made her giddy with excitement. She took such a sudden and serious interest in her new role of ranch matriarch that I drew back in alarm, too young to recognize what having the bond of extended family could mean to her in this community. I had always had that connection. Before my marriage, when she confided in a girlish whisper that mine would be the only wedding she would ever help to plan, I sighed and added her suggestions to the list of those compiled by me, my mother, John and John's birth mother, Nellie. As I recall, only a lavish amount of broad hinting dissuaded her from wearing a white dress to the wedding, but hers was the widest smile there.

In my first dealings with them, I sensed that she and Frank shared an Old World view of family. As modern as ranching corporations were with respect to tax and inheritance laws, their structure reflected an ancient patriarchal model. In every case it seemed, the father and son became the president and vice president, Mom was named secretary, and all generations worked for the common good of the ranch. They could deduct the costs of doing business, with income derived from the division of profits based on the ownership of shares. The extreme example would be one multigeneration household where Papa directed the sons in working the land and Mama directed the wives in preparing communal meals, and the earnings all funneled into a common purse. That sort of lifestyle was not unknown during the settlement days, when immigrant families worked together to establish their footing in the New World, and later in the Depression days when a couple might live with one set of parents or the other while they saved for a place of their own. A few of the county's larger ranches still supported two or three generations of family headed by the patriarch of the clan. But more familiar to me were the husband-wife partnerships like that of my parents, couples who bought improved land in the forties and fifties and worked it together, an arrangement that often rewarded a woman's strength and independence. It was left to young women of my generation to discover the vast difference between entering a marriage partnership like our mothers had and becoming the daughter-in-law in a ranching corporation.

I was not caught totally unaware. With Frank and Rose as the major shareholders, I assumed they would control the purse strings to a certain extent. John would draw wages, the bulk of our expenses would be paid by the corporation. But never in my wildest dreams had I expected to run my life as an extension of Frank and Rose's. We were married in 1973, not 1873, I assured myself. Somehow I pictured a corporation as just like a marriage partnership, but with two households serving as the members of the team, both sides working respectfully and cooperatively, but separately.

After allowing us the first week to "get settled," Rose had arrived on my doorstep one morning without warning, her round face beaming, eager to caution and advise my first steps on her old stomping ground. She had arrived nearly every morning since on the pretext of packing, though the cartons often sat unused in the porch while she addressed the arrangement of my cupboards. I was nearly a foot taller than she and tended to use the high shelves for storing everyday items. She seemed determined to break me of the dangerous habit of placing glasses and heavy pots where she had to stand on tip-toe to reach them. I listened patiently as she shifted items from shelf to shelf, victim of an upbringing that allowed no sassing of elders. After she left, I would move everything back. A day or two later she would open the cupboard doors and stand with her plump hands on her hips, tsk-tsking. She must have thought me terribly slow. As the days progressed, the sound of her car pulling up filled me with dread.

Stung by Frank's words that morning and confused by his silence at lunch, I warily poured Rose coffee from the still-warm pot, watching her closely. Her usual cheerful greeting had been dampered. She pulled out one of the new kitchen chairs, hefting it in her hand, then lowered herself toward the seat with exaggerated caution, as though testing the heat of a bath. When it held her satisfactorily, she leaned back and squinted through the living-room doorway at the brown-plaid couch, her mouth a moue of disapproval. She hoped I wouldn't have trouble keeping the couch clean. It was pretty now, but the fabric didn't look practical. She rummaged through her purse while I talked about the new soil-guard treatment, the lifetime warranty, my voice trailing off as she drew out the long receipt from the grocery warehouse. She spread it on the table and settled herself more firmly. So here it is, I thought wearily. From where I stood braced against the counter, I could see several of the items had been circled. Beer. Cigarettes. Kotex. Soda pop. Five pounds of bacon. A gallon can of pie cherries. My throat tightened with humilia-tion. I took my time, pausing a second with my eyes closed, hoping to hear truck or tractor approaching from down the creek. Where the hell was John in all this, I wondered. He had helped pick out every stick of furniture, had trooped down the grocery aisle adding to the pile on the huge cart and had written the checks without a murmur.

We went through the list item by item as Rose pointed out which of my purchases could be had for less in other stores and the rash of brand-name products I had wasted money on instead of opting for less-expensive store brands. Her manner was serious but sincere, not angry as much as disappointed that I had managed to triple their food bill in one trip to the store. After all, she said as though reciting a clever saying from memory, my joining the family added only one more mouth to feed and we all expected the grocery bill to reflect that. I waited for her to finish, careful not to interrupt, though I was fuming. "We" meant Frank. Frank expected the grocery bill for two households to be almost the same as for one. Frank, the man who bragged that he'd never cooked a meal for himself since he settled on this place. Lord, the injustice. I sputtered, I flushed, I explained, voice shaking, that the bill reflected the cost of setting up a kitchen, not replenishing a pantry. I had had to purchase some of everything all in the same bill, rather than spaced out over months. Like spices— here I pointed to the list—you have to have them to bake, but they last forever.

She studied the circled items around my fingertip as I rambled on, the pleasant smile on her face never dimming. When I stopped, she went on as though I had never spoken. Some, like the breakfast meats and that strawberry jam, were a waste of money to feed to hired men. Pancakes and eggs were good enough. My eyes must have widened at that, as she went on for some time about the economic wisdom of pancakes and eggs. I bit my tongue and focused on the list, as though reading it one more time might offer enlightenment. John. It had been John, victim of that same breakfast menu for a year, who had selected the jam and bacon. Some items she'd both circled and checked—the gallon of cherries, the case of soda pop—as too indulgent. One item, a carton of cigarettes, she had crossed off altogether. I was, she explained calmly, forbidden to buy these with corporation money.

I waited for her to make her way to the end of the list, conscious of the pent-up thump at the base of my skull, the wash of self-pity that pushed me to the brink of tears. She must have mistaken my mood for remorse, for she patted my hand and smiled her understanding. I would do fine, she said kindly. I just had to use my common sense. She finished her coffee, tucked the receipt back into her purse and left without packing a single box. I waved her to her car, then dropped into my chair at the kitchen table and gazed at the neat list of items she'd written on a sheet of notebook paper. Crib notes for grocery shopping, the mustn't-dos and can't-haves, the good-enoughs. At a complete loss, I sat in the silence of the ranch kitchen, trying to read the lay of this land. Where did I fit? Where was my place in this business, in this kitchen? How could it be that the one person expected to make most of the household purchases for the ranch was the one person not allowed to write checks, the one person with no say in budgeting or bank drafts?

Caught up by exhaustion, I slipped into the bedroom and closed the door. If the men came in for coffee that afternoon, I never knew it. I was still sleeping when John shook my shoulder hours later. I had slept past dinnertime, he whispered as I struggled to sit up. The men were in from the field, waiting.

We talked far into the night, my outrage returning as we lay each to his own side, hidden in the darkness of the bedroom.

Learning the Ropes

I had not married his father and I sure as hell hadn't married Rose, I told him. I had one of them looking over my shoulder and the other breathing down my neck, and it was going to come to a screeching halt. We were going to have a sit-down with Frank and Rose and get some things straight. With a long sigh, John shifted from his side to his back and lay still, as though settling under the weight of one more problem. I brushed aside a twinge of guilt as he stared at the ceiling. He was so tired. He had problems coming at him from dawn to dark, hired men screwing up or slacking off, his father second-guessing his every move. But my sense of urgency was bolstered by absolute righteousness. If I knuckled under now, when would it end? Surely I could not be expected to tackle this issue on my own. As far as I was concerned, his duty was clear. I needed him to back me up.

John answered with what I came to know as "the voice of reason," a tone both sympathetic and evasive. Of course they were wrong, he said, but at this point all we could do was ignore their meddling, let it run off us like water off a duck's back.

"How am I supposed to ignore them when they're parked in my kitchen half the time?" I hissed. He gave a wry laugh and his head wagged against his pillow.

Ah, hell, things will settle down. He pulled me close, reassuring me. Just don't let them get to you. The old man doesn't believe the place can run without him. Once we prove ourselves, he'll back off. We just have to tough it out another few years and we'll be running things the way we want. As for this thing with Rose, he went on, a bit wary now, if he got in the middle of that it would just cause hard feelings. We'd have to work it out on our own. He dozed off in the quiet that followed.

When Rose yoo-hooed from the front door the next morning, I kicked the bedroom door shut and sat on the bed, waiting for her to leave. Instead, the soft squeak of the floor mapped her progress as she began to putter about the kitchen, moving the rug to the space in front of the sink, pulling the curtains tight across the west window. Then the floor squeaks were joined by the clink of dishes as she moved from drying rack to cupboard. Unable to stand it, I eased open the bedroom door and stepped out. A bit hard of hearing, she stood with a dish in each hand, gazing up at my cupboards, unaware of me until I appeared at her elbow.

"I can take care of that, Rose," I said firmly. "I know where they belong." She jumped like a deer, nearly staggering with the fright I had given her. Her whoop of surprise gave way to uncertainty when she saw I was not smiling. She didn't like leaving dishes in the rack, exposed to dust and flies, she explained, holding up two plates. Her voice trailed off. "I'll take care of it," I repeated. Chastened, she handed the plates to me and wiped her hands carefully on the towel.

"Do you need help packing?" I asked. Oh no, she replied. She'd just get a few things and be on her way. She brightened—unless I wanted help with lunch? I assured her I had lunch all figured out, no problem. She labored upstairs to the attic with a box in hand and was gone within the hour.

Her next visit caught me with my hands in dishwater. A "Good morning" full of smiles lilted across the room. I washed and rinsed, my stiff back and the rough jerk of my arms offering the only clue that I had heard. She stood quietly by the counter, waiting until I pulled the plugs to drain the dishwater. Intent on my game, I avoided her eyes, imagining her stony glare following me as I carefully wiped the sink and rinsed the dishrag. Shifting my face into neutral, I turned toward her, finally, ready for battle. Had she stood before me naked, I could not have been more horrified. Instead of anger there was pain, her mouth open in a soundless cry, her eyes swimming. When she spoke, tears dropped at once, as if shaken loose by the tremor in her voice.

"Can't you even say hello?" she quavered, and under the weight of silence that followed, her face crumpled in a final plea, stark and simple as the cry of a child. "Don't you like me?"

I felt all the shame and cowardice of a bully, and still could not bend to comfort her. My answer fell like a chill on her upturned face and her head bowed as I finished. "We'll get along fine, Rose. We just need to get settled in our own places." When her car pulled out, I sank into a chair, barely able to think. Muscles in my arms and legs crawled and ached with fatigue. I made it to the bedroom and slipped under the covers with my clothes on. With my last ounce of energy, I reached over and set the alarm for 11 a.m. There was enough ground beef in the refrigerator to make spaghetti sauce or a hot dish. Whatever. I'd think of something.

The middle of that summer has gone from my memory, though I retain a gauzy image of events occurring, a gray stretch of days shot through with moments of clarity when panic cleared the cobwebs and I worked frantically to avoid being caught sleeping. I slept ten, twelve, sixteen hours a day. In bed by nine and up to fix breakfast at five. Back to bed until the intrusion of another person, another meal dragged me up, afternoons of oblivion that ended with the rumble of returning pickups, the mad dash to wash dishes from one meal and set out another. I kept a damp washcloth and a hairbrush on the dresser, my subconscious tuned to the sound of the porch door opening, the stomp of feet as the men took a break for coffee. Rolling off the bed, I would cool my eyes with the cloth and smooth my hair, then scoop up a pile of clothes and emerge from the bedroom as if caught in the midst of laundry chores. Quivering with adrenaline, I would dump coffee grounds and start another pot with blood thumping through the cotton in my head. Like acting out a dream. I barely remembered my brother Kenny's wedding, a month after my own, though I cringe at how I must have looked in my rumpled pantsuit, my hair pulled back in a greasy ponytail. I had not bathed for days.

At some point a week, perhaps several weeks, into summer, John roused me from sleep and led me to a chair by the kitchen table. He sat and pulled me onto his lap. My resistance was visceral, a dread born so far below the surface I was helpless against it. I leaned against his chest quietly, aware of trying to wake up the same way I would try to run in a dream, the awful labor of dead weight and slow motion. We sat. A blanket of flies lifted and settled around the stove and table where dishes from the noon meal remained, and around the sink where breakfast dishes waited in a pond of stagnant water. The garbage stank. I burrowed my nose into his collar, hushed by the sweetness of dried grass and sweat, sunshine trapped in a cotton shirt.

Gently, he pushed me upright and held me at arm's length, his face kind and determined. Unable to meet his eyes, I closed mine before he said a word. He didn't understand what was going on, he said, but there was no margin for error here. I would have to do my part if we were going to make it.

I knew I was not doing my share, and I shriveled around the truth of what he said. No one had learned the truths about work better than I had. What was wrong with me that I had forgotten this, I wondered. What is wrong, what is wrong? I watched him from the porch window as he walked to the shop, his sadness palpable, visible in the weary slope of his shoulders. Leaning against the sill, I began to shake like a wild animal. Whatever this madness was, it felt bottomless.

I reclaimed myself slowly, throwing myself into hard physical labor and fighting back with pots of coffee when exhaustion seemed overwhelming. I shoveled out the chicken house and worked the late garden we'd planted below a reservoir a quarter mile from the house. I poured out a basement full of canned goods abandoned since Frank's second wife had lived there, burying gallons of spoiled sauerkraut and age-softened pickles under the lilac bushes out back and washed the jars with their crazed rubber rings and zinc lids. I kept myself moving as best I could and gradually felt better. Riding horseback became one of my substitutes for sleep, though in light of the chores I could have accomplished instead, it was no more worthwhile than a long nap. Cream Puff was getting old, but she was still nimble enough to negotiate the unfamiliar trails of this new ranch, and guiding her along I felt the same thrill I felt as a child, afternoons when my sister and I would make our getaway to the horse pasture, then ride like fury beyond the sound of our mother's voice. The irony of being a married woman and sneaking out of my own house to avoid the grown-ups was not lost on me.

Such was the difference in landscape that I found myself renewed by discovery. My parents' hard gumbo flatland with its musk of cured grass and sage gave way to the strong, sweet pitch of juniper and pine, the jagged landscape of the Missouri River Breaks. Awed in some private way, I found the places that matched names I'd first heard in stories. For the first time that fall I rode roundup in the pines above Beauchamp Creek, learning to balance my horse as we slid down steep ravines, a river of soft gray shale pouring around his hooves until we reached the bottom. The cattle we sought to corral at Summer Camp were branded "WV," the remains of a herd that came with the recent land purchase. They bore little resemblance to my father's herd of sturdy, amiable Herefords. Appear on the skyline, and these creatures threw their heads high in the air, sniffing the wind, then light and nimble as goats, they ghosted away through the trees, following game trails. Their calves hid the way fawns do, lying still under a low juniper with their necks stretched flat on the ground, nearly invisible, and the adults were not above "brushing up" themselves, burrowing into brush and going as flat and still as coyotes. Occasionally, when the blowing wind obscured sound, we would surprise them bedded down or grazing in a clearing. We called this "jumping" them, as in, "I jumped six or seven head of WVs out of Karsten Coulee." You had to be fast to get an accurate count. We joked that only their short horns and their superior speed separated the WV cattle from the elk they grazed with.

So it happened, whether through accident or design, that I came to know and love the land that was my new home. I walked the Prowdy Pines and drove the trail to Beauchamp Creek to mine the shale banks for marine fossils and buffalo skulls washed out by spring floods. I rode horseback up the slope and down the length of Stouts Coulee and Pea Ridge, following an unbroken string of hay meadows tucked into the bends and curves of Fourchette Creek all the way to the Fields Cabin. I learned new directions that went with the new land— up the creek went west and down the creek went east. I found tepee rings, graves of dead homesteaders, the dugouts and cabins of those who had sold out and moved on.

Learning the Ropes

For the sake of time stolen from daily duties, I often took the pickup on these expeditions, but only when I rode horseback could I see the true contours of the land, the ravines hidden from any road. The Breaks, I thought, had all the rugged stature of mountains, except the peaks went the other direction—down into the earth. The ranch sprawled for miles along the northern edge of the Breaks where the shortgrass prairie began to roll, then plunged abruptly into steep gullies. Animals, whether wild or domestic, followed the same network of trails down to the narrow grass-lined strips at the bottom, tracing drainages carved into the shale of an old seabed, held down by the gnarled roots of juniper and greasewood, the sort of forage that required little encouragement to thrive.

Looking for chokecherries one afternoon, I came upon the Andrews place, the long-abandoned buildings now part of Frank's holdings, and stopped to explore. The board barn stood agape at the prairie sage that grew to its threshold, the corrals long gone, either fallen or torn down. Nearby, a crumbling two-story shack stood in the shelter of a bleached cottonwood. The front door had buckled across the opening, hanging by one bottom hinge, and I straightened it until it could be propped open or wired closed. We would be turning cattle into the field around it soon, and old buildings like these could be death traps for animals. Where cattle had free range, especially herds of curious yearlings, landowners made an effort either to fence off the abandoned homesteads or to clean up around them, often filling the buildings with the litter of broken glass, rusty tin cans, nails and barbed wire they found scattered around the grounds.

I was curious enough to go snooping, for I had met the owner, Shaw Andrews, while I was working as a waitress. He was one of many quiet old bachelors who had retired from homesteads in the area and had taken rooms at the Fifth Avenue, a residential hotel in Malta. Shaw was distinctive to me because he wore a black patch over one eye, but in all other ways he was like any of a dozen old-timers who came into the Sugar Shack Café once or twice a day for meals. He wore the same clothes, ate the daily special, was unfailingly polite, and tipped a dime.

I recalled only one time when Shaw had not eaten alone, but entered the restaurant with a young man in tow. I hardly recognized him with his hair wet down, his rusty suit and cloth tie, his excitement. Rather than take a stool at the counter, Shaw chose a booth. He introduced his guest to Elsie, the owner of the café, and she waited the table herself. "Give us some of that fried chicken," he boomed with all the pride of a good host. "We'll take the works!" I watched from behind the counter as the feast was laid, and I remember his careful wrapping of a chicken breast in a paper napkin as they prepared to leave. The extravagance of this dinner was likely lost on his guest—a great-nephew, perhaps, someone who had taken time to trace the last of a family line to this booth, this one day. I remember how we waitresses pitied these old men their empty lives.

Shaw was long dead the afternoon I pushed the door open and stepped into the old house where he'd lived for decades with his spinster sister. A nickel-plated wood-burning range still held the place of honor in the kitchen, though most of the three downstairs rooms were filled with moldering boards and junk. Up the narrow stairs, a second bedroom and an A-framed attic of sorts lay much the way they'd been left. Boxes of tattered farm receipts and string-tied bundles of old correspondence were scattered across the attic floor. A large, bird-spattered window at the peak end highlighted the dust motes I stirred up as I sorted among the piles of bank statements and Christmas cards, collecting the old stamps, feeling my skin crawl at the rustle and creep of invisible little feet along the perimeters of the room. Pack rats sorted through the boxes along the walls, and I did not challenge their claim.

In one pile near the door, I found a large bundle of bank calendars, the ones with every month's page made into a pocket to hold receipts. My mother used these until they quit making them. Shaw had kept years of them tied together with string. I popped the bundle open and fanned them out on the floor, wondering what sort of vital record they held, to have been collected like this, but my search through pockets came up empty. On the face of each page, in the corner of each square, beside the date, someone had written numbers, pencil marks starting sharp and getting fatter as the days progressed— I imagined a pencil on a string dangling from the same nail that held the calendar. I knew these numbers, or ones like them. They were the careful milk and egg records kept by someone who sells a few eggs, a little cream, keeping track of business.

Month after month, year after year, the calendars painted our seasons by number. Spring days produced "2 dz egg, 2 gal milk" far into June, then the numbers gently tapered off as the hot weather set in. Here, the bump in egg numbers in late August, early September—Shaw's pullets have started to lay. The old hens will be butchered then, as soon as cool weather allows. Here, at the end of September, where the eggs go from "3 dz" to "2 dz" again; that's when the old hens are gone and the young ones have come into full bloom. Two dozen eggs. Probably thirty hens, maybe a few more. That's a good number for the bigger breeds of chicken. They don't lay every day, but the egg breeds, the leghorns, are too scrawny to be popular as farm hens.

In December the egg counts dwindle and the milk numbers disappear, replaced now, by another number, another sort of record as the temperature sinks to the depths of winter and stalls. The milk cow is dry, her calf long weaned. Chickens won't lay much when they're chilled, just enough for the table. "−12 snow, −17, −25 and wind, −34." The new year dawns with rows of manila squares that testify to the cold, spilling the length of January without break and into February. The weather breaks in March, early or late, and there are a few eggs beside the dates. By Easter, they're back in production. The cow comes fresh in April, "2½ gal" and all her calf can drink, and more as the weather warms and the grass greens. The hens are let out to range in the sunshine, the yolks of their eggs going from pale butter to rich orange as they gorge on bugs and weeds. "2 dz, 2 gal." Year after year, bound tightly together amid an ocean of loose paper, the calendars had survived the elements, telling their tale in numbers instead of words.

I wired the door shut and climbed into the pickup, rolling down the window to let the breeze cool the cab. The weather-burned legacy of Shaw Andrews sat before me, a shrunken cluster of buildings returning, one year and one board at a time, back to the prairie they had sprung from. Stories of the homesteaders were the stuff of my childhood. What they told were the big storms, the births and deaths, the clever or outrageous or humorous. No one talked about what was important, the way they made it day to day, season to season. Did they, too, settle for small victories in the face of overwhelming odds? Were they happy?

If "ranch wife" was a job, I'd spent my entire life in training, surely. But never had I felt more childlike and more alone than I had in these first months of being a ranch wife. It seemed I had learned nothing. Then I thought how these past weeks would look on the old man's calendars—one page, two pages in a knee-high stack. Everything I knew seemed small in the measure of Shaw's years, his simple story of patience and perseverance told in dozens and gallons. I felt no need to take the calendars with me when I left. I knew the numbers. All I needed was faith—faith in myself, and faith in the seasons to come.

Winter Kill

"What in the hell do you *do* out here?" The woman ran a finger across her brow, tucking in the lank strands that fell across her forehead. I glanced over from the stove as she settled her bright orange cap and shrugged out of her coat, sliding it carelessly over the back of her chair. The hunting party she belonged to was camped on our hay meadows about a mile down Fourchette Creek, her husband and three other men.

The question she'd asked was as familiar as the worn tiles under my feet. I studied her as I poured the coffee. She fussed at layers of long johns and woolen shirts now, opening buttons, rolling sleeves, adjusting to the warmth of the kitchen. Maybe thirty, trim. The long dark hair snarled under her cap would be pretty when she washed it. The guys had dropped her off on their way to scout for deer on the other end of the Breaks, two riding in the cab, two who hadn't yet filled their tags perched on the fender wells in the back of the pickup, guns at the ready. Eyeballs spackled with red veins, and not a shaved chin in the bunch. They were having a great time.

I snared a quart jar of cream from the refrigerator and slid a knife through the thick slab that formed on top, pouring the

246

lighter cream into a pitcher. She gazed moodily out the window. The clean center of her face faded to a sooty patina where cold water hadn't reached. I plunked the cream beside her coffee, pulling my tenth cup of the day in front of me as I slid into a chair across from her.

"Sugar?" The woman turned as I spoke. Her eyes were smoky, distant.

"No, really." She waved her spoon at the bowl and I set it back in the center of the table. "I mean, what do you *do* out here all day, you know? You must go nuts." She was leaning forward, more outrage in her voice than interest. I smiled at her over the rim of my cup.

"I keep busy," I said, evenly as I could. "You get used to it."

The first zillion times I answered that question, I was tempted to tip the polite cover and let a little sarcasm ooze across the table. What I did was everywhere around me, falling off the countertops, stacked to the rafters, visible to the naked eye. I knew what she was saying, this disillusioned hairdresser from the coast, even if she didn't. Others posed the question as an honest statement. "I don't know how anybody can live out here," they would say, sweeping one hand to describe some endless barren arc beyond my kitchen.

Only once did my patience snap when I heard that question, my victim an older woman named Carol who dunked a homemade doughnut in her coffee with one hand and spread the other in that same wide gesture that denoted ice floes and bottomless pits. She'd stopped at a bad time, dishes still piled in the sink, canning jars and late-season tomatoes filling the countertops, three preschoolers mewling around underfoot, ready for naps.

"What does it *look* like I do?" I sputtered, mocking her wide stare. She laughed as I caught myself, cringing in embarrassment. Carol loved to hunt, one of the handful of women I met who packed rifles and filled their own tags. Each fall, when her deer hung from a tree by her camper, she spent the balance of her time hiking and photographing the Missouri River Breaks. But she couldn't shake the desolation she felt after a few days and nights of our solitude. Spooky, she called it. Yes, she admitted, she had been asking not about me but about herself: *What would I, a college professor, do on this cattle ranch at the end of this dirt road seventy miles south of a nowhere little town? How would I fill my time two hundred miles from anything resembling a decent restaurant or shopping mall or library?* She shook her head at my apologies, chuckling over the trade of insults, amused that I had brought it to her attention.

"Show me around," she said, draining her cup. We toured the barnyard while the children slept, and then the enormous garden that surrounded the house on three sides. When I moved there, the yard held a couple of scrubby lilacs, a cottonwood and some bunchgrass fenced with woven wire, typical of a region that boasted ten or twelve inches of moisture a year, most of it snowmelt. The deep artesian well provided drinking water laced with fluoride and alkali, salty enough to kill some plants outright and sour the soil permanently if it was used for irrigation.

That first year we had leveled the hillside in our backyard with terraces, stealing rocks from the tepee rings that dotted the bench above and building two stone retaining walls thirty feet long and three feet high. The second year, the men laid pipe from a deep reservoir a quarter of a mile away to a feedlot near the house. Almost as an afterthought, they extended a branch to the yard and rigged up a hydrant. To have rainwater easy as lifting a handle and moving a hose was an unheard-of luxury. I tore up the sod and planted lawn grass around the house, mulching the new seed with a layer of straw. Rattlesnakes had taken over an old wolf den up the hill decades before, and whether they moved down to the yard for the mice the straw attracted or the moist shade it offered, I never knew. For a while it seemed I was growing a layer of snakes under the straw. Hoe in one hand, hose in the other, I would spray the seedbed twice a day, listening for a buzz through the rustle of water. But the grass grew. When the lawn could be clipped and the straw raked away, the snake population dwindled to an occasional migrant I'd catch napping in the flowerbeds.

My daughter was born at the end of the second year. In the five years since then, my garden spot had doubled and doubled again, and still when the seed catalogues arrived in the spring, I grew restless for more space. As soon as the ground thawed, I was outside, moving a fence back, digging up rocks and sagebrush, spading out cactus. There was never a shortage of manure: cow, horse, chicken, wet or dry, we had it all. My harvests were spectacular, even in the drought years— bean crops measured in five-gallon buckets per picking, corn and cucumbers by the wheelbarrow, spuds, onions and carrots by the gunnysack. Flowers, more than fifty varieties, bloomed along the foundation of the house, in rock gardens and tractor tires filled with topsoil, though fewer than half of them really thrived. I kept moving the perennials, digging new beds, looking for a corner with just the right shelter, just enough sun.

The skill was not so much in the planting, I told Carol as we walked the rows of frost-singed vines, but in selecting the seed stock. Only specially developed hybrids could stand the heavy gumbo soil, the late springs and harsh winters. While I dug potatoes and sorted them by size into buckets, she talked about her own work, teaching English at a community college, how she'd cut down to one semester when her husband retired but couldn't quite give it up. As we talked, a pickup load of hunters topped the hill above and began inching down the rutted road that led past the garden and around to the front of the house. I recognized the truck and waved them on from the garden, permission granted. Carol looked back toward the trail that led up and out, silent for some time.

"So then there's winter," she said, turning back to my harvest operation. "What happens in the winter?" The soil had packed rock hard between rows of plants, and her question caught me jumping on the spade like a pogo stick. Stepping off, I wrenched the handle back and down. The bush lurched into the air and red potatoes boiled up through the dirt with a dull pop of roots. I stabbed the spade back into the loosened ground and leaned on it with crossed arms, not as winded as I seemed to be. Her question, the wise look in her eyes, unsettled me.

"Well, winter's winter," I said lightly.

"Can you get out, then, after it snows?"

"Most days," I said, slowly, wondering what getting out meant to her, exactly. Visitors tended to see social life connected to town. We had many acquaintances in Malta, some good friends, but going to town was a different trip. More often than not, I traveled alone, John unable or unwilling to tear himself away from ranch work. On a routine trip to Malta, I would orbit the streets for hours, my three children growing dingier and crankier with each pass, no time or place to sit down but the cab of the pickup. I had business in Malta, a long list of vet supplies to find, repairs for broken-down machinery, bills to pay, banking to be done, checkups and immunization shots and a month's shopping to fit around feeding, watering and pottying a trio of excited preschoolers.

Winter Kill

In winter, groceries were the last stop. I grabbed something fast to fix for supper and whatever fresh produce would fit under our feet in the cab of the truck. The rest fit in back, packed to survive the wind chill of the ride home. Store clerks insulated the cardboard boxes with items that could freeze and not be damaged, saving the center for canned goods and glass jars. Stopping to visit in town meant unloading the boxes into someone's kitchen or porch, and loading them back up when we left. In milder weather, it was simply a long, late drive, kids asleep in frazzled heaps, arms flung limp over siblings and laps and sacks of oranges, all the unpacking to face at the end of the trail. We could get to town a hell of a lot more often than we did.

"If you have to get out, generally you can," I said. "It depends on the wind, if the snow's deep or hard or whatever. The roads can change from one day to the next."

Carol raised one eyebrow, shifting her weight to one hip. "So when do you have to get out?" she asked. A thrill of irritation puckered the skin on my arms. Visitors usually wanted details of a pioneer lifestyle, questions I could answer. What if someone gets sick? They don't, I'd say. When you're snowed in, you're not exposed to anyone else's germs. I could tell about blizzards, close calls. I took pride in my "tough guy" stories, and most city folks gasped and cooed in awe. "Weren't you afraid?" they'd say. "Don't you worry?" I'd bluff it on through. I had a favorite. "Well," I'd say, "when you're stuck in a drift you can either get out and shovel or you can sit in the cab and wring your hands for a while and *then* get out and shovel."

I slid my hands down the handle of the spade and rested one foot on the blade. When did I have to get out? I looked at her blankly, a silence that should have changed the subject.

Carol pressed on, oblivious. Her voice took on a persistent tone as she approached the question from another angle.

"What if you just wanted to have dinner, see a movie?"

I laughed. "Yeah, what if?" I pressed my foot down on the shovel to start it, then jumped and lit on the blade with both feet. Balancing, I began working it back and forth, cutting deeper and deeper into the packed clay.

"You mean you could, but you don't," she said with a nod, as if she'd made her point once and for all.

"No, I mean we could if we had to," I replied, still bouncing back and forth. I leaned back on the handle and another hill of potatoes erupted from the row between us. Carol moved with me, two paces to the right, as I set the spade at the base of a new plant with a solid *chuck*.

"Most people would have to," she said simply. "I don't care where you live, a woman with nobody but babies and men all day, I don't know." She touched her forehead with one finger. "I suppose it's all up here, how you look at it, but I'd need time for myself. I think anyone would to be happy."

Even as I felt the clean heat swell through my chest, I knew it was wholly out of proportion to what she'd just said. Hers was the fantasy world I read about in *Good Housekeeping* and *Ladies' Home Journal,* "Finding Time for You," "Take Care of Yourself First," articles that applied to me about as much as "Office Wear—How to Dress for Power." The shovel bit savagely into the dirt, too close to the plant, and I swore at the sound of metal grating into flesh. Moving back, I stomped once and unearthed the split potato. A film of dirt clung to the exposed meat, and I rubbed the halves down my pants leg before hurling them into a bucket.

I looked at this woman, her legs so solidly planted in the broken earth, and I wanted to swing the shovel. If it wasn't courage that let me live out here, what was it? Apathy? Igno-rance? Struggling to keep my face empty, my jaw loose, I opened my fist and dropped the spade, my silence another sacrifice. No. Carol was not like me. This was all part of our strength, dealing with these clueless outsiders.

If I opened my mouth, where would I start? With the wind? Well, Carol, when the wind blows, a few inches of pow-der can drift the roads shut in an hour. Sure, we could shovel out—if we had to. Fifty miles to the highway, and when it fills back in behind you, you can shovel the same fifty miles back home. Before dark, if you're smart. Then there's the kid equa-tion. Mine are five, four and two. Only an idiot would take a bad road with a kid too little to walk in deep snow or head for town when it's below zero with more kids in the rig than arms to carry them. Unless they have to. In winter, getting stuck is only one worry. A frozen fuel line, a broken fan belt, an engine failure at thirty below zero on a road where someone may or may not pass by for hours or days—for what? A movie? If no one ever froze to death on our county road it was not because it couldn't happen, I thought furiously. We didn't let it happen.

But even as I assembled my defense, my anger faded. I was sick of the taste of lies. The truth was harder than that, more complicated. There were times we couldn't have gotten out if we had had to, monthlong stretches in the winter when the roads were plugged solid with drifts, weeks during spring thaw when travel was done on the frost—early morning or late at night—or not at all. Other times the roads stayed passable all year. Good weather, you live here because you want to, I'd tell visitors. In bad weather you live here because you have to.

Sometimes it was the not knowing that kept people close to home, a fear that passed for caution or common sense. A storm might blow up in the middle of a clear day, a few hours of wind, an inch of snow, and by suppertime a road the county plows took two days to clear might be socked in or blown bare. You never knew. A shift and the mercury might rise, a chinook wind gust in from the west, and the cattle humped up by days of bitter cold would turn to face it, arching and stretching as the snow melted from their backs. The drifts would settle and glaze, but by night the air could grow still again. Sounds dulled by warmth all day turned sharp and brittle as the temperature followed the sun, sliding past zero and down, ten below, fifteen, twenty below.

Thirty-below-zero cold threw the senses out of kilter. The loose stretch of shale ridges above the creek bottom puckered into sharp pleats, drawn up in a common thread, squeezing closer as if the land itself were shrinking. In the eerie twilight of midwinter I could listen to chores from the doorstep, sounds looping the barnyard, chasing their own echoes—the ring of axe against ice in water troughs, the creak of boots on snow at the far end of the feedlot, the pop of a neighbor's tractor as loud as the slam of our shop door. We traveled on educated guesses then, calculating the risk. Could we put off the trip? Did we really need to get out? Wanting had so little to do with it. The whole business wasn't about "me" anymore.

At age thirty, John had been eager to start a family. Having been raised with a twin sister and no other siblings, he began our marriage with rosy visions of a large family—four children, maybe five. Having the experience of the large family to draw on, I was less enthusiastic but willing to go along. When Jeanette arrived two years after our wedding, he became a papa in the deepest sense of the word, a man enchanted by this tiny, marvelous creature who ran to meet him and saved her best smiles for him alone. He remained distanced only in the areas of diaper changing and discipline. When Jason followed seventeen months later, my struggle to manage two babies along with the ranch wife's workload caused him to rethink the large family. Two seemed quite a lot of worry and work, and he found it difficult to get used to the chaos and mess that went with babies. And then our little surprise, James, arrived a week before my twenty-fourth birthday, and I headed into that next long winter with a newborn, a two-and-a-half-year-old and a four-year-old to tend, in addition to cooking and washing for a husband, a father-in-law and a hired man.

As my family grew larger, my activities outside the house shrank in equal measure, a natural result, though I struggled against it. For the first two years, I had reveled in the freedom and status of outside work, getting to know the expanse of prairie and badlands that was my new home. The spring before Jeanette's birth, I rode in the branding roundup, using rubber bands to expand the waist of my Levi's. Even when I stood in the stirrups, my belly cleared the saddle horn by a safe margin, but the neighbors were aghast, especially the men. A week later, while I was gathering yearlings from a creek pasture, the bog-sour gelding I rode hit an alkali sink hidden by weeds and pitched a fit. He reared, freeing his forefeet from the sucking mud, and the momentum carried us both over backward. As his head tipped past that center of balance, I cleared the stirrups and shoved off from the pommel with both hands, landing full length on my side. The saddle gouged a deep scar in the ground a few feet from my head where the horse hit and rebounded, twisting to find his feet in the instant he touched down. The wreck was minor, no injuries but the hoof-shaped bruise on my forearm where he trampled me as he scrambled back to his feet. A close call, nothing more.

It was nearing summer when I snubbed a range cow to a post, trying to convince her to feed her starving calf. Twice, after stretching the cow's hind leg back with a lariat, I straddled the calf and shoved him toward her tight udder, and twice she fought the ropes, choking, losing her balance and falling. The third time I left slack in the leg rope and she stood, panting and rolling her eyes. Already I'd felt the first butterfly kicks of my unborn daughter and I'd grown thick enough through the middle to feel clumsy as I leaned forward to push a hard, swollen teat into the calf's mouth, squeezing to give him the taste of milk. In a few months I would have a new appreciation for how that might feel, but at the time I was unprepared. With a bawl, the cow lunged forward, bowling the calf and me over in a tangle, then sat back on her neck rope, giving that one hind leg enough slack to drive like a piston. She caught the calf first, a solid knock that spun his head in a half circle, then nailed me twice in the second it took to unsnarl my legs and roll free. The first blow grazed my thigh, the second bounded off my hipbone and caught me solid in the lower belly.

Lamaze breathing got me through the pain, but as I crawled upright against the corral, a gout of bright blood flowed toward my boots. I made deals then, with God or the devil, whichever was listening, as I walked carefully toward the house, uncertain if what I felt was bruise pains or labor. I would stay away from the cattle; I would quit trying to do everything I'd done before, if only I could have another chance. The bleeding stopped as quickly as it started, and I kept my end of the bargain, finally convinced that I couldn't have it all. In my determination to prove I could do anything a man could do, I'd lost sight of the fact that I was already doing the one thing no man could.

Winter Kill

The next year, with one toddling and another on the way, I slowed a little more, raising chickens and one hell of a garden, sometimes calving the night shift. I still got out to help with riding and branding when I could justify asking some equally burdened neighbor woman to keep two babies, but with the birth of James, even that became logistically impractical. Helping outside was a one-way street, and when I finished there, my own work waited back in the house. Boredom wasn't the same as having time on my hands. My days were full to exhaustion with the garden, the canning and freezing and butchering, three kids and three men, and when hunters invaded the Breaks and the weather turned, the boundaries drew even closer.

In October I would carry the pressure canner to the base-ment and pause to take stock. Wooden shelves lined the con-crete walls, and I could run my hands along the rank and file of quart jars, hundreds of them touching shoulders in precise rows, arranged so the colors came to life in the dim light. Tomatoes bloomed between the corn and sauerkraut. Pickled beets rested the eye between the dills and the 224-day sweets, rich purple plums livened the space between pears and peaches.

Up the stairs in the porch, the bulk of our winter's meat lay in huge freezers, two steers or dry heifers butchered and hung in the walk-in cooler, cut and wrapped on the kitchen table. The roasts were weighed on my baby scale, the largest a fifteen-pound standing rib or top round selected from the fattest carcass, double-wrapped and tagged with grease pencil. I centered that one in the bottom of the second freezer, where it remained buried through the winter. My first glimpse of the branding roast through diminishing layers of burger and steak signaled spring as surely as the crocus.

Outside, past the untidy mountain of split cottonwood and across the road, the root cellar jutted from the base of our hill, facing south. The double doors built of bridge plank reeked of creosote where the sun hit, but inside the air hung so rich and heavy I could take it up by mouthfuls. I never breathed the earthy smell of the cellar without thinking of my grandmother Pansy, a story she told me the first summer I was pregnant. Where my grandparents homesteaded, the land was flat, and their root cellar had a trapdoor entry with steps leading down to an earthen chamber deep below the frost line. She didn't recall which pregnancy it had been, the sixth or seventh maybe, when she made her way down the stairs with a pail to get a mess of spuds for supper. Something in the smell made her stop, she said, and she sat on the pail in the gloom of the cellar for a long time, breathing in the damp odors of roots and earth. A pale vein midway up the dirt wall had shed a litter of bone-colored rocks and without thinking, she picked one up and slipped it onto her tongue. The rock crumbled into powder against her teeth, and her mouth watered at the taste, the taste of the air.

When she left the cellar she carried the chipped enamel pail heaped with potatoes and tucked in her apron pocket, a handful of brittle white stones. She nibbled them in secret, lest her half-grown daughters or her husband catch her eating dirt. "I just felt I wanted it," she told me, still grimacing with wonder at her own behavior, still wanting it secret after fifty years.

There'd been a time she spent four years on the homestead between trips to Malta, back when the trip was two days in a buckboard, too much for the baby still in diapers, too rough for the mother heavy with another. She shrugged. Trips to town were rare, the wagon often loaded with grain to sell, no room to ride; Alfred, my grandfather, was impatient with stopping to feed children or rinse diapers in the potholes along the creek, impatient with the nonsense, the inefficiency. "Well, the kids was too little," she'd say, as if that said everything.

The oldest books on my shelf belonged to her, Pansy Robinson McNeil Blunt, and to my other grandmother, Pearle Watson Aikins. Both raised their children, my parents, on homesteads in Phillips County. Pearle had kept her own mother's book, my great-grandmother Mary Ann Deffenbaugh Watson's Civil War–era guide to the practical household. *Mrs. Owens' Cook Book and Useful Household Hints* tucks medical information here and there around notes on the management of servants, instructions for building roads, making hair mattresses and dyes for cloth, curing windgall in horses and caked udder in cows. Between pages of printed recipes are blank pages covered margin to margin in a glowing script, records of milk sold to Mrs. J. L. Ball in 1894 crowding into later entries I guess to be my grandmother Pearle's, recipes and notes that become cramped and jagged as the arthritis that finally crippled her begins to show. She was dead before I was old enough to know her. My other grandmother lived to know my children.

On the back of a recipe for Nannie's Cake, my great-grandmother records one to cure cholera. *Mix well, equal parts of Cayenne, opium, tincture of rhubarb, essence of peppermint and spirits of camphor. Dose 10 to 20 drops in a wineglass of water. Give according to age & violence of attack, etc.*

Grandma Pansy fills the flyleaf of her 1908 edition of *The Practical Guide to Health* with a recipe she has gotten from another source, perhaps passed on to her by a neighbor or sister. *Diphtheria. At the first indication in the throat of a child, make a room close, then take a tin cup & pour into it a quan-*

*tity of tar & turpentine equal parts. Hold the cup over a fire so
as to fill the room with the fumes. This will loosen the mem-
branous matter & the disease will be thrown off thru the
mouth.*

The cures my grandmothers believed in were as useless in
their time as they were in mine, but they had the mercy of not
knowing. At least recipes were possible then, when tinctures
of this and spirits of that were kept in corked bottles and any
woman who had a tin cup and the steady hand to hold it over
fire had all she needed, all she could hope to have. No one
knew better than tar and turpentine, and no one expected
more. They lived where they lived, a simple notion of "just
being" that set the moral for every story. "We didn't know any
different," Pansy would say, or "that's just the way things were
then," always with her palms spread, balancing the good with
the bad and coming up even. For her, isolation and solitude
were a meaningless complication of terms. The rules were the
same: wanting what you could not have was the worst form of
foolishness.

Born in the seventies, my babies came with a modern set of
standards for immunizations, well-baby checkups and prompt
medical treatment for illnesses, store-bought vitamins and
cereals, fresh fruits and vegetables year-round. To be a responsible parent now meant getting out. Travel was easier for me
than it ever had been for my grandmothers, or even my
mother, what with modern vehicles and graded roads. But the
distance was still there, and the new roads were all built of the
same old soil.

My grandmother would have found comfort in my root cellar, carrots layered in clean sand, onions and potatoes sacked
in burlap against the stone walls, Hubbard squash wrapped in
newspaper on shelves near the ceiling. There was security in

food, the gathering of all we needed and more, the preservation of body and soul against whatever might come. There was peace in all this plenty, somewhere. But as I made my rounds in the early autumn, from basement to freezer to root cellar, the sheer abundance of the harvest felt threatening, a measure of the months ahead.

Carol talked a lot longer than I listened that autumn afternoon, but for all my stoic silence, my face must have flickered like a neon sign. The next fall and every year after that, she and her husband pulled up on opening day of hunting season and unloaded their truck on my doorstep, boxes and grocery bags filled with paperback books, hundreds of them gathered at rummage sales over the summer. "Just in case you get five minutes to yourself," she'd say, brushing aside my thanks. My husband greeted this windfall as he might have a crowd of slick-haired rivals who appeared on his doorstep each October, wearily accepting the affairs he knew would play themselves out by spring. I got acquainted with them all as I sorted them, reading covers with a tingle of expectation, arranging long rows on the floor of the attic, best-sellers and murder mysteries first, spy thrillers and horror novels in the middle, bodice-rippers and romances pitched into a far corner, something to sneer my way through around March.

For months I lived inside stories as strange as my own, emerging guilt-ridden to do what needed done in spasms of speed and efficiency. I pushed away thoughts by reflex, learning like my mother and grandmothers the cautious shutting down of self to any needs beyond those provided. Making do, we called it. No one gave us orders. We were partners in an uncertain business, responsible, hardworking, self-limiting. I understood it as I did no other way of living. The change was gradual, but slowly over the years, as I sacked the last spud and watched ice film the reservoir, the solitude I treasured took the shape of isolation. With the first blizzard of the season came a shift in perception, a mental shutting down as quiet and predictable as that final December day when frost stitched through the center of the last windowpane, and I no longer looked outside.

Sunday, May 15, 1977. Eight p.m. My daughter's screams bounce off the walls of the bathroom, inspiring wails from her baby brother on the bath mat by my knees, drowning out the plaintive notes of her father's fiddle in the next room and the murmurs of comfort I direct first to one, then the other, as I kneel by the tub. The water in the tub is tepid, though on the phone the doctor said cold—cold water, fifteen minutes. Even so the bath is agony, her grip on my wrist so tight I have to pry her fingers loose to palm the water over her chest and neck.

Jeanette weighs just over twenty pounds at nineteen months, a perfectly proportioned little dynamo who scales cupboards like a monkey and can stand flat-footed under the kitchen table with inches to spare, a pixie compared with the angry, hungry boy on the floor. At five weeks, Jason's long past the ten-pound mark, and the fists waving on either side of his mouth are nearly as big as his sister's. The milk he wants trickles unheeded down my stomach, my breasts pressed against the edge of the tub as I hold as much of Jeanette's body in the shallow water as I can manage with only two hands. She arches, each scream going silent as she runs out of air, jaw chattering so wildly I'm afraid she will bite her tongue between breaths. Her dark eyes remained fastened on my face, her arms outstretched, begging.

Two hours have passed since I spoke with the doctor, and

in that time I have forced unwanted liquids down her throat, stripped away the solace of her blankie and wrapped her head in wet towels. I have invaded her rectum with thermometers, aspirin suppositories and cool-water enemas, so deaf to her protests that she has taken to protecting herself, clinging frantically to the edge of her diaper when I unpin it for the cold bath, pleading for her papa over and over—the parent who does not hurt her. He has retreated in anguish, unable to help or hurt, covering her pain with his headphones, volume cranked up, bow flying over the strings. He's learning to play by ear, a little over a year since he started.

Numbers clear my mind, keep me calm and methodical. The watch balanced on the edge of the tub marks three and a half hours since Jason's last feeding, his cries intermittent now, muffled by the noisy sucking of his fist. After eight minutes, Jeanette quiets to hiccups, exhausted, compliant. Through the wall, the fiddle strains at a hoedown, and I croon the familiar words like a lullaby:

> *Never marry an old schoolmarm*
> *I'll tell you the reason why—*
> *She'll blow her nose in old cornbread*
> *And call it pumpkin pie!*
> *Oh, boil them cabbage down, boys, boil*
>   *them cabbage down. . . .*

A bath thermometer shaped like a turtle floats by my arm, rocking on the waves. Outside, it's 45 degrees and steady under a clearing sky, the rain slowed to a sprinkle, over an inch in the gauge when John came in for supper. When I last looked, the moon had risen over the east meadows, and the barnyard shone like foil, water glistening in the ruts, a riotous night for the coyotes. The bathwater has cooled to 79, down 6. At last reading, the little body balanced on my arm registered just over 105 degrees and rising.

"Are you sure you're reading the thermometer properly?"

"Yes, I'm sure." There was a pause on the other end of the phone, and I drew a deep breath. I'd left a call for the doctor in Malta early that Sunday afternoon, and he'd finally gotten free to return it at 5 p.m. His voice sounded distracted as he thumbed through the notes the nurses had jotted. Though he'd been in Malta for two years, Dr. Ramaiya was still the new guy, the topic of neighborhood gossip. He would not prescribe over the phone or write penicillin and sulfa prescriptions for people who wanted to keep these medicines on hand and dose themselves as needed. Old-timers regarded him with some suspicion. He was a vegetarian, for one thing, an "India-type Indian" whose wife made timid appearances in local store aisles wrapped up to her chin, even in summer, a red spot painted on her forehead. Worse than that, he didn't appear to take his job seriously, the old cowboys complained. Not a group to run to the doctor for every sniffle, they expected some serious attention when they finally felt rotten enough to go. But those who dragged their virus-ridden bodies to Ramaiya rather than wait hours to see the old doctor often left empty-handed and insulted. He would not dispense antibiotics for routine colds and flu, and most ranchers weren't "bed rest and fruit juice" kinds of guys. They wanted a pill, and the bigger it was the better.

The new doctor was most popular with the young women in the county, because he approved of drug-free births and was less resistant to fathers in the delivery room, something the older doctors had seldom allowed. Although he'd been educated in England and spoke with a clipped British accent, Ramaiya had doctored in remote African provinces, experience that came in handy in Malta's ill-equipped little hospital. In 1975, when my sister-in-law required an emergency cesarean, there was no time to call an anesthesiologist from Havre, ninety miles west. Dr. Ramaiya performed the surgery with local anesthetic, using injections to deaden her skin like a dentist before pulling a tooth. For Karen, the procedure was neither pleasant nor cosmetically rewarding, but she survived and Kurt was born bright and healthy. Ramaiya had delivered both of mine.

He had Jeanette's chart in front of him, and I waited for the rustling of paper to stop, already ticking down the list of questions he would ask. Half a dozen books lay facedown on the coffee table, all opened to the chapter on fever. In addition to several standard baby-care books, I owned nursing text-books, a medical encyclopedia and a prescription-drug desk reference, the last being the only one I had not read cover-to-cover more than once. No, I repeated to every question, no congestion, no cough, no diarrhea, no vomiting, no behavior that would indicate the pain of an ear infection or sore throat. Just the fever.

"She was hospitalized last August . . . ," he began, and I interrupted impatiently. I knew her medical history. It was my job. Steady temp of 104 with diarrhea and vomiting. I'd driven her to the hospital because she was less than a year old, and I was concerned that she would dehydrate. She spiked 103 with her DPT immunizations, 102 with any cold she caught. These were on the chart as notations, reported when I took her in for regular checkups: Fever of Unknown Origin. We joked that she had a faulty thermostat. This late-spring afternoon she had gotten up from her nap with a fever of 101, and in the two hours since, it had spiked to 104, in spite of aspirin. The number worried me less than the speed.

"I should look at her." The words were muffled, and I imagined the doctor hunched over the desk in the tiny cubicle of the nurse's station, rubbing his face with one hand. "Oh, you're . . ."

"It's raining." We spoke at the same time. For all his time in the outposts, Ramaiya had a hard time grasping our connection between bad weather and no travel. He hissed under his breath. I wondered if he was thinking about the case in Glasgow a few weeks before, a baby younger than mine diagnosed with meningitis. I had pored over those chapters, memorizing the symptoms, and had watched Jeanette as she slept between tortures. Did her head arch back toward her heels instead of bending forward in the curl of natural sleep? Did her neck seem stiff? Yes, no, maybe. I couldn't tell.

Ramaiya gathered his thoughts and rattled off a series of orders. Ice packs at the base of her skull, cool-water enemas, no clothes, fluids, a cold bath if her temperature rose above 104. In the two-hour lull that followed the phone call, the fever neither rose nor fell. When John came in for supper, he had mud caked to the second buckle of his overshoes. The hired man had quit in the middle of calving, disappearing up the road the first day of spring, the day Jason was born. So far, no one was beating down the door to take his place.

"Jesus!" Jerking his hand from Jeanette's forehead, he looked up at me. "Does she need to go to town?"

"Can we get out?" I jiggled the baby, trying to get him to settle for a pacifier. Jeanette's temperature had shot to 105. The bathwater was running. He rose from the edge of the couch, steadying his daughter as the cushion lifted, then

266

cupped that hand against his chest with the other. "Jesus," he said softly. "I don't know." I followed him into the kitchen, retracing a route I had paced every hour, waiting as he tapped the barometer and shaded the glare of indoor light on the east window to read the outside thermometer. Even a light frost would have helped firm the mud, but it wasn't going to happen. An inch of rain on gumbo softened by snowmelt, and the inch had come slowly, soaking in instead of running off the high spots. A good grass rain.

Turning from the window, John shook his head as if shifting information from one side to the other. Our soil was rich with bentonite, a pale clay that swells to several times its volume when saturated with water. It will stick to anything. It dries hard as flint and can be ground into a fine gray powder, a dirt of many commercial uses, like lining the molds in foundries and sealing the walls of oil wells drilled in porous rock. At a certain stage of drying, the mud would build up on the chickens' feet until they looked like they were wearing shoes. Fat hens would stagger spraddle-legged through the barnyard, heads bobbing to gain momentum against the weight, pausing every few steps for a baffled, head-tilting examination of their own feet. In that same stage, what we called "balling up" occurred, mud gathering on the pickup tires in thick rinds and piling up in the fender wells until the wheels could no longer turn. Roads with the top inch wet were merely "greasy," something that happened with a couple tenths of rain or when the surface began to thaw in spring.

The cold bath finished and the baby fed, I stood in the shadows by the living room window, rubbing the last burp from Jason. The top of his head pulsed against my cheek. His sister dozed naked on the couch, a plastic bread sack framing her face. Out of ice cubes, I had scraped a double handful of frost from the inside of the chest freezer and wrapped it in a wet washcloth. The bath brought her down to 104.5. I hoped it had peaked and would continue to drop. Dr. Ramaiya had gone home, the nurse reported briskly, but she had orders to call him if we showed up at the hospital. The music had stilled. John leaned in the doorway.

Turning away from the window, I laid the baby on the floor in the center of a quilt—dry, warm and full as a tick. Released from my hold, he roused and stretched, lips pursed in a brief dreamy suckling. Beside the quilt squatted a nylon duffel bag I had readied in the late afternoon while the rain sill washed down the hills. Packing, I had felt a twinge of fear, as if preparing for the worst might trigger it. Now the bag seemed solid and essential, something safe to grab. John moved aside as I stepped past him. Calving season was over, but the weeks of long days and broken nights showed in his face, his eyes red-rimmed over a three-day stubble.

"What do you think?" His voice pushed at me. I began to clear the supper dishes, shoving food uncovered into the refrigerator. It was my call. How sick was she? Was she better off here than on the road? How long could we wait? I was tired of thinking, my body already counting hours to the next feeding, and the next. Tonight, the road would not be greasy. Tonight would be tough roads, probably somewhere between damned tough and pretty damned tough, like driving on a twelve-inch layer of cold lard. A trip would mean nearly fifty miles of grinding and sliding, fighting the wheel to keep the side-to-side slew within the narrow range of road top. We stared at each other for a brief moment. Mud didn't shovel like snow. If we slid off the road, we were stuck. No one could be traveling tonight.

When a digital timer beeped from the countertop, less

than an hour since her cold bath, thirty minutes since the last dose of aspirin, he followed me back into the living room. I knelt by the couch and shook the thermometer down with rapid snaps of the wrist. She lay on her side facing me, knees tucked up, tufts of honey-brown hair dried askew against one ivory and rose cheek. I worked quietly, reluctant to wake her. She shifted in her sleep, turning her head. The exposed cheek was the dry, deep color of old brick. Alarmed, I lifted the edge of the blanket and rolled her onto her cool side.

Heat radiated from the flushed skin where she had pressed against the blanket, and like testing a banked fire, I slid a practiced palm down her back, feeling the delicate feather of her ribs, the rapid breathing. She was too hot to be real. I felt my heart begin to pound in my throat. The decision was made, but I waited the full two minutes for confirmation. The thermometer I twisted to the light showed a slim red streak that disappeared under the pinch of two fingers. 106. I leaned forward, trembling with the effort to stand up, and finally spoke from my knees, voice shaking. "Get the pickup."

John jerked like he'd been shot and was out the door in three long strides. By the time I pulled myself up and reached the freezer for more ice, I could hear the bawl of the big Ford pickup churning through the mud to the gas pumps. I diapered Jeanette quickly, then slipped a fresh ice pack behind her neck. She squirmed against the cold, but she did not wake as I bathed her head, white frost melting where it touched, evaporating as it trickled toward her ears. Her hands were drawn up, resting on her chest, the tips of her fingers quivering in a pale imitation of my own.

From the hay yard by the barn, a tractor popped, and I followed its progress with a numb detachment, the slap of giant chains growing louder as they neared the house and swung around at the base of our hill. If we got bogged halfway up, John would have to drag the pickup over the top with the tractor, a slow, nerve-racking process of inching the tractor around the 4x4, then backing down the steep incline to the nose of the pickup and clawing away mud to hook up the tow chains. The tractor had no headlights, and on the blind crawl up the hill John would steer by feel, guided by the pickup lights that swept on either side of the tractor and marked the shoulders of the narrow road.

Her lethargy, the tremors I saw in Jeanette's hands, were symptoms, facts I reported to the hospital switchboard clearly and precisely, hanging up on the overly patient voice that suggested I just stay calm and try a different thermometer. Seconds after I hung up the phone, a thin, bleating cry rose and wavered, raising the hair on my arms, a cry designed to erase a mother's sanity and send her flying at the beast that threatens her child. In a way, the textbooks had prepared me too well. I had memorized definitions, descriptions and treatments. I knew about epileptiform, tetanic and hysteroidal convulsions, how they were characterized and the difference between colonic and tonic contractions. Nothing prepared me for the child to be mine, the clawlike curl of her fingers, the eyes rolled, bulging white against the clenched blue skin, blood-streaked foam bubbling between her bared teeth, the jerky paddling of limbs, like a clumsy dog caught dreaming. I heard the sounds, the choking and grunting of something wild snared by the throat, at another level of reality, and for a single heartbeat, instinct won. I saw the beast. And I caught myself in mid-reach, ready to yank her off the couch and shake her with my bare hands.

Something solid gathered and took hold as I found my breath, something colder and more practical than anger. The pickup idled out front. I drew myself up at the sound of John's footsteps, bracing for the questions he would ask. Jeanette's thrashing had slowed to jerks and quivers, but at the sight of her, his face would grow helpless and still. When calves convulse they are dying, that's all he would know—all he had ever needed to know. He had no other reference, no doctor's voice or nurse's handbook telling him that fever convulsions weren't, in and of themselves, fatal. He would look to me for answers I didn't have, strength I wasn't sure I could spare.

My parents' ranch lay fifteen miles up the road, the fifteen worst miles for mud. John was on the phone to them, calling ahead as I changed clothes and made a final pass through the house, checking lights, pitching the cat out the door. I shoved the checkbook in the duffel bag, cocooned the baby in his quilt and strapped him into the car seat, moving both in one trip to the kitchen where John could grab them from the door. Jeanette lay rigid, her body straining against touch as I folded the blanket around her and lifted her gently against my chest to carry her out. When the pickup door slammed behind us, she arched backward and stopped breathing. I let her head fall back on my arm to open her airway, pulling the blanket to one side as she caught a ragged breath, and her legs began their ethereal gallop.

John eased the pickup toward the barn, then gunned the engine and swung in a wide circle facing the hill. We had a fifty-yard running start. I braced my feet against the floorboards, my right elbow cushioning Jeanette's head from a sideways jolt against the window. Without slowing, he slammed the gearshift into second, and fed it gas. The big Ford twisted through the barnyard, gaining speed like a sidewinder, and we hit the hill with the engine wound tight, mud thundering against the floor, the front wheels throwing clots higher than the cab roof. As the pitch tilted us back, our headlights searched the sky in slim arcs, fishtails tapering off to a slow wag as we passed the halfway point, shuddering as we hit the final stretch. Toward the top, the road angled up like a greased chute with steep shale banks on either side. When the engine lugged, John finessed the gears, a smooth clutch-shift into compound, and the truck settled to a dull grind, straining, wallowing by inches up the slope, to the very top, and over.

On level ground, we stopped for a moment, both of us breathing fast. John turned loose of the steering wheel, wiggling his fingers, and sat back against the seat. I forced my legs to relax their rigid push against the floorboards. Jason slept unperturbed, and I loosened his wraps with one hand, trying not to jiggle his sister. With the window rolled down a few inches, I opened her blanket to let the damp chill fan the heat from her face as we pulled away, lurching in steady mud-slinging rhythm to the right, to the left, to the right. Cornering from our lane onto the raised county road, the tires growled against the fender wells, kicking out boulders of packed gumbo. Dried in the sun, they could tear out an oil pan. I leaned my face against the door, into the breeze that smelled of wet roots and sweet grass, of spring. Stars snapped in the wide arch of sky, and the hills crouched over the coulees in the clear night, bristling with new-growth sage. Jackrabbits flinched and bounced from the barrow pit, bounding madly alongside the pickup.

John never wavered, his face serious and steady, his hands lifting and gripping, passing each other on the wheel as he corrected the slides. I looked at Jeanette's face, quieter now as the breeze cooled her, the moon a thin blue glow in the whites of her eyes. How many close calls would it take, I thought, before we could no longer justify the choice we made to live where we lived, the quarrel we took up with the land and passed along to this baby who tightened like a claw with every bump and sway. In the side mirror, the road closed grudgingly behind us, plowed into bloody furrows in the taillights, fading into bruise-colored shadows as we fought our way north. Ahead, as far as I could see, the road lay swollen, smooth as wet concrete.

We made it to the bench lands, out of the Breaks, when I saw the first light. Word had gotten out. Off to the right, a mile, two miles from the road, headlights bucked over the sod to the top of a rise where the driver could see us coming and watch us pass. The lights blinked once, like a nod. Good luck. Safe journey. Past the little school it was dark again, but over the next hill my father's mailbox was braced with a pair of battered four-wheel-drives, the road torn where the men turned to wait. They stood silhouetted, one in front of each pickup. John's mud-spattered window squealed down, grit against glass, as he pulled up. Dad's shadow stepped away from the truck and moved toward us. On my side, Fred Veseth hesitated. I slid my window down a little farther and he came forward, a tenderhearted man whose boys were nearly grown.

"How's it going?" he said quietly, almost whispering, as though the small blue child in my arms was sleeping.

"So far okay," I replied. "I guess."

He gazed at Jeanette's face, the blank eyes, rictus grin, and turned away to look at the ground, his hands sliding into the pockets of his jeans. Dad had called ahead. "Watch Lonesome Coulee, less rain the farther you go. Beaver is flooding but the Midale road is still better than the Regina road, still the way to go." Dad peered in through the open window for a second, then slapped the hood and turned back to his own. At the sound, Jeanette jerked in my arms, one leg drawn up, quivering. When we pulled out, spinning, finding our footing, two pickups fell in behind us, watching our back all the way to the highway.

I remember the hours of that trip with more clarity than the days my babies and I spent in the Malta Hospital, Jason in one crib, Jeanette in another, my fold-out cot in the aisle between. We pulled onto the highway two hours after we took off, and as John jumped out to turn the hubs, it was easy to imagine the pickup blowing and trembling like a winded horse. Twenty miles of highway we took in fifteen minutes, bombing the pavement with clods of mud that tore loose from the under-carriage and rolled for a hundred feet behind us. John dropped us off at the hospital and turned for home.

The nurse who checked us in wrote down the temperature I gave her and the word "convulsions," both with question marks in the margins. Within minutes, Jeanette vindicated me with another strong seizure as she lay in the glare of fluo-rescent lights, and again the next night when her fever spiked to 106.1. Dr. Ramaiya appeared at the hospital and stayed, pulling a chair to her bedside and watching her closely through many of the miserable hours she spent encased in ice packs. Jason remained healthy, protected by breast milk and newborn resilience. The nurses carried him around like a doll and let me sleep sometimes. On the third day a fine red rash all over her body suggested a diagnosis of roseola, and she had recovered enough to climb my leg like a squirrel whenever she saw a white coat. Dr. Ramaiya waited until her appetite and energy level returned to normal, then let us go. I called the ranch. The roads were drying. John came for us on the fourth day.

"You're not taking her back out there?" Our bags were piled on a bench in the waiting room, ready to load in the pickup. In them, I had packed her new seizure medication, new thermometers, aspirin suppositories. At the sound of the head nurse's voice, Jeanette straight-armed her brother to one side and clambered on my lap, burying her face against my neck. The nurse squinted her eyes in disbelief, as if searching me for some glimmer of maternal instinct. It was not the last hospital campout the kids and I took, not the longest we would endure, but it was one of the hardest, and I remember the physical effort it took to gather strength, to pull up one more answer to one more well-meaning question.

When I close my eyes and try to call back the dark of that night, mostly what I see are the lights. We're crossing from the breaks to the flatlands, churning sideways up a hill, and at the top, the night comes alive with lights, pickups waiting by mailboxes, lights like stars in the distance, moving across the prairie toward the road, zigzagging like penlights held in shaky hands, neighbors fighting slowly up their lanes toward the county road, every one of them called from bed, come to see us safely by. And I remember thinking we wouldn't dare ask people to do this. And I remember believing it was enough, knowing that they would come, tired ranchmen already turning back as we pass, a flash of lights handing us ten miles down the fence line to the next set of lights facing south, watching. What could we ever give our children except uncertainty and a place to belong, the quiet strength of a community that would see them by?

I was waiting to go home when the nurse asked her question. And I answered her the only way I could, juggling my babies on either arm, offering her my grandmother's evenhanded shrug, weighing the odds.

Night Shift

Spring happened overnight that year, and the coyotes couldn't get enough of it. Calls shot up from shale banks and bloomed over the barnyard, sharp yaps and strings of *eee*'s that met the icy pulse of northern lights overhead. Walking to the calving shed for the three o'clock check, I had to remind myself and the chickenhearted bird dog bumping against my heels that they were farther away than they sounded. Everything seemed closer and sharper those first few weeks when snowdrifts drew back in clean lines and the land rose through. Even the breeze seemed urgent with the smell of wet prairie and new sage, the swollen rumble of the creek. Or maybe it was me.

I ran my fingers over the pack of Marlboros in my jacket pocket, thumbing a matchbook from the cellophane sleeve. The breeze was steady northeast, perfect. John slept with the window open, and he had some pretty firm ideas about the sort of woman who smoked. Actually, he'd borrowed them from his father, or maybe it was a genetic thing, I didn't know. She was a vision of sin, this woman, and in the first years of marriage I had come to love her like a sister, the way she sat that barstool like she owned it, eyelashes drooping with mas-

cara, cigarette fused to her lower lip. Definitely not wife material. "Probably can't cook," I said aloud.

Katie waved her tail and laughed up at me. A registered
Gordon setter in a country seething with beady-eyed blue
heelers, she had to appreciate a good joke. She pressed against
my legs as I juggled the oversized flashlight and the chain
latch on the corral gate, then dropped her ears and flopped
down to wait.

Pinching a filter between my teeth, I pulled a cigarette
from the pack, drawing air through the dry tobacco. My muscles were taut with exhilaration that had less to do with nico-
tine than the solitude that went with it. I had hours before the
ranch woke to be fed—kids, husband, and hired hands. At first
light the pop of tractors brought cattle bawling up the creek to
the feed ground and John's dad rattling down the hill to the
shop. The smoking issue went back to the beginning of my
days on this ranch. It was Frank who had issued the ultima-
tum a couple of months after the wedding—quit smoking or
get out. I had abstained from smoking around him and Rose
since before the wedding, and tried to be considerate at social
gatherings when we were all together. But I was also a child of
the sixties who had insisted on having the word "obey" stricken
from the vows. When Frank put his foot down, I stuck my chin
in the air on pure principle. I was not taking orders from a
father-in-law.

John was sympathetic, up to a point, because he also
chafed under Frank's iron rule. He was a newcomer to the
ranch and to the ranching community, the guy with all the
responsibility and none of the seniority. He'd spent very little
time with his father before moving to the ranch at age twenty-
seven, and they still weren't easy together. John backed me for
a while, trying to josh both sides into getting along, until the

day Frank walked into the kitchen unannounced and spotted my cigarettes lying on the table. He grabbed them and pitched them at my head.

"Are you still smoking those sonsofbitches!" It wasn't a question, and he was still swearing as he slammed back out the door, nearly running into John. They faced off in the shop. John grabbed a crescent wrench from the bench inside the door, his dad gripped a ball peen hammer and they squared.

"You take care of your own goddamn nest and I'll take care of mine," John said, his words so tight they barely moved his jaw. His father's face looked stretched, and it shone with rage.

"Then you'd better goddamn take care of it," he hissed, "or get up the road."

That night when his dad left, John laid down the law as gently as he could. My smoking had raised more hell than it was worth. He must forbid me to smoke. There was too much at stake to stand on principle. If I loved him, I would do this for him. There was more, and I sat silently and listened. Everything he said made sense. I couldn't defend smoking, I found, without sounding selfish, a spoiled teenager. John vowed to help me quit and I nodded, and in a way the matter was settled, mapped out in clear lines. All I had to do was keep both feet on the right side. All I had to do was be good.

True to his word, it became a "we" project. Every hug began as a sniff test, ending abruptly if my hair held the faintest trace of smoke. His nostrils flared when I walked by. The hired men tattled. Cigarette butts I stashed in the weeds found their way indoors, sometimes scattered like seed on the kitchen floor, sometimes dropped in my coffee cup. I cleaned them up and never said a word. I was bad, and I knew it. Why couldn't I just not smoke? I didn't know. Before long, John's patience gave way. The smell of cigarette smoke brought him roaring out of a dead sleep. I bought them with egg money, untraceable. I smoked one, maybe two a day, and when the men hung around the buildings all day, I seethed. They had me on the run. There was the time I leaned out of the wind against a granary to light a cigarette, feeling secure with the men off fencing. Suddenly the wind caught a shop door and slammed it. I nearly wet my pants. The electrical shock of adrenaline left me weak and shaking. And angry.

This was the game we called smoking, just one leak in a mile-high dam. If John and I recognized the issues that lay behind it, we didn't let on. We spent a great deal of time and energy keeping confrontation at a safe level. The anger I felt at being forbidden and the anger he felt when I defied him were manageable angers; they passed and left a blank spot where we could write "normal" or even "happy." We shared a history, a love of our children and the land they grew on. We were careful with each other. But there were times we slipped, times I pushed too hard and defenses crashed. One time I argued for the power to sign bank drafts when I paid the ranch bills every month; another time I wanted a small wage check for field work, something in my own name. John listened. The last time I pressed him for an answer, he rose to his feet and grabbed his hat from a shelf by the front door. He turned, pointing the hat at me, straight-armed.

"Don't think you're going to run this ranch," he said, and for once the truth lay between us, flat and unmoving. In the stillness that followed, his expression never moved, and my gut twisted with the finality I read in those clean straight lines. Old rules do not break; they simply stretch and snap back like a well-made fence.

Inside the corral, I cupped my hand around the match flare and leaned against the gate, dizzy but mellow. The heifers were up and anxious again tonight, their ears swiveling forward to test the darkness, then back to the row of babies bedded down against the windbreak. The lantern beam swung a lazy arc across the pen, stroking down the backs, pausing a moment on the tail end, moving on. I smoked while counting the heads I could see from the fence. We started with 125 heifers in mid-March and in a month had calved all but 35. "Got a good catch on those heifers," John's father would say. I grinned around the last inch of Marlboro. What can anyone say to a man who takes personal credit for a cow's heat cycle and a bull's virility? The herd shifted to watch me fieldstrip the cigarette butt and stomp a clod of half-frozen corral mud over the pieces. They parted easily as I began talking and clucking my way among them.

The past week had been slow and I wasn't surprised to find a heifer down, secluded against one end of the hayrack. She grunted softly as my light played over her ribs and down her flank to the fluid-filled membrane that bulged beneath her tail. The hay was wallowed flat where her head had rolled back with each contraction; she'd been at it for a while. Stepping closer, I could see no sign of feet in the bubble of opaque fluid glistening in the flashlight's beam. She clambered up awkwardly as I approached. The gates were set in the calving barn, and I hazed her toward the doors at an easy jog.

We had built a high wing fence of lodgepole pine that narrowed like a funnel to the barn doors, a system used by the Indians who had built wings of brush and boulders to guide buffalo off the cliffs that loomed over the creek. The bottom layers were white with bones. The heifer fell into a high-headed trot with the pole fence on one side and me on the other. As she swung through the doorway, I raced up behind her to close the gate before she changed her mind. She stood panting amid a labyrinth of smaller pens, ignoring her labor to watch me enter and flip a switch that activated the series of flood lamps along the rafters. I urged her down the alley to the far end, where a square catch pen bedded with straw waited. This gate swung both ways, and when pushed to the inside formed one side of a narrow chute that ended in a head-catch. A small duck-through door opened to the warming room, where we kept vet supplies, gunnysacks and a space heater. The delivery area had a cement floor beneath the straw, and water ready at a hydrant outside the warming room. It was a state-of-the-art system, more modern in its own way than my house.

Bales stacked along the walls absorbed outside noise, and the interior seemed unnaturally still as I rustled a nest in a pile of loose straw and settled in to watch the heifer. Nose to the ground, she circled the pen with a growing sense of urgency as her labor resumed. Had anyone been there I would have given him ten-to-one odds that she would lie down facing me so I couldn't monitor her progress. I would have won my bet, too. Front legs folding under her brisket, she settled to her side with a grunt. The membrane had broken in her dash to the barn and I had seen the bottom of one hoof peeking out at the height of a contraction, comma-shaped pads soft and puffy from the warmth of the womb. There was still a chance that the other foot would follow. Sometimes we had to pull calves—help the heifer by wrapping chains around the calf's legs and pulling as she pushed. But more often than not, they figured it out.

Stretching my legs in the straw, I relaxed in the luxury of silence. Waiting for her to calve flew in the face of general ranch policy, but to John, exhausted by the pace of spring work, free help was free help. I could do pretty much anything within reason, and he wouldn't flicker. Frank was another story. The sight of me with a cow brought him loping across the barnyard. It made him crazy. Had I followed a common ranch wife custom, I would have checked the heifers and fetched the men immediately if I found one calving. The first time his father caught me up to my armpit in a cow he slammed through the gate and grabbed my shoulder, pulling me to one side. "Here, here, wait wait wait . . ." He was sputtering, winded, jerking at the band on his wristwatch, popping the snaps on one cuff. Elbows up to ward off challenge, he thrust both dry, grease-blackened hands into the cow.

When the chains were secured on the calf's front legs, he hooked up the puller, a steel Y-shaped contraption. The forks of the Y fit below the birth area and a wide band went over the cow's back to hold it in place. The leg of the Y was about four feet long, and at the end a powerful winch controlled the cable we hooked onto the calving chains. He pulled the calf while the cow stood caught by the neck in the calving chute, working the winch like he was hauling in a trophy fish, so much torsion on the line I half expected the calf to cannon out and land in the straw behind him. It was the last time I could stomach watching Frank in the calving shed.

I quit helping with calving during the daytime mostly to avoid Frank, but there were other reasons. Three kids were a handful, too young to leave alone, too many to take along. And the hired men seemed to have more to prove if I worked outside. These were men's men, most of them, used to working undisturbed in a man's world—which scenario did not include women in the calving shed. The last time I calved the day shift I ran two heifers in to watch, both barely started, and went back to the house to check on the kids. The hired man saw me leave, and when I returned half an hour later, he had just finished pulling the second calf.

"What took you so long," he yelled, grinning as I walked into the shed. Then the cow staggered up, gave another heave and her uterus landed in a slick purple mass at his feet. He'd been trying to show off and had pulled the calf before it was ready, causing the prolapsed uterus—an outrageously stupid mistake, as far as I was concerned. But when he complained that I had "spoken up" to him, I got no support beyond another worn lecture about trying to boss the hired men. "You might be dead right, but they're not going to take orders from you," John reminded me for possibly the tenth time. His voice matched the sag of his shoulders, forever the mediator, and hating it. It was difficult to keep hired hands this far from town, and Frank was notoriously difficult to work for. Where hired men were concerned, John played the "good cop" role to Frank's "bad cop," and could generally keep everybody working happily, as long as I didn't jump in and piss someone off. It was a basic rule: wives didn't give orders. It wasn't that I didn't get it. I flat refused to.

Most ranchers I knew pulled calves in the early stages of labor rather than lose sleep or waste daylight. They treated birth like a disease that was cured by quick action. Complications were obstacles that they treated with the same finesse with which they tore stumps from productive fields. In Frank's day, calves had been winched from the womb with fence stretchers or pulled free with a farm tractor or pickup linked to the chains on their feet. The uterine prolapse that frequently followed this rough treatment was blamed on a defect in the cow's anatomy or heredity. She would be hoisted by her hind legs from the tines of a buckrake or an overhead winch while her fifty-pound uterus was rinsed with soapy water, dusted with sulfa powder and reinserted. The process triggered strong contractions, so the vaginal opening was sewn shut with a large curved needle and twine to prevent a relapse. Survivors of this first stage were given massive doses of antibiotics to curb the infection. Survivors of the second stage were shipped with the canner cows in November, hamburgers on the hoof.

I had this theory of birth as a natural process that worked best at nature's own speed. It was considered a pretty harebrained idea in a community where the only "natural" human birth in decades took place in the backseat of a car bucketing down the road toward the hospital. Stranger yet, I insisted that my own experience with birth transferred to the calving shed. The methods I argued for were common sense to me—giving the cow time, pulling with the contractions as they occurred, easing off when they quit. Birth is birth, I reasoned, human or bovine—same process, different product. Most often my argument met with offhanded dismissal. If a woman's knowledge of birth gave her insight into an animal's experience, what did that make her? If a man could calve a cow did that mean he could deliver a baby?

I knew my own experience, flying solo through three Lamaze births in four years in the sterile shelter of the twenty-eight-bed hospital seventy miles north of us. Behind that were the stories of my mother and her generation, drugged labors, forceps, women kept flat in bed for days after birth. One of my aunts made the long ride to Malta sitting on my cousin's head but was prevented from delivering by two strong nurses who crossed her legs and held her down until the doctor arrived. Intrusion was normal, and the fewer challenges offered by the mother, the more smoothly things went.

Night Shift

In my family, only my grandmother remembered when birth depended on women working together, mother and midwife, neighbors who helped one another through birth and stayed on to cook a few days. She bore eight children. She told me of a time the midwife didn't come, of having both hips nearly dislocated by my grandfather, who panicked at the slow crowning of his daughter's head, folded my grandmother's knees against her stomach and pushed, until the screams of a ten-pound baby joined those of his wife. He was easily forgiven. Childbirth and children lay within the boundaries of a woman's world. Men knew livestock. There was all the difference in the world.

Inside the barn I checked my watch again and then rose to walk around to the other side of the pen. The heifer rolled her head to watch me, and I spoke to her in a soothing tone. Her labor was hard now, drawing her in taut, extended arches with little rest between. If something hadn't moved by now, it wasn't going to. Our heifers were bred to Angus bulls six months after being weaned from their own mothers, and were still losing baby teeth and growing when they gave birth the next spring. Calves were sold by the pound, and the rancher's only control over his paycheck in the fall was to build bigger calves. It amounted to keeping big cows, buying big bulls and breeding early to get as many calves as possible out of each cow. It was a matter of pure business, dollars and cents, profit and loss; the smaller picture was the nine-hundred-pound heifer that stared through the fence at me, straining to give birth to a ninety-pound calf. It was like a hundred-pound woman having a ten-pound baby—not impossible, but it wasn't going to be easy either.

The heifer still had a single black hoof showing and it looked half-grown, facts that I related to her in a steady monotone as I moved back around to prepare a bucket of antiseptic soap and water. Lifting the calving chains from their nail on the wall, I ran out of things to say. I stood there slowly pouring the stainless steel links from hand to hand like coins, pulling hoof-sized loops and letting them slide empty through my fingers.

I dropped the chains in the bucket of soapy water and stripped off my jacket. A few hours a night, six weeks out of the year, I did things my way. The heifer had decided to ignore me. There was a slim chance that she would allow me to ease up behind her—another ten-to-one shot—but this time the odds were against me. Unlatching the gate, I began pushing it forward and she lurched to her feet, moving unsteadily along the chute I created until the head-catch closed around her neck. She attempted to back up, fighting the metal bars that held her. I pushed up tight against her so she would not have room to kick hard, slipped a loop of lariat around her hind leg, then jumped back out of the way and snubbed the free end to a pole behind me. She stood quivering, not quite resigned. Swinging the gate back to give us room, I pushed up my sleeves and tossed my watch over beside my coat, rinsing my hands and forearms in the bucket as I fished out the slippery chains. I had quit wearing my wedding ring when calving started, but my left thumb still slid down to check. Forming loops at both ends of the chain, I slipped them over one clean wrist. Her ears flipped back as I eased up from behind, but she stood.

I began talking again, more for my own sake than hers. The calf was big. The little cow lunged forward when she felt my hand on her back, but settled down and began to strain against the intrusion as I slid the other hand along the calf's foreleg and into the birth canal. The head was right there and a thumb against its nose produced a satisfying flinch. It was alive. But the other foot was not where it belonged. I shifted to the other hand and groped for the second front leg, turning sideways and pressing against the heifer to wedge my hand flat along the calf's neck to his shoulder and down. The angle of the shoulder blade told me that the leg was flexed and not extended straight back. That could have been big trouble. My soothing tone disintegrated as her uterus seized like a vise, pinning my arm. The calf's left foot was somewhere under his chest, and every push drove his knee hard against the bony arch of the cow's pelvis. I eased my arm out and rinsed in the bucket, rolling my sleeve up to my shoulder. To straighten the leg I would have to go deeper, deep enough to cup the toe of the foot and bring it forward over the ridge of bone.

The only songs I knew by heart were old Simon and Garfunkel. We started out with "Bridge Over Troubled Water." My voice shook and I took a few deep breaths. The little cow stood fast, hams trembling as I pushed in, palm up, under the calf's chin, but the fact that she was standing meant the weight of the calf rested right where I needed to go. By the time I had worked my way down to his brisket I had forgotten the words to "Troubled Water" and started on "Sounds of Silence." The heifer shifted, nearly squatting with the power of her contractions, and I switched from song to Lamaze, focusing on the root of her tail, breathing deep and slow to control my own pain as hundreds of pounds of pressure crushed my arm between the calf's body and hers. As each spasm ended, I pushed farther into the cow, triggering another.

By the time I had the foot in my left hand, the heifer and I were locked together in an intense cycle. I heard nothing but panting, felt nothing beyond the thud of the calf's heartbeat on the inside of my wrist, the heifer's pulse answering, pounding against the back of my hand. In some dim part of my mind I knew that in a matter of seconds I would have to quit, pull out and change hands, or go for help. With my free hand I reached in and grabbed the calf's nose and shoved with all my strength, pushing him back against the tide as I pulled his left foot forward. When it happened, it happened all at once. The cow paused for breath, the uterus relaxed, the calf slid back and the hoof cupped in my fist popped over the pelvic bowl. The heifer tensed to push. I made a fast shift, grabbing the leg with my good hand, jerking it straight before it could slide back down. It was done.

I fell back against the fence, crouched against the rails cursing my own weakness as the shakes took over. My right arm was coated with blood and mucus and numb to the shoulder, and I worked at it, flexing and rubbing until nerves began to sizzle and heat swelled in my fingers. If the umbilical cord had been pinched or broken when I pushed the calf back, I had about two minutes to get him to fresh air before his heart stopped. The calving chains still hung from my right hand. I made a pass through the bucket with them and worked a loop over each rubbery hoof, pulling a noose snug on each foreleg. The calf puller rested just outside the fence, and I hauled it over and lowered it into place.

The puller is designed to fit a standing cow. I had a side theory that cows were not designed to give birth that way, any more than women were designed to give birth flat on their backs with their feet in the air. I hooked the cable to the chains on the calf's feet, then winched up the slack, already reaching, one-handed, to hit the release on the head-catch. When it sprang open the heifer staggered sideways and knelt in the straw, held only by the lariat on her hind foot. There was no resistance when I grabbed her front leg and rolled her on her side, leaping back to grab the long end of the puller before the whole damned mess came unraveled.

The cow and I worked together, her pushing, me pulling as hard as I dared, but by the time we got the head clear it didn't look good. The legs were stretched tight by the puller and the head sagged down to the straw, eyes open, tongue hanging swollen and limp. I could put more pressure on the cable, maybe enough to break the calf's legs or pull him in half. I could work the handle left and right, up and down, hoping to change the angle enough to jar him loose faster. I could scream every foul word I knew. I could run to the bunkhouse and kick the hired man out of bed. I could get John up and tell him to calve his own goddamned cows. I could drive seventy miles to town and sit in a bar and smoke like a whore.

I swore and hauled on the winch, going up on my knees to shove the handle toward the cow's hind legs, both of us straining until the calf finally burst free in a wash of thick fluid. He wasn't dead, quite. I squeezed his brisket between my palms and found a heartbeat. But when I ran my hand in his mouth to clear it, there was no gag reflex. I pulled the chains out of the grooves they had made in his forelegs, jerked the loop off the cow's foot, then grabbed the calf by one hind leg and dragged him backward to the oil drum I kept in the warming shed. I rolled him up on it until his head hung down and his lungs drained. John would have picked him up by the hind legs and held him upside down. I hated not being able to do that, but physical strength was one difference I couldn't ignore. I slapped on the calf's ribs until he sorted out a ragged job of breathing, then dragged his limp body over where his mother was struggling to stand, her back legs as wobbly as a newborn's.

When she caught scent of him, her ears snapped forward, and I felt my throat swell. Cows have a language for their newborns, eager, anxious groanings and mutterings they make at no other time. I watched her nose him over, his ribs rising, falling in a shallow pattern, then begin to wash him with tentative swipes of the tongue. He would live or die by morning. If he lived he'd be crippled for a few days, bones bruised from the bite of the chains. We'd have to milk the cow out and feed him by hand until he could stand. If he died we'd peel his hide and make a jacket for one of the orphan calves in the barn, convince the cow it was hers.

Blood and mucus had dried to a thick glaze on my arms, pulling and flaking like another skin as I set the pen in order and dumped the water down a floor drain. It would take a brush, hot water, soap. I rolled my cuffs down over it and grabbed my coat and watch. Quarter to five. The calf still hadn't moved when I hit the main light switch and let myself out through the warming room door and into the spring night. The moon was bright. I squatted in the square shadow cast by the shed, easing my shoulders against the rough boards. There was movement on the path to my right, and the red end of my cigarette wobbled in my fingers for the second it took to place the sound and settle back. I took another drag and closed my eyes, waiting for hot breath to hit my cheek. "You goddamn ignorant dog," I whispered. Katie plunked herself down and made both ears available, grunting with pleasure as I described her own humble faults and those of her ancestors. I lit another cigarette off the end of the first and closed my eyes again, drifting.

There was a level of tired I learned to welcome, a place where everything rose and passed without mattering, hairpins or harness rings, benign sex or winter storms. Words skipped across this flat place without sinking. Hate and love filled the same space, the same need. From here I could observe myself objectively, peacefully. I could change, but I ignored the old rules at my own peril and on my own time. I was the daughter of a good rancher, wife of another, daughter-in-law on a corporate ranch. I could do it all—I could play their game until I dropped—but I would never own a square foot of land, a bushel of oats or a bum calf in my own name.

When Katie lifted her head, I opened my eyes. The yard light was flashing on and off. John was awake. I stood for a moment limbering the chill from my legs, then started for the house, already thinking the routine of breakfast, remembering the flashlight still in the calving shed, set down on a straw bale so long ago. Days. Hours. The breeze had died in the predawn chill, but behind the barn the creek full of spring runoff roared on and the stars flared against the imperfect black to the east. Nothing out here stood still. Walking this prairie at night I could believe something rippled just beneath the sage, something immense and quiet. I could imagine the land crouching, pushing up a new hill each night, snaking a network of roots and rhizomes through the soil, then settling back innocently as the sun rose. Who would notice? At first light John would step out to have a look at the day, and the change would niggle at the edge of his vision. There would be a moment of searching, checking the clouds, checking the set of gates, the lay of buildings, of meadows and fields. Something. Something his mind would not register, could not imagine. He'd hold for a second, then stretch and pull on his gloves. And the day would begin.

Afterword:
Leaving Home

It has taken me thirty years to recognize the infinite patience of the land we lived on, how a way of life can consume people from the inside out. Always we waited for next year, hope whispered on the east wind, snatched away by the west, trusting as blood turned to dust that the rains would come. And they did. Sometimes too late, when the wheat stood like straw, other times in a wide swath that buried crops in a mire of roots and mud. But always they came, just enough to stir the imagination of more.

For more than a century, the people living this marginal lifestyle have warmed to their own mythology and basked in the admiration of the world. We are ranchers, cowboys—a special breed. We are feeding the world in the face of all hardship: *The latchstring is always out.* Our investment in this image of independence and generosity is visceral. The truth is more complex, however, and not nearly as popular. Farming and ranching is a business, and people living in the wide-open West are just as concerned with turning a profit, making a living and raising their kids as any other group is. It's always been that way. Where the romantic idea of cowboy life paid off was the point at which it set us apart from other businesses: we didn't have to make a profit to be doing a good job—we were in it for deeper, more soul-sustaining reasons, like freedom and autonomy.

When public opinion turned, it seemed to happen overnight. Third- and fourth-generation ranch kids like me received no introduction to the land and the forces that govern it. The land was simply there, a network of place names we came to know like the names of the people around our dinner table. In the daily talk of work and range planning, my parents did not speak differently of the deeded land they owned outright and the public lands they leased. But by the seventies, stories began to surface of hunters and streamside anglers who stood their ground and argued their right to access. Terms such as "multiple use" and "environmental impact" became common. As the pressure grew, families who had tended those acres since the turn of the century and before began to bristle at the invasion. These are lands passed down in families. These are leases that sell just like deeded land; the new owners pay the same amount per acre of leased land as they do per acre of deeded, and when the lease is transferred, they continue to pay the annual fee. Asking a third-generation rancher what of this land is his and what is merely leased is like asking the parent of a blended family which children are adopted, which are his own. The correct answer, stated with dignity, is, "We don't remember."

America's love affair with the mythical West has held strong for more than a hundred years. We need to believe in it, for if a frontier exists just over the horizon, those of us asleep behind bolted doors in cities are not trapped. We can imagine that somewhere a community of our own awaits us, a life on the land under the big sky. Since the 1980s, tens of thousands of families have relocated to the inland west, searching for the promised land and changing it irrevocably as they go. Like the first pioneers, more than half pack up their disillusionment and leave after a couple of years. They move to small towns and find them staggering under increasing burdens of unemployment and poverty, crime and alcoholism. They're dismayed when the modern-day Shane drives through town with a lip full of chew, a rifle rack in the back window of his pickup and a bumper sticker that reads: "This Land is MY Land— (Yours is in California)." They go to court to stop the Cartwright boys from running cattle on Forest Service land or leasing their mineral rights to an international conglomerate that wants to punch a gold mine or a gas well in the North Forty. They discover that the cowboy hero will shoot any wolf, coyote, bear or bison that threatens his livelihood, as he always has, and some that don't as well. *A varmint's a varmint.* But now he posts the land against human trespassers as well, and spends as much time defending his business as he used to spend running it. The latchstring is no longer out. There are two dreams being destroyed here, and on both sides the outrage is palpable.

As the new century begins, I am fortunate to still have my family on the land where I grew up. I can drink coffee in the kitchen where I learned to bake bread, bathe in the same shallow cast-iron tub of sulfur and salts, visit the lopsided outbuildings where I once fed chickens, scouted new litters of kittens and roped milk pen calves. I can ride through a herd of cattle descended from cattle my grandfather knew. When I'm done, I get in my car and drive back to Missoula, secure in my sense that the landscape of my childhood remains intact, in place. For fifty years my parents have held the line, grubbing a marginal existence from marginal land, preserving the heart of ranching tradition even as the lights of the community winked out around them. They've paid dearly for my privilege.

≠

In August of 1986, I left Phillips County with a new divorce and an old car, with three scared kids and some clothes piled in back. We followed the sun west for hours, climbing mountain passes, crossing river after river, until we spanned the final bridge into Missoula. The kids started school the next morning, and within days I started my freshman year at the University of Montana, the four of us holding hands and stepping together into a world of mountains and shopping malls. Even the air smelled different—the rotten-egg stench of pulp mills blowing in from the west, or, as often, the clean, rich redolence of the Clark Fork river. I savored the mornings most, when the chill lingered and the air lay crisp with dew and the fragrance of alpine vegetation. Missoula lives under a canopy of trees, and I found myself half ducking the first few weeks, conscious of feeling something always hovering overhead, turning to look up and up through the limbs of giant firs, sprawling maples and oaks. And, of course, there were people. More people than I'd ever seen before.

Finding a job that fits around kids and classes is hard. After a year of trying to adjust our lives to unpredictable schedules and late-night shifts in restaurants, I settled into the construction trades like coming home. Dale Thom, an industrial arts instructor returning to the university, became a dear friend and teacher for the years he spent in Missoula. Under his tutorship, I learned painting, power tools and the ABCs of woodwork. In 1988 I began my apprenticeship with Cliff Cain, owner of Custom Wood Floors. A master craftsman who had apprenticed in Hollywood, Cliff found the patience to humor my schedule, and the integrity and compassion to pay me union scale, even though I was in a position to demand neither. He took my trade schooling the next step.

For years, I sanded and finished hardwood floors around classes, and worked full-time summers and holidays, balancing my trade and my education as best I could. By my junior year at the university, a reputation for intensity began to precede me into the classroom and onto the job site. Scholarships would put me through, and I went after them with deliberate, humorless attention to detail. I strode into classrooms with my hair stuffed under a baseball cap and my sweatshirt dripping sawdust, trailing the reek of acetone and formaldehyde. I sat in the front row where I could hear the lecture over the residual ringing in my ears.

Summers the kids spent with their father, I ran a bootleg painting crew manned by graduate students in addition to full-time floor work, jamming sixteen to eighteen paid hours into every day, banking time and money against the start of the school year, when I had to cut back and be a mom and a student again. By then I was ready to slide back into my kid routine: home by 5 p.m. to arrange supper, shopping, errands, laundry and music lessons; my own homework and class preparation from 9 p.m. until midnight or later; and up again at 6 a.m. to read the paper and get the household percolating through the single bathroom and off to two or three different schools. When I left the house in the morning, I carried my toolbox, a backpack full of books and a stainless-steel thermos of coffee so black it threw daggers. I did not own a purse. I did not own a dress. I did this for eight straight years. And gradually, in the hours before dawn and after dark, I found my voice again as my children slept. I began to write.

In June of 1997, I made the long drive to south Phillips County accompanied by a tinge of sadness. Second Creek School had been without students for years, and with no children waiting in the wings, the decision had been made to close it permanently. All its contents were to be sold at auction. In addition to its own thirty-year accumulation of books and materials, it held all the books, desks and materials we'd moved over from South First Creek School in 1965, as well as collections from the long defunct Robinson, Rock Creek and Fourchette Schools. The sale would mark the end of an era. The First Creek Community Hall was falling into disuse and disrepair. The 4-H Clubs had folded or moved to Malta. With the rural schools closed, the Regina and Sun Prairie communities had little to offer young families.

I turned south onto the Midale Road, rolling my eyes at the latest road-improvement project. Some land-managing arm of government had thought to string wooden signs south like a trail of bread crumbs, every reservoir and creek, every branch and fork in the road posted with place names, arrows, mileage. Public lands were suddenly popular, and in an effort to accommodate visitors, the boggy gumbo grade had been fortified with gravel in a few places, too. Our end of the county had made a name for itself with big-game hunters, some miracle of water, forage and isolation combining to produce a number of trophy mule deer and elk. Varmint hunters had been welcomed, too, as a means of slowing down the prairie dogs in the absence of enough natural predators. South Phillips County, alone, supported 26,000 *acres* of prairie dog towns, occupied by around a half a million prairie dogs. By the early nineties, the combined efforts of state and federal agencies had succeeded in planting a small, fragile population of black-footed ferrets among the prairie dogs on the CMR Wildlife Refuge south of John's ranch. From my home in Missoula, I'd kept an idle ear to the ongoing soap opera of the endangered species experiment, the chest-thumping among local/state/federal officials over who was in charge, the tiny ferret radio collars tracked to mounds of coyote crap as the big predators ate the little predators, the official intervention when the plague began decimating the prairie dog population—once considered nature's way of controlling overpopulation. Now, with the ferret project at risk, officials set about dusting prairie dog towns with insecticide to kill the fleas that carried the plague that killed the dogs that fed the ferrets . . . and on and on.

The prairie rolled along as it always had. On an unfenced stretch of road we called the Veseth Pasture, a small band of antelope crossed in front of the car, and I pulled over and stopped for a moment to watch. Overhead, a pair of red-tailed hawks coasted on a lazy round of air, the dip and glide of pronghorns chasing the shadow of their wings on a landscape largely unchanged since the day I left. But I knew better. The changes had occurred over the rise, back from the road a ways, where the people lived. Fewer than half the families I grew up knowing still lived in the Regina and Sun Prairie communities, and fewer still had another generation beginning on the land. Although still locally owned, many of the ranch buildings I'd passed on my way south from Malta stood vacant, their secret given away by the stripe of tall weeds that grew down the center of the lanes leading in from the county road. Some, nearer to the highway, had strands of wire stretched across the cattle guards, a deterrent to hunters and joy-riding high school kids, but no real defense against thieves and vandals in four-wheel-drives—the sort of outsiders ranchers worried about now.

The school's sale day began with a cool rain shower that cleared the air and stopped before the roads became too slick to get around. My sisters, Margaret and Gail, drove with me to Second Creek School in the morning to thumb through the amassed boxes and make up auction lots of our own choosing. Midway through disassembly, the schoolroom and the teacherage were chaotic. Larger items were already moved to the auction site, while supplies and materials with mostly sentimental value had been pulled from shelves and piled in heaps. The offerings ran the gamut from worn turn-of-the-century primers to the little Apple II computer the community had helped acquire in the eighties by collecting and redeeming Campbell soup labels. The old brass handbell our teachers had rung to call us in from recess had disappeared from the school one hunting season years before, but some obvious plums—like the old Red Wing drinking crock—were expected to draw spirited bidding. I searched for the alphabet story cards we'd used in first grade, but they were missing, perhaps buried under tons of books and materials, but more likely discarded in favor of the more modern, cartoon-style ABCs in primary colors that circled the schoolroom.

All the boxed lots accumulated by neighborhood volunteers in the morning were numbered and moved to the auction site at the First Creek Community Hall that afternoon. Margaret and I drove over together, and in the end bid ten dollars for a box we'd handpicked that included a dented tin globe, a couple of sets of Winston readers, and a dozen storybooks from the thirties and forties that I remembered reading as a child.

Driving back to the ranch from the Hall, we paused, with time to kill, at the site of our first school. Only a jog in the barbed wire fence told us where South First Creek School had been; no sign marked the spot and no man-made artifacts remained visible from the road. The grass had grown up thick and green where our feet once trampled it to bare dirt, and recent rains had set the prairie blooming with the small, close flowers we both remembered. The wild parsley we called cat's-paw, curlycup gumweed and broom snakeweed glowed yellow and gold. Here, the lick of scarlet globe mallow and pincushion cactus, there, a sprinkle of cool lavender and pale blue in the low mounds of moss phlox.

We poked around through the grass, keeping one eye and one ear tuned for rattlesnakes, and quickly found the concrete step that once led into the school's entryway. With that to center my gaze, I could see a vague outline of the building in the vegetation, and on the south side, a couple of shallow, parallel troughs in the grass where our swing set had been. We laughed at how tall the grass had grown at the western end, where the outhouses used to stand. The old South First Creek building had been sold to a Sun Prairie rancher to use for storage, the outhouses relocated to Second Creek School the summer it was finished. We'd just watched them sell for a few dollars apiece. Little else remained.

It was a beautiful afternoon, and we were in no hurry. I smiled as I shook off the buzz of town life and breathed in the absolute silence, the rich smell of spring sage after a rain. I was back in the cradle of my childhood, surrounded by everything, and nothing. Blank horizons marked north, Malta some fifty miles away, and south, where the Missouri River Breaks lay invisible, tucked below the surface. To the east, a slim blue streak marked the Larb Hills; to the west, the Little Rocky

Afterword: Leaving Home

Mountains stood in silhouette, and though the profile had changed gradually since the seventies, I found my eyes drawn back to the huge bite dredged from the center of the range by Pegasus gold mines, the missing peaks visible a hundred miles away.

It was on the prairie itself, a short distance from the schoolyard, that I found a solid piece of my past. There, half buried in sod, were the rock houses built by a generation of grammar school girls in the fifties and sixties. Not three-dimensional except in concept, a rock house was made like a floor plan, with a rectangle of large, same-size rocks outlining the exterior "walls" and smaller ones marking off the interior rooms; gaps in the walls denoted doorways. The rest of the house existed only in our imaginations. For years we had played rock house during recesses when the weather was mild, returning to the same small plot when the snow drew back in spring, as a bird might return to its old nest. Every autumn when school began, we reseated any rocks dislocated by grazing cows over the summer, then scoured the prairie for more to expand and improve the walls. The best rocks were quite difficult to find, like the highly prized pink granite and the darker green-flecked field stones, and more than once I sneaked rocks to school from home in the back of the pickup.

I recognized my house at once by the layout, though I recalled it being much larger. The living room and kitchen made up more than half the house, and the three small "bed-rooms" alongside were just large enough for an adult to sit in cross-legged. Some old lessons survived with the stones—one did not step over the wall of a rock house. On that June afternoon, thirty-odd years after I had last done so, I walked around the perimeter and entered through the front door. Inside these rooms, we had enacted the social rituals of our grandmothers and mothers, the formal invitations crayoned one recess, guests assembling the next. We younger girls took our cues regarding proper rock house decorum from our elders, the seventh and eighth graders. The older the girl, the bigger the rocks used in her house, and the more impressive her collection of broken crockery and glassware scavenged from the homesteader's dump over a rise to the west. Bits of prairie foliage, even an insect or two, served as imaginary luncheon on the salvaged china. I'd been a fifth grader when the school closed, one of the last to serve "air tea" and grasshopper drumsticks on broken Depression ware to a circle of ranchwomen-in-training.

How I had grieved for this land, that first spring in Missoula. Gardenless, landless, craving anything secure and familiar, I had bought seeds and planted an edge of the alley to bachelor's-buttons, the hardy, familiar flowers of my childhood. I did everything the same as I had done at the ranch, but I barely recognized the results. Plant varieties that grew a few inches tall in compressed gumbo grew waist-high here, their blossoms twice the size of their eastern Montana cousins. My neighbors did not understand my enthusiasm for this back-alley plot of pink and blue monster-flowers. When one after another took me aside and explained how bachelor's-buttons spread like dandelions in this climate, I could only nod, unable to give an accounting for my poor judgment. Everything about my former life seemed so odd, then, so hard to explain.

In the years that followed, I would find other elements of my old world growing in this new one, with no less surprise. I came to recognize the landscape of my life in the lives of many women. Their stories and the places they spoke of spanned a world beyond my experience, from mill towns to suburbs, from logging camps to ethnic neighborhoods, from inner cities to Indian reservations. Few shared my place of origin or the events of my life, but many, it seems, shared my experience. Listening to their stories, I came to understand how women can be isolated by circumstances as well as by distance, and how our experiences, though geographically distinct, often translated into the same feelings. Away from the physical presence of my past, I found it easy to argue that what mattered most was the story, the truth of what we tell ourselves, the versions we pass along to our daughters. But as I stood in the living room of my rock house that afternoon, I was again reminded of the enormous power of this prairie, its silence and the whisper I made inside it. I had forgotten how easily one person can be lost here.

I left my house as I found it, settling into the sod a year at a time. The prairie will reclaim its squared corners and straight walls as it has gradually, patiently, taken back the tepee rings left centuries before. Driving the narrow, familiar road back to my parents' ranch, I felt a sense of peace, imagining my house hundreds, thousands of years from now, suspended far below the surface of the shortgrass plains, five stone rooms that hold a part of me, still.

A NOTE ABOUT THE AUTHOR

Judy Blunt spent more than thirty years on wheat and cattle ranches in northeastern Montana, before leaving in 1986 to attend the University of Montana. Her poems and essays have appeared in numerous journals and anthologies. She is the recipient of a Jacob K. Javits Graduate Fellowship and a Montana Arts Council Individual Artist Fellowship. *Breaking Clean* was awarded a 1997 PEN/Jerard Fund Award for a work in progress, as well as a 2001 Whiting Writers' Award. She lives in Missoula, Montana.

A NOTE ON THE TYPE

This book was set in a typeface called Primer, designed by Rudolph Ruzicka (1883–1978). Mr. Ruzicka was earlier responsible for the design of Fairfield and Fairfield Medium, Linotype faces whose virtues have for some time been accorded wide recognition.

The design of Primer makes general reference to Linotype Century—long a serviceable type, totally lacking in manner and frills of any kind—but brilliantly corrects its characterless quality.

Composed by NK Graphics,
Keene, New Hampshire
Printed and bound by R. R. Donnelley & Sons,
Harrisonburg, Virginia
Map by Mark Stein Studios
Designed by Virginia Tan